THE RED ONE

by Harry Harris

THE INSIDE STORY OF JOSÉ MOURINHO AT MANCHESTER UNITED

G2 entertainment

Published by G2 Entertainment Ltd

© G2 Entertainment 2016

ISBN : 978-1-78281-836-6

AUTHOR: Harry Harris

EDITOR: Sean Willis

DESIGNER: Paul Briggs

PUBLISHERS: Edward Adams and Jules Gammond

PICTURES: Action Images

PRINTED IN EUROPE

SPECIAL THANKS TO:
Bryan Robson and Ray Wilkins for providing their forewords.
Alan Brennan and Mike Farnan at Red Strike.
Ant Verill at Footba11Legends.

CONTENTS

"The fact that José Mourinho has been successful wherever he has been fills me with enormous confidence he can bring back the steel to the team that has been missing for a couple of years now.

I believe he is the right choice. There are not many managers in the world who can fill Sir Alex's boots, and we have seen this over the past few years now. Again, to be fair to David Moyes and Louis van Gaal it was a very difficult task to come into this job immediately after Sir Alex, the intensity is something quite different given the aspirations of the club itself and the tempo of the Premier League which is quite a unique combination.

You really do need someone with a big character like José Mourinho at Old Trafford, as it is a big, big job, and it takes a big, big manager to tackle it.

The boys have done quite well, to be fair, in winning the FA Cup, and we do need trophies at Old Trafford and the FA Cup carries on that tradition of winning trophies. But there is no doubt that in the modern game it's about winning titles and challenging in the Champions League that counts, and we have been well off the pace of both of those for a few years now.

José has a great record and it's remarkable that he has virtually come from nowhere as Bobby Robson's interpreter to having one of the greatest coaching careers of all time, and long may it continue at Old Trafford. One thing is certain, this is going to be one of the most interesting, challenging and defining seasons in the history of Manchester United, and that's saying something."

Bryan Robson

LEGEND, CAPTAIN MARVEL AND CLUB AMBASSADOR

"I love José. Love him because he is great for our game, and he is fantastic for Manchester United.

I am now really looking forward to this season, mainly because José will be at Old Trafford.

I'm looking forward to his tenure at United, because he is the man who could turn things around, and make them one of the game's greats again.

I'm often associated as having worked with José at the Bridge, but that was Steve Clarke. I've worked under Luca Vialli, Claudio Ranieri, Luiz Felipe Scolari, Ancelotti, Guus Hiddink but not José. As you can imagine, having worked with these guys for so long, I speak to the likes of JT (John Terry) and Frank (Lampard), and they loved him, and they have told me what makes him tick, and how he makes them tick. It's all about his man-management, and that aspect of his repertoire is simply superb. JT and Frank tell me he is the best manager they have ever played under, and they have played for some of the biggest and best managers in the world at Stamford Bridge.

It's all about how he manages the players on a personal level. Invariably at the clubs he has managed the players are at such a high standard that they know how to play the game, how to organise themselves on the pitch and how to manage the game on the pitch, so it's a question of the art of man-management. What astonishes me is how brilliant José is at this aspect of management considering that he never played at a high level himself, which contracts starkly with say a manager of equal world renown such as Pep Guardiola. For me that makes José a genius. When you look at the level that Guardiola played at, he was a superb footballer, you would know that he understands players at the highest level, he is on their wave length, gets into their psychic. Yet, Mourinho still understands his players every bit as well as Guardiola, and of course he is a serial winner, and that makes him, in my book, the best that there is.

I know how much the Chelsea fans adored him, and how much he is associated with the west London club, but it really doesn't matter now he's at United. There have been a only a handful who have played for both clubs, myself included along with Juan Mata, Mickey Thomas, Mark Hughes, Juan Sebastián Verón, Paul Parker, Mark Bosnich, Alex Stepney, Mal Donaghy, and George Graham being the others. But even fewer who have managed both clubs, Dave Sexton and Tommy Docherty are the only ones who spring to mind, and José makes the third. What is important is that José Mourinho is back in the Premier League and has not been lost to English football. We now have all the world's best coaches here in the Premier League, and it is slightly worrying that we are talking about them and not the players, but with Conte joining Chelsea, Koeman moving to Everton and Pep and José in Manchester, this is going to be one helluva season!

But if we are discussing players, then it will be an absolutely thrilling combination of José and Zlatan Ibrahimović. José is going to return United to their glory days, and this player is going to help him to achieve that. He is 'Cantonesque' in his qualities of style, arrogance and class; he will have an enormous influence on the team, he is a proper character, and he can do for United what Cantona did for them. He is a phenomenal footballer and he scored 50 goals in 51 appearances for Paris St. Germain last season, that's some going. He will light up Old Trafford, he's got balls.

The fans might have been thinking 'is José the right man for us?' My message to the fans is 'don't worry', he is tailor made for Old Trafford."

Ray Wilkins

LEGEND WITH MANCHESTER UNITED & CHELSEA.

#WELCOMEJOSÉ

Manchester United, @ManUtd May 27: We are delighted to announce José Mourinho is our new manager! #WelcomeJosé

MOURINHO APPOINTED
UNITED MANAGER

Portuguese coach has won 22 trophies since 2003.

José Mourinho will take over as manager of Manchester United from the 2016/17 season, signing a three-year contract with an option to stay at the club until at least 2020.

José, 53, has managed at the top level of European football for over a decade and in that time has won league titles and cups in four countries (Portugal, England, Italy and Spain), as well as winning the UEFA Champions League twice - in 2004 with FC Porto and in 2010 with Inter Milan.

Announcing the appointment, Ed Woodward said: "José is quite simply the best manager in the game today. He has won trophies and inspired players in countries across Europe and, of course, he knows the Premier League very well, having won three titles here. I'd like to take this opportunity to welcome him to Manchester United. His track record of success is ideal to take the club forward.

José Mourinho said: "To become Manchester United manager is a special honour in the game. It is a club known and admired throughout the world. There is a mystique and a romance about it which no other club can match."

"I have always felt an affinity with Old Trafford; it has hosted some important memories for me in my career and I have always enjoyed a rapport with the United fans. I'm looking forward to being their manager and enjoying their magnificent support in the coming years."

Source: www.ManUtd.com/WelcomeJosé

Chapter 1

JOSÉ: THE GREATEST

In terms of managers, who is The Greatest? Ask José Mourinho and he will probably tell you José Mourinho.

Statistically Mourinho is the most successful current club manager in world football.

He has won league titles in each of the four countries where he has managed, Portugal, Italy, Spain and England. He has won the Champions League twice.

I asked for views from experts; coaches, footballing legends, top sports writers, and even some football-mad celebrity fans. The conclusion: two managers stood out above all others, Sir Alex Ferguson and José Mourinho.

And while Mourinho has some way to go to catch Fergie, the one-time Manchester United 'hairdryer' is now switched off. Mourinho, however, remains very much in his prime, has a renewed hunger and is clearly energised to prove he is still indeed 'The Special One'. If anyone is going to catch and overtake Sir Alex in terms of trophy haul, it is going to be Mourinho.

Glenn Hoddle, the former England, Chelsea and Spurs manager told me: "Mourinho has won the Champions League in different countries. Mourinho has challenged himself in new countries, and like never before has proved himself in every country he has managed whatever the conditions with all different types of clubs and different types of players. And it's not taken him 10 years at each club to do it, he comes in and does it straight away, that takes some doing, so whatever managerial methods he uses it works wherever he goes."

Roberto Di Matteo, the only Chelsea manager to have won the Champions League, put Mourinho ahead of Sir Alex. Why? "He is a great coach, communicator and motivator. One of the best in our generation."

Paul Elliott, while casting Sir Alex as No. 1, placed Mourinho third in his all-time list but he explained: "Mourinho in my view is currently the best modern manager in the world; modern day coaching and tactical methodology. Brilliant man manager, delivered championships in Portugal, England, Spain, and an unprecedented treble in the unlikeliest of environments in Italy with Inter Milan, similar to the amazing achievement with Porto when winning the Champions League. Only 52 with hunger and desire to achieve much more."

Ben Rumsby, sports correspondent at the Daily Telegraph, said it was "tough" picking his top five, but went for Mourinho over Fergie as he explained: "Mourinho always wins, all the time, everywhere he goes. If Ferguson had done it overseas as well as in the UK, he'd be top."

I have to declare my position here. I have written four books on Mourinho. Yes, four. Now to follow his managerial career that closely, I have either become his stalker, obsessed with his every move, or, in truth, I am genuinely fascinated by his character that I have often likened to Brian Clough in my writings about him.

Brian Clough would be third in my all-time list of 'Greatest Ever' managers, just ahead of Sir Matt Busby because of his charisma and unique character. My top two are Sir Alex and José. But, if there is more to management than trophies and success then I'd argue that Mourinho is in a league of his own.

"Mourinho is also the most divisive manager in football", Mick Brown suggested in an extremely intuitive piece on Mourinho in the Daily Telegraph, "watching Mourinho is almost a spectator sport in itself" he observed.

Jamie Carragher in his Daily Mail column commented: "Spain might have the best players and by Saturday night they will have won both European club competitions after the all-Spanish Champions League final, but the invasion of the great managers will electrify the Premier League and confirm it as *the* place to be. The Manchester United manager José Mourinho (22 trophies) battling it out with Manchester City's Pep Guardiola (21 trophies). Then there's Chelsea's Antonio Conte (three Serie A titles) slugging it out with Liverpool's Jürgen Klopp (a dual Bundesliga winner and Champions League finalist) and Arsenal manager Arsene Wenger (17 trophies). It means no other competition can rival England's big league for expertise and swagger. Whether you are a fan of his ways or not, you cannot deny that Mourinho is box office and will get United challenging for silverware straight away. The man is a serial winner."

It is hard to compare like-for-like when managers were in charge of vastly contrasting dressing rooms in different eras with different standards, just as Pelé and Maradona played on some churned up grassless pitches wearing heavyweight boots and using those hard leather balls, compared to the snooker table like surfaces and light weight everything the modern players can use to make him look better and faster, and much better protected by the officials with massive changes in the rules to protect the flair players.

Jim Lawton, one of my favourite all-time writers, gave me his considered options "It is easy to despise Mourinho for his vanities and his cynical tactics but so much harder to deny that he is a one-off football genius. His Champions League win with Inter was a triumph of football's black arts. He did more than park the bus. He out-thought Guardiola and disabled the team that was supposed to be the best in the history of club football. For what it is worth, (Jock) Stein was the master of man management and motivation, getting eleven Glaswegians to pick off the cream of the European game and destroy the mystique of the legendary Inter coach Helenio Herrera. Fergie had the nerve to build on Busby's legacy - and an astonishing drive to win - and Clough was a forerunner of Mourinho, a man who had a rage and an instinct to finish on top."

Ivor Baddiel, brother of comedian David, and the man who writes the X-factor scrips, certainly believes that Mourinho has the X-factor among managers. Ivor placed Mourinho as No. 1 in his list of 1-5 greatest ever managers with this explanation: "José Mourinho is a manager who actually manages as well as coaches. In a game that is now dominated by massive egos, here is a man with possibly the biggest of them all, and one that he uses to deflect attention away from his players, allowing them to get on with their job. It's a master stroke, beautifully simple, yet effective."

"He's a man who is obsessively thorough and regimented. If you play for him you know exactly what is expected of you and you're prepared to do it to the best of your ability. Once again there's a brilliant simplicity to this. In any walk of life, clarity is vital. If you give someone absolutely clear instructions, they will know what is required of them. They can be focussed, a vital part of the game. Ultimately though, José Mourinho is a man who knows how to win. He doesn't bottle, he sees the job through, no matter how hard that might be. He knows that tough decisions are part of it, but he doesn't shirk and will do what is necessary to succeed."

It is often thrown back into his face that he never made the grade as a player. He was a defender in the second tier of the Portuguese league, but made little progress and decided to move into coaching, enrolling at the Technical University of Lisbon to study Sports Science, and then becoming a teacher. Mourinho's father - also José - was a goalkeeper, who made one appearance for Portugal before becoming a coach. The young José accompanied him to games, sometimes running the line, passing on instructions from his father to the players.

His first job was teaching children with Down's syndrome and severe mental disabilities - "a big challenge", he admits in an insightful Daily Telegraph interview, "I wasn't technically ready to help these kids. And I had success only because of one thing, the emotional relationship that was established with them. I did little miracles only because of the relationship. Affection, touch, empathy - only because of that. There was one kid that refused all his life to walk upstairs. Another one that couldn't coordinate the simplest movement - all these different problems, and we had success in many, many of these cases only based on that empathy. After that I was coaching kids of 16. Now I coach the best players in the world, and the most important thing is not that you are prepared from the technical point of view; the most important thing is the relationship you establish with the person. Of course you need the knowledge, the capacity to analyse things. But the centre of everything is the relationship, and empathy, not only with the individual but in the team. And to have that empathy in the team we all must give up something. It's not about establishing the perfect relation between me and you; it's about establishing the perfect relation to the group, because the group wins things; it's not the individual who wins things."

Mourinho believes in family values. When he wins, he is on the phone to his wife, the first person he calls on his smart phone. They are well connected. He and his wife, Matilde, were teenage sweethearts, growing up a street away from each other in the coastal town of Setúbal, now married for 26 years with two teenage children, also named Matilde and José.

Mourinho's first managerial job came in 2000 as the manager of the Portuguese side Benfica, having worked as a translator and then as a coach under Bobby Robson at Sporting Lisbon, Porto and Barcelona. He lasted only three months at Benfica, just nine league games in charge, before resigning after a row. A subsequent brief but successful spell at União de Leiria earned a move to Porto, where he won the Portuguese Primeira Liga twice, the UEFA Cup and, in 2004, the Champions League. That was equivalent to Brian Clough winning the European Cup with humble Nottingham Forest. That sort of thing isn't supposed to happen. The European elite tournament should be for the European elite, surely; Real Madrid, Barcelona, Bayern Munich and before that the likes of Ajax, Liverpool and Manchester United. That totally unexpected triumph, with the running down the touchline and celebrating on his knees knocking out Manchester United on the way, announced his arrival on a global basis.

Mourinho remembers his old mentor, Sir Bobby citing the Old Etonian ethos of his Ipswich Town owners, the old school Cobbolds. "Bobby Robson used to say - and I disagreed with him - when we lose a match, don't be so sad, just think that in the other dressing room the guys are so happy. Don't be so sad, it's not the end of the world."

That might be something to go against the grain, yet in his own career he has learned to "respect the guy who deserves to win," and cites the example of Crystal Palace, who inflicted a painful league defeat on Chelsea at Selhurst Park in March: "I wanted to kill my guys. But they (Palace) were amazing. And they needed those points to survive. So, in the middle of my unhappiness, I was mature enough to say - hey, these guys were brilliant, because they did very well. I told the (Palace) guys 'congratulations' one by one."

Mourinho first locked swords with Sir Alex in 2004, when Porto knocked Manchester United out of the Champions League. "That was when I felt the two faces of such a big man. The first face was the competitor, the man that tried everything to win. And after that I found the man with principles, with the respect for the opponent, with the fair play - I found these two faces in that period, and that was very important for me. In my culture, the Portuguese and the Latin culture, we don't have that culture of the second face; we are in football to win and when we don't there is not a second face most of the time. But when we beat United in the Champions League I got that beautiful face of a manager which I try to have myself. I try."

Since then they forged a very close friendship and share a love of fine red wine, it is often stated, but it just happens to be true. Yet, one wonders how much Sir Alex pushed for his appointment at Old Trafford considering he backed David Moyes as his successor.

Reminding him of that iconic moment, sliding down the Old Trafford touchline, Mourinho recalled, "When I remember that (knee slide), the good thing for me is that last year I did the same," he says. "So it was not something from a young coach, it was not something from somebody who feels that moment was my moment to change my career. Last year I did exactly the same against Paris Saint-Germain and hopefully this year I will do another one. So this is part of me. This is part of the way I sometimes don't control the emotion, the happiness. But going back to that day, I think I was already in important contact to leave Portugal so it was not because of that game and that moment I had the interest from Chelsea. I was already in on that."

That Champions League triumph over Sir Alex made Roman Abramovich sit up and take notice as he bought out Ken Bates having watched Champions

League football at Old Trafford wanting to build his dream team capable of winning it at Stamford Bridge. So, with Claudio Ranieri knowing he was a 'Dead Man Walking' even before his Champions League tie with Monaco, Mourinho was to be installed for his first stint at Chelsea, where he won back-to-back Premier League titles 2004-05, 2005-06, the FA Cup and the League Cup, again twice. As the manager of Inter Milan he won the Serie A twice, and the Champions League for a second time. In 2010 he moved on to Real Madrid, where he won the Copa Del Rey and La Liga in consecutive seasons. In June 2013 he returned to Chelsea and after one barren season, landed the Premier League and League Cup double.

Mourinho, whilst during his second stint at Chelsea, interestingly ran through his CV: "I had a career project. Many times you cannot follow your career project. I want to leave Portugal and come to England. Clear. When I leave England I want Italy. I'm mad to go to Italy, where people are talking about the mentality of the Italians, the tactical aspect of the game. And after that I want Real Madrid. Spain - but I wanted Real Madrid. This circle - I want very much to do it, and I did it. When I did it came the (question): where do you like more, where are you happier? Which is the biggest challenge? I made the choice. I keep saying the same. In every club I was working and thinking about that club, but I always have my next movement. This is the first time where I don't have my next movement. I want to stay. I want to stay till the moment Chelsea tells me it's over, because the results are not good, or they want to go in another direction, or they don't agree with my style of management - for any reason. This period at Chelsea is going to hang by their decision, not my decision. That was the objective, but to make that movement I had to be very sure what I was doing, especially because I didn't want to come back to my club - because I can say Chelsea and Inter are my clubs - after a very nice period I had here, and not be happy again. And not to make good things again. Mr. Abramovich gave a lot of time to think about that. Also when he invited me to come back it took time for me to analyse the situation. The Chelsea team we started building in 2004-2005 is finished. We have just two or three boys from that time. We need to rebuild the team. And the perspective now is different from 10 years ago, because the perspective then was about spend not-in-a-controlled-way. So me and the club found each other in a very good moment. I think the club was waiting for a manager like me, and I was waiting for my Chelsea to have this new profile. Hopefully we can hold together for many years."

It came as quite a shock to the system to have ended up sacked for a second time.

Mourinho's future began to dominate the media agenda as he suffered meltdown on the touchline, and an uncharacteristic sequence of poor results. He felt it necessary to have discussions with the board following a shock 3-1 defeat at home to Southampton as there was something fundamentally wrong within a few months of being crowned champions with four losses in eight games. Also of concern was the state of their Champions League position, third after two matches in Group G.

Some newspapers reports suggested Mourinho's prospects at Chelsea were in serious doubt, but it was premature, and there was a deep resolve within the club to end the damaging headlines which were beginning to have a negative impact within the dressing room; the club released a surprise statement on the Monday afternoon after the defeat by Southampton in an unprecedented attempt to quash any speculation.

This was an unusual step, and clearly had the ultimate approval of Roman Abramovich, who would have sanctioned it in consultation with his inner sanctum of friends and advisors. Normally Abramovich prefers to ignore media speculation, leaving it to his in-house communications department to deal with it, sometimes with briefings, sometimes to play a straight bat and refuse to rise to the speculation and treat it with utter disdain.

To have issued the dreaded 'vote of confidence' in a manager was something I had never experienced since Abramovich bought the club from Ken Bates and I had set about writing a series of books, including a detailed account of the takeover from former chairman/owner Ken Bates, and of the inner workings of the Abramovich regime.

For me there were two main reasons for this; the manager's insecurity, and the club's determination to end the speculation. Mourinho felt it was undermining the dressing room and his ability to hold it together and the club's board agreed; even though Abramovich actually doesn't sit on the board he authorises all major decisions.

For those two key reasons it was imperative to act, and a statement was duly released, and because it was extremely out of character for Abramovich it had the desired effect in quelling the speculation, if only temporarily as it turned out.

It read: "The club wants to make it clear that José continues to have our full support. As José has said himself, results have not been good enough and the team's performances must improve. However, we believe that we have the right manager to turn this season around and that he has the squad with which to do it."

When asked by Sky Sports reporter Greg Whelan for his thoughts on the Southampton defeat, Mourinho spoke for seven minutes that involved a number of accusations and a declaration that the club would have to "sack the best manager in their history" to get him to leave.

"People can say what they want. I think you should go straight to the players," said Mourinho, who had already received public backing from club captain John Terry, "Get a table at Cobham next week - John Terry doesn't go to the national team, Diego Costa doesn't go, Ramires doesn't go. Ask them. If they tell you they don't trust me, that is the only thing that can make me resign. The only thing. But not fake sources. The players at the table."

Mourinho had already confessed a week earlier that he was experiencing the "worst period and results" in his managerial career, while Terry was happy enough to the defend his under-siege boss over the weekend despite being phased out by him. Terry said: "I have been here a long time and I have seen managers come and go and if anyone is going to get us out of this hole it is going to be José Mourinho."

Gary Cahill believed it too, well, at least publicly as he commented while away with the England squad. "(The statement) is important," he said. "I think everybody knows the situation we're in at the moment. It has been a very, very difficult start. The Southampton game, for me personally, was a real low and I've come away here totally determined to make that right when I come back. That's the kind of attitude I've got towards it all and I am sure my other teammates are probably feeling the same - pure determination to turn it around and make sure that when we have the good times again, they're even sweeter because of what we've been through. I think that's important. I think in terms of backing the manager, of course we all back him, of course we are all around him. Dare I say, he doesn't even need backing. When you've done so much in the game, got the CV and been through everything that he has been, not just in this league or what he has done for Chelsea but in other leagues. I don't even think he needs backing, but obviously it is nice to have that and he has certainly got that from the players and the club."

At the beginning of November came a hugely significant result for Mourinho to create a renewed credibility rush as he put the clubs Champions League campaign back on track.

While Chelsea continued to survive in the Champions League, their season was being held together by the glue that this elitist competition can provide. The knock on effect was a compelling reason to shelve discussions on the manager's future.

It seemed to me, at least, inconceivable that Chelsea could contemplate sacking their manager while they remained in this competition, and funnily enough working on my football website zapsportz.com with Glenn Hoddle, the former Chelsea manager, I was confidently predicting that provided they could get through the group, they might just come good in March and be the Premier League's main hope in the Champions League. The impetus that would provide could yet propel them on a run of results in the Premier League that would make it possible to sneak into the top four.

An emotional Mourinho praised the show of support by Chelsea's fans, claiming "this is my moment" as his team beat Dynamo Kiev for a second win in nine matches. Willian curled in a stunning winning goal, his fifth free-kick of the season, seven minutes from time as Chelsea moved above Kiev into second place in Group G.

The temperamental and tempestuous Mourinho drew huge encouragement as his name was chanted regularly by the majority inside Stamford Bridge. After less than cooperative post-match appearances in recent weeks, Mourinho was effusive, as he spoke in his post-match conference of his deep and sincere gratitude to the fans for sticking with him.

"What the fans did for me is not normal or they don't read papers, listen to television, pundits and commentators - or they have a big heart or they recognise that I am a good professional that gives everything to the club," Mourinho told BT Sport. "I brought great moments for the club and they have a great memory. But it's not normal for such support - with not just such a bad run of results but fundamentally due to what people read in newspapers, listen to on television - and I don't know how to thank them. The only thing I can say is that until my last day with this club - be it four years, 10 years, 15 years it doesn't matter how long, I will give everything for them. To have the whole stadium supporting me in a difficult time is an unforgettable moment in my career," he said. "When I came back to the club and we played the first match at home against Hull City, the way the stadium welcomed me was amazing. But not comparable to today. Today came in a moment where the results have not been good. It comes in a moment where people are asking for my 'end'. The fans read newspapers. They watch television. They listen to pundits, commentators, opinions, read blogs, and this was quite unbelievable what they tried to say today. They tried to say: 'We want you here.' And, probably, they want to say: 'All of you, let him work. We want him. Let him work.' It was fantastic. The players showed they wanted to win. Today they did. Last week, no, but they showed again they wanted to win. And the fans showed their passion for the club. Fundamentally, that's what they showed. Passion for the club. And then to support the club's manager, that's a way to show respect and passion for the club. Amazing, really. With Chelsea, I think this is my moment. It was amazing. The club should be proud of their fans. I can only thank them by giving everything I have, to thank them for this reaction. To win after conceding a goal with 15 minutes to go, it's important…it's something I spoke about with the players. 'When the difficult moment arrives,' I said to them, 'face the difficult moment. Don't collapse. Keep the belief.' The fans recognise I'm a good pro and have brought them great memories."

The significance of the tie was that Mourinho was watched by his family from just behind the dugout. It was a demonstration of family unity, of those closest to him, acknowledging the strain, and his determination to put it right and to survive.

The manner of the win was also grounds for encouragement, to silence the hawks within the Abramovich inner circle who would have wanted Mourinho out.

Mourinho had seen his side collapse in similar situations as Aleksandar Dragovic conjured a late equaliser. Chelsea wilted against Southampton and Liverpool, but not this time, and that gave Mourinho enormous grounds with which to convince Abramovich that a revival was in sight; something Mourinho was cock sure he could engineer given time, but this is an industry where time and patience is always in short supply.

"I was impressed when I saw Liverpool at Anfield, when we beat them 4-1 (in October 2005) and, in the last 10 minutes, Anfield was singing for that team," added Mourinho. "In good moments you see the streets full of people celebrating in a buzz, and it's easy for kids to go to school in a Chelsea shirt when Chelsea win every match. But it's not easy for 10- or 12-year-old kids to go to school with a Chelsea shirt when Chelsea are losing matches, when probably they are bullied by other kids whose teams are winning. The win is a big relief. To qualify, we didn't need a win. So, at 1-1, it was not a drama. But, from a mental point of view, it was important to provide a reaction to a negative moment. In other matches we've played well, but when a negative moment arrived the team felt it too much, and it was difficult to emerge again in the game, to have control in the game. The team was strong mentally and kept trying, and I'm happy with that."

On the back of the result against Kiev, the manager thought much the same as Glenn Hoddle, that his position was secure while he continued to make headway in the Champions League, and that a string of results in the league to propel the team back into the top four was not out of the question.

There was "no chance" of him leaving, according to his agent Jorge Mendes, even though still 15th in the Premier League. Mourinho's side had leapt to second in Group G, and despite six domestic league losses in 11 games and a stadium ban coming up for their next outing at Stoke, there was certainly a feeling that there was a turning point in sight.

The omnipotent manager's representative Mendes was confident his high profile managerial client could turn it around. "He doesn't need to prove anything to anybody," Mendes told BBC Sport. "He knows what to do. Many people are saying these things but there is no chance (he will leave). He will solve the problem. He is the best."

Again that statement smacked of being approved by Mourinho, or at least Mourinho knew that Mendez intended to speak out on his behalf. This was another indicator that Mourinho knew he was under intense pressure and the slightest thing might tip the balance against him.

But the feel good factor wasn't to last very long.

The shock home defeat to promoted Bournemouth, who were deep in a relegation fight themselves, was Chelsea's eighth in the Premier League, bringing to an abrupt end a recent improvement in results. Not surprisingly, reports in the media were again gathering pace that Mourinho's job was under threat if they failed to progress in the Champions League, despite a vote of confidence from the board back in October. The media have never been fooled by such votes of confidence. Abramovich would not have been pleased at how badly wrong that vote of confidence had gone.

Around this time Bobby Campbell had been taken seriously ill and soon died of cancer. Bobby was a dear friend of mine, and, give him his due, never leaked a single piece of information to me as he stayed rock solid loyal to Abramovich. Bobby was a former Chelsea manager who craved a foot hold back in the game, and we worked together on a football legends project along with Glenn Hoddle. He had met Abramovich by chance in the Chelsea gym and forged what seemed an unlikely friendship; the abrasive Liverpudlian became a trusted member of the Abramovich elite inner circle.

"If I told you want I know, I'd have to kill you", he often told me, and anyone else, with one of his huge deep throat chuckles.

However, knowing his football philosophy inside out and knowing the man on a personal level, I know for sure that he would have advised Abramovich against sacking Mourinho for a second time. He would have recommended allowing the team, at least, to have run their course in the Champions League and, possibly, the FA Cup too.

Old school was Bobby, very much in the mould of Sir Alex Ferguson, whom he knew very well.

Sir Alex commented that Chelsea would be sacking "one of the best coaches of all time" if they got rid of Mourinho, and I am convinced Bobby Campbell would have shared this view.

Sir Alex said: "(Roman Abramovich) has sacked so many coaches in the last 10 years that I am sure he has learned by it. He has to trust and have confidence José can turn around. There is no point in sacking one of the best coaches of all time, he's won the European Cup twice, he's won the league in each country he's managed in, he's won the big trophies."

Mourinho suffered a stadium ban in November, but the wily old fox Fergie believed his old rival had recovered his cool and was close to reviving Chelsea's season. Speaking at the TechCrunch Disrupt London event, he said: "I have been watching José recently and spoken to him a couple of times, and this is the first time he has been confronted with non-success. If you look at his whole career there has been nothing but a rise all of the time so for the first time in his life he has had to deal with bad publicity, adversity and that is a challenge for him, but there are signs he is getting back to a balanced level although they lost on Saturday. I watched the match on Saturday and they could have won by a few goals, but they lost and then he has still has to face that sort of negative publicity and it is never easy for a manager in present-day football because the media attention is huge. Football today is such a big financial industry, the television deal is (worth) billions, there is the press involvement, there is pressure from their own fans, it is a very high risk industry today. The sort of average time a manager lasts now is a year throughout the whole country and that is not a big time. For José, I think all good leaders will eventually find a solution. I think he will find a solution and will get back to normal (but it) is not looking great at the moment. But I know the guy and I know the work he has done in football and I can't see it lasting long, I can't see it."

Despite wise words form Sir Alex, there were forces within the camp that wanted Mourinho out.

Once again the whispering campaign came from those who were getting it in the neck from Mourinho behind the scenes and were happy to put the knife in, while there were those even closer to Mourinho who never wanted him re-hired in the first place.

Mourinho could emulate Roberto di Matteo and win the Champions League while failing to make the top four, but there was now a feeling that it was time to bring down the curtain on the Chelsea career of their greatest ever manager.

Mourinho misjudged the mood when he publicly declared in a press conference that Abramovich would not "change with the wind" and would stick by him, despite being 14th, having lost eight of their 15 Premier League matches, had yet to clinch Champions League last-16 qualification and were out of the League Cup.

Asked why he would be retained, Mourinho said: "Because I think I did lots of good things for this club. I don't think the owner is a person to change with the wind. Abramovich believed in me twice: one, when he brought me back to the club, and the second time when he gave me a new four-year contract in the summer. I know the wind of results is an important wind and I know this wind is really strong because the results in the Premier League are really bad."

Mourinho was speaking at the news conference previewing the Champions League match against Porto. The club had to avoid defeat to confirm their place in the last 16. It was crunch time, no more margin for error as they went into the match on the back of that surprise home defeat by Bournemouth and before meeting league leaders Leicester on the Monday.

It was confidently reported that Mourinho could be sacked if Chelsea lost their next two games.

Yet, Chelsea forgot their domestic woes by easing into the Champions League knockout stage with a victory over Porto enjoying some luck, for a change, for the opener as Diego Costa's low shot was saved by Porto keeper Iker Casillas and rebounded in off Iván Marcano.

Porto, needing to win to join Chelsea in the last 16, but Mourinho's defence looked far more solid.

Willian ensured Chelsea advanced as Group G winners by thumping in a rising shot from 20 yards after the break. Eden Hazard struck the post from a tight angle, while recalled striker Costa wasted two clear opportunities as Chelsea threatened a third

Mourinho insisted before the match that he retained the unwavering support of Abramovich, and winning their group meant Chelsea avoided Barcelona, Real Madrid and Bayern Munich giving the club every chance to progress toward the Final.

Mourinho was able to restore Terry following injury but, more significantly, summoned Costa back after leaving him on the bench against Tottenham and Bournemouth. Costa drew the save from Casillas which led to Chelsea's opener and linked up neatly with Hazard for Chelsea's second, holding up the ball to bring in the Belgian, who played in Willian for his seventh goal of the season. Costa failed to score himself and was bundled over by defender Danilo when clean through in the final 15 minutes. He received a standing ovation when he was replaced in the final few minutes - and a warm embrace from Mourinho.

Porto, who were second in the Primeira Liga, arrived with 10 wins in their previous 12 matches, Julen Lopetegui's side had only lost once in 19 matches during the season, and beat Chelsea 2-1 in September's reverse fixture.

As you are only as good as your last game, last result, the Porto tie had bought him valuable time.

Chelsea then travelled to Leicester, 17 points behind them. The Leicester City coach, Claudio Ranieri, had been sacked by Abramovich whilst at Chelsea. The Russian owner had instead wanted the new kid on the block, Mourinho, to replace him; his attention being drawn to the young José's incredible Champions League exploits at Porto. Ranieri had gone into the semi-final clash with Monaco knowing he was already a 'Dead Man Walking' and his tactical tinkering was, in part, responsible for Chelsea's shock defeat.

Now Mourinho's very survival depended on getting a decent result at high-flying Leicester, the surprise team of the season but, arguably, no bigger a surprise than Chelsea, who were in an embarrassing position just above relegation. It was a lively build up as the media refused to give up their belief that the manager would be fired if they lost to Ranieri's team.

Mourinho's terse exchange with a journalist:

Journalist: "If you lose your next game at Leicester, do you expect to lose your job?"

Mourinho: "There are no ifs. I win, or draw, or lose."

Journalist: "But what about..."

Mourinho: "You are a pessimist guy, I am an optimist guy."

Journalist: "Let's say you lose, if that happens do you expect to lose your job?"

Mourinho: "There are no ifs."

When Leicester returned to the top of the Premier League with victory over Chelsea at the King Power Stadium, Abramovich's patience snapped.

Jamie Vardy's 15th goal of the season put Leicester ahead before half-time and Riyad Mahrez's brilliant curling strike just after the break sealed the win. Substitute Loic Remy pulled one back, but Leicester survived in relative comfort to move back ahead of Manchester City at the top of the table.

The reigning Premier League champions, in contrast, were just a point off the relegation zone in 16th place.

The pace and movement of Vardy and Mahrez exposed John Terry in the style that had troubled so many teams on Leicester's remarkable rise to the top, but this was the champions playing like chumps.

Terry replaced by Cesc Fabregas after only 53 minutes was a sign of the times. Terry had been a magnificent servant for Chelsea, but the aging captain, who turned 35 on 7 December, looked like he had run his race. Mourinho recognised as much when Chelsea bid £40m for Everton's John Stones, only to be met with resistance at Goodison Park. One of the key reasons for the current position could be traced back to the failure to sign Stones and secure the back line, plus the sale of Petr Cech and the early injury to Courtois. Terry, making his way to the bench so early on in the second half, emphasised Chelsea's defensive plight.

Ranieri's side were buzzing, high on confidence and adrenalin, the reigning champions fearful and tentative. Seven months earlier Chelsea were crowned champions and Leicester were pulling off a remarkable escape from relegation. Leicester's best start to a top-flight season in their 132-year history, compared to Chelsea's worst ever as defending champions. This was Mourinho's ninth defeat in the Premier League this season - the same number as in 2013-14 (6) and 2014-15 (3) combined. Chelsea lost 9+ of their opening 16 top-flight games for the first time since 1978-79, a season in which they were relegated. Ninety-six teams have gained 15 points or fewer from their opening 16 games,

50 were relegated and the average finishing position of those 96 teams was 17th. The stats were powerful ammunition with which to fire the bullet at Mourinho's head.

Not long after, it was announced in Germany that Pep Guardiola was leaving Bayern Munich at the end of the season. His destination was obvious: Manchester City.

Chelsea's loss is now Manchester United's gain, and let battle commence in Manchester, the Premier League and Europe: José v Pep.

Chapter 2

THE APPOINTMENT

The not too unexpected email popped into my inbox. Not long after Manchester City had hired Pep Guardiola, Manchester United acted to ensure they weren't left in the shadows of Manchester football, let alone European and world football.

While Pep Guardiola was a momentous signing for City, United trumped them with José Mourinho. The appointment of Mourinho to succeed Louis Van Gaal, who in turn took over from David Moyes, has given the United faithful their belief back.

Press Release:

27 May 2016

José Mourinho appointed manager of Manchester United

Portuguese coach has won 22 trophies since 2003.

José Mourinho will take over as manager of Manchester United from the 2016-17 season, signing a three year contract with an option to stay at the Club until at least 2020.

José, 53, has managed at the top level of European football for over a decade and in that time has won league titles and cups in four countries (Portugal, England, Italy and Spain), as well as winning the UEFA Champions League twice - in 2004 with FC Porto and in 2010 with Inter Milan.

Announcing the appointment, Manchester United executive vice-chairman, Ed Woodward, said: "José is quite simply the best manager in the game today.

He has won trophies and inspired players in countries across Europe and, of course, he knows the Premier League very well, having won three titles here. I'd like to take this opportunity to welcome him to Manchester United. His track record of success is ideal to take the Club forward."

José Mourinho added: "To become Manchester United manager is a special honour in the game. It is a club known and admired throughout the world. There is a mystique and a romance about it which no other club can match. I have always felt an affinity with Old Trafford; it has hosted some important memories for me in my career and I have always enjoyed a rapport with the United fans. I'm looking forward to being their manager and enjoying their magnificent support in the coming years."

José Mourinho GOIH:

Full name: José Mário dos Santos Mourinho Félix

Date of birth: 26 January 1963

Place of birth: Setúbal, Portugal

Playing position: Central midfielder

Honour: GOIH - Grande Oficial, Ordem do Infante Dom Henrique (Portuguese Knighthood), 2005

Playing Career:

Years	Team	Apps	(Goals)
1980-1982	Rio Ave	16	(2)
1982-1983	Belenenses	16	(2)
1983-1985	Sesimbra	35	(1)
1985-1987	Comércio e Indústria	27	(8)

Managerial Career:

Years	Team
2000	Benfica
2001-2002	Leiria
2002-2004	FC Porto (win percentage 71.65%)
2004-2007	Chelsea (67.03%)

2008-2010	Internazionale (62.04%)
2010-2013	Real Madrid (71.91%)
2013-2015	Chelsea (58.82%)
2016-	Manchester United

José Mourinho has indicated that he was born to be a manager and has no regrets about not making it at the highest-level as a player.

Widely regarded as one of the finest coaches to have graced the game, Mourinho played for Portuguese sides Rio Ave, Belenenses and Sesimbra but ended his playing career in his mid-twenties and began focusing on management.

Speaking with comedian David Baddiel for the Radio Times, asked whether he tried to make it as a player, the then Chelsea manager said: "I didn't try. As every young kid likes football, I don't think at ten years old a kid wants to be a manager. A kid wants to be a player. The feeling I was getting was that I can play - at the professional level. Low level, second division. But that's not what I was born for."

By 23, he had realised his limits as a player. "I'm an intelligent person. I knew I was not going to go any higher. The second division was my level."

Having retired from the playing side of the game in his twenties - just as Brian Clough had (albeit due to an injury), another managerial legend - Mourinho was asked whether failing to make it as a player spurred him onto become a great manager.

Unequivocal in his response, the former Real Madrid and Inter Milan manager said: "No. I never felt that. I never felt any kind of frustration for not be a… no, never, never."

Trophies won:

Porto:

Primeira Liga: 2002-03, 2003-04

Portuguese Super Cup: 2003

UEFA Champions League: 2003-04

UEFA Cup: 2002-03

Chelsea:

Premier League: 2004-05, 2005-06, 2014-15

FA Cup: 2006-07

Football League Cup: 2004-05, 2006-07, 2014-15

FA Community Shield: 2005

Inter Milan:

Serie A: 2008-09, 2009-10

Coppa Italia: 2009-10

Italian Super Cup: 2008

UEFA Champions League: 2009-10

Real Madrid:

La Liga: 2011-12

Copa del Rey: 2010-11

Spanish Super Cup: 2012

José Mourinho is a headline waiting to happen, and it has indeed happened many times in the past but, arguably, nothing compared to his dramatic return to the Premier League with Manchester United.

It created a whirlwind on social media and generated more column inches than even Mourinho himself had managed in the past.

Associated with Chelsea for so long where the fans idolised him to the extent that they sang his name louder and more often than any of the superstars who passed through the Bridge under his command. While he was welcomed with glee in the red half of Manchester to counter the imminent arrival of Pep Guardiola at City, there were Chelsea fans left broken hearted.

The little old lady who lives nearby in the flats, whom I meet most mornings on her way to Waitrose, looked most definitely a broken hearted Chelsea fan as she told me: "I won't be able to stand it next season, I cannot believe what has happened."

My wife Linda is a true life-long Blue, hence our house is called Bridge House, and has very similar sentiments.

#WelcomeJosé:

Twitter users were gripped as the drama unfolded at The Theatre of Dreams. So much so in fact that, according to figures provided by the social media site, discussion around the managerial change at Old Trafford had generated more than six million tweets in only two weeks. Half a million tweets came in the hours following United's confirmation of their new manager, with a peak of 6,200 tweets per minute as the news broke.

The anticipation of Mourinho's arrival at Old Trafford had been ongoing for as long as everyone knew that Pep Guardiola was heading for the Etihad.

It was the worst kept secret that Pep was replacing Manuel Pellegrini, as indeed it had been speculated for almost as many months that Mourinho would be heading to Old Trafford.

A vacuum had been created during the days when it was clear that Louis van Gaal was out and Mourinho was in. Lengthy discussions were going on with all the usual peripheral figures normally associated with this type of deal; an army of lawyers, accountants and agents. It was widely assumed to be about loose ends in the contract negotiations. But, these issues are sorted out by the middlemen and advisors months beforehand.

So, new speculation centred around Chelsea still owning the "Mourinho" name as a trademark and whether Roman Abramovich's club were demanding a six-figure sum from United before any deal was concluded, something that remained high on the agenda for 48 hours, but later dismissed as a red herring.

In reality the deal to bring Mourinho to Old Trafford was largely complete, but discussions between his agent, Jorge Mendes, and United officials entered a third day and media agendas had to be filled with something to while away the time.

But it made for an interesting side show, as it was aired that Chelsea registered 'José Mourinho' and his signature as a European trademark in 2005, to use it to sell merchandise such as toiletries, technology, clothing and jewellery. Yet, it didn't really add up as Mourinho had managed both Inter Milan and Real Madrid since the trademark had been registered; a big hint here that this really was not much of an insurmountable problem at all, whether in fact it even had been an issue at all.

Despite the complexities of Mourinho's commercial agreements with the likes of Jaguar and Hublot Watches, which could potentially clash with United's deals with General Motors and Bulova (watches), and the manager's image rights being held by Chelsea, Woodward and the manager's agent Jorge Mendes unpicked the off-field complications of Mourinho's personal portfolio of sponsorship deals long before when first finalising his package with United, so the holdup was not to do with image rights and Chelsea owning the Mourinho trademark name.

Ironically, it was Jaguar who first broke the news of Mourinho's appointment hours ahead of the official club announcement, although they had to embarrassingly delete the tweet.

Jaguar UK: - "Congratulations to José Mourinho on his @ManUtd appointment. He'll always be #TheFrozenOne to us."

Other brands were falling over themselves to welcome José Mourinho back to the Premier League:

BT Sport Football: "Welcome back to the @premierleague, José. We'll see you on @btsport next season."

NOW TV Sport: "What will José Mourinho call himself in his first #MUFC press conference?#WelcomeJosé

6% The Grumpy One, 4% The Angry One, 31% The Handsome One, 59% The 'Not Van Gaal' One"

Rightmove: "Found this one for you José!
http://www.rightmove.co.uk/property-for-sale/… #WelcomeJosé
#ManchesterUnited"

Ryanair: "Special fares from Manchester. £9.99 - one-way José #JoséMourinho #WelcomeJosé #Mourinho"

Soon his first interview, carefully choreographed on the club's internal TV station MUTV, was released to the media. No possibility of any accidental or enforced bloomers with the in-house station making sure Mourinho would be word perfect. His unveiling at the Bridge in 2004 witnessed Mourinho coming out with 'The Special One' line that has stuck with him ever since. On this occasion, however, his media debut was totally controlled, so no slip ups or one liners that could come back to haunt him.

But, nonetheless, it was riveting stuff from the old maestro, who had clearly regained his mojo after the calamitous goings on at the Bridge that precipitated his departure from Chelsea at the turn of the year. Mourinho called on his new players to erase the memories of the last three years and restore a 'giant club' to its former glories. So much for Moyes and Van Gaal then!

He signed a four-year contract, with the option to cut ties after three years, but in reality management was no longer going to see the likes of Sir Alex, Wenger at Arsenal, and even Moyes at Everton again. It was a couple of days earlier that the League Managers' Association released their usual fascinating statistics showing that the average life span of a manager these days in English football was 1.3 years. The £10m-a-year, contract was double the £5m-a-year paid to his predecessor. He will also secure bonuses of £5m and £2.5m respectively if he guides United to the Champions League and Premier League titles during the length of his contract.

United won their first trophy since Sir Alex's retirement in 2013 by bringing home the FA Cup but both David Moyes and Louis van Gaal paid with their jobs for a lack of major success. The FA Cup was enough to fill Van Gaal with pride, albeit for a precious small amount of time before it became apparent it was insufficient to save him from the axe.

But let's be fair, the FA Cup no longer carries the status or significance it once did. I was around when Manchester United were the first club to question the FA Cup's position in world football when they abandoned the Cup to controversially participate in the World Club Championships in Rio, which I travelled to with the team, and was bitterly opposed to at the time in my capacity as chief football writer at the Daily Mirror. The FA Cup was worth fighting for then, and I still do believe it is now, but it won't carry the proper weight until the winners gain automatic qualification for the Champions League which the Premier League are adamant won't happen. I agree with Van Gaal that the FA Cup makes you a champion, but not in the modern game where the Champions League is the Holy Grail and the FA Cup and other domestic cups are relegated in importance.

Therefore had Van Gaal not failed to gain that elusive fourth spot and also win the FA Cup, it might have proved more difficult to jettison him with one year left on his contract. The fact that Mourinho was available, though, was also virtually impossible to ignore.

The sub-plot, of course, was that Mourinho and Van Gaal worked together at Barcelona from 1997 but that has not stopped the new boss looking to rewrite the recent history books to erase the memory of his former colleague.

Mourinho, a winner of three Premier League titles, is determined to bring back the regular silverware that United fans were so accustomed to in the past. "We can look at our club now in two perspectives," Mourinho told MUTV. "One perspective is the past three years, and another prospective is the club's history. I prefer to forget the last three years. I prefer to focus on the giant club I have in my hands now and I think what the fans are expecting me to say is that I want to win. I think what the players need to listen to is I want to win. And more than that I need the supporters and the players to feel that I say that, not just for the sake of saying it, but because I think we really can. I want to focus on the history of this giant club and give what I have and what I don't have, so I will give absolutely everything to try to go in the direction we all want."

MUTV asked: "You seem to have had a good rapport with Manchester United fans when you've come back with Inter Milan, Real Madrid, with Chelsea, with charity games. What is your message to United fans?"

Mourinho replied: "I know what they can give me I think also they know what I can give them. Obviously the most important thing is the players and the relationship with them. It's very important and curious that I play so many times against Man United and I play so many times at Old Trafford with other clubs and there was empathy, no problems, and in fact I was pushed by that feeling to say things sometimes that my clubs were not happy with. I remember for example when I won at Old Trafford with Real Madrid, I said that the best team lost and not many people were happy at Real Madrid."

Mourinho is planning a summer full of transfer activity with the former Chelsea manager being handed £200million to spend in his bid to create a squad able to challenge for the title. He was initially linked with a number of big name players, and while he won't get them all, it was clear that he had been planning a complete overhaul of his team, notably right through the spine to create his new look United.

That spree could include moves for Zlatan Ibrahimović, John Stones, Henrikh Mkhitaryan, Nemanja Matić and possibly former United player, Paul Pogba.

But after the initial excitement of the unveiling his main focus was on a return to the action he had so badly missed since his Stamford Bridge sacking in December. "I feel great, I think I'm in the right moment of my career because Manchester United is one of these clubs you need to be prepared for, because it's a giant club," the 53-year-old said. "Giant clubs must be for the best managers. I think I am ready for it so I could say I'm happy, I'm proud, I'm honoured, I'm everything, but the reality is that what I love is to work and I cannot wait for July 7 to go on the pitch."

Mourinho was already eagerly working towards taking charge of United for the first time when the club face Borussia Dortmund in Shanghai on July 22 on the first leg of a two game tour of China. Ahead of that, though, he was due to sit in the Old Trafford home dugout on June 5 for the biennial Soccer Aid charity match, supporting UNICEF.

Chapter 3

THE REACTION

José's wife, Matilde, and son, José, gave insights into the new United boss's home life as they uploaded pictures of his office onto their Twitter accounts, which included a Manchester United home shirt draped over his chair - captioned as "Mourinho is a Red Devil."

The 53-year-old boss also took to Instagram on the day of his appointment, to post the message: "Manchester United Football Club, Old Trafford, The Theatre Of Dreams" alongside a photograph of his service agreement.

Mourinho Jnr. is a 16-year-old footballing scholar at Fulham, while Angola-born Matilde met the United manager when they were teenagers in Setubal, Portugal, and the couple married in 1989; their first child, daughter Matilde, was born in 1996.

Their photographs could have been taken at Mourinho's central London home, where he was spotted wearing a grey t-shirt earlier in the week of his appointment. Storage boxes were photographed being moved outside the house.

Mourinho was also pictured returning home the day before the big announcement, when everyone knew it was a done deal, carrying a bag from 'Hedonism Wines' located in Mayfair. Mourinho is a wine enthusiast and had a tradition with Sir Alex of sharing a glass of red after their teams played each other. Once he gifted a bottle to the Scot who described it as 'paint-stripper', but made amends by sending over a bottle of Portugal's finest wine.

After days of walking around looking like a scruff, he was pictured in a dark suit, white shirt and patterned tie as he left his house in the capital, carrying a small leather folder as he got into the passenger side of a Range Rover, parked outside his home, alongside a driver. There was little doubt he was studying the small print of the three-year deal worth around £45million.

Michael Carrick welcomed the arrival of serial winner Mourinho. The vastly experienced midfielder hoped the Old Trafford side can claim trophies under their new boss playing the sort of football for which the club has been synonymous down the years, but winning is all that matters. Mourinho's winning mentality will bring the glory days back to Old Trafford after just one trophy in the last three years. Asked for his reaction to Mourinho's appointment, Carrick told Sky Sports News: "His track record speaks for itself. I think it's a good fit. It's about winning at the end of the day. I know there's a lot of talk about styles and playing this way or that way. But it's about winning, it's about being No. 1. It's about winning trophies and if we can do that with a bit of style and a bit of flair then obviously that's the perfect match. But first and foremost it's about winning and getting back on top."

Carrick would like Mourinho to bring back the Sir Alex style of success but accepts life will be very different. "There is going to be change without a doubt," Carrick added, speaking at the Monaco Grand Prix. "He is coming in and he's his own man. He's got an unbelievable track record. Everyone is looking for quick results and that's how it is. I'm not sure exactly on the situation of who he's bringing in or anything like that just yet. We'll have to wait and see on that one."

Carrick hoped the Wembley victory can be the start of United returning to past glories. "For the players, for the backroom staff and for the whole club it (the FA Cup) was a massive stepping stone. We hadn't won anything for three years and you don't want that to carry on for too long. We were desperate to win something. After assembling the new squad over the last two or three years, you want that trophy to give everyone that feeling (of success). Hopefully that feeling will drive everyone on and we can win a lot more in the future."

Mourinho was expected to undertake a major overhaul of his squad, but despite being out of contract, Carrick was keen to stay, having been at United since joining from Spurs in 2006. "I'm hopeful. There's no news as yet but we'll have to wait and see what happens next week. I haven't got a timescale on it to be honest. This week has been a bit crazy with the new manager so I've come away to get away from it. We'll take it up next week."

Even before Mourinho's arrival was officially signed and sealed the probable outcome was welcomed by Bastian Schweinsteiger - the former Bayern Munich midfielder signed by Van Gaal last summer. Schweinsteiger, on international duty with Germany, claimed it will be "special" to play under Mourinho at Old Trafford. "Should Mourinho join Manchester United, I believe everyone would love to be coached by Mourinho," Schweinsteiger said. "Then it will be something special."

Manchester United legend Eric Cantona had just turned 50. He still symbolised United - flair, flamboyance, silverware, and excitement. "They miss me," Cantona observed, "I think they have lost something. You can feel it. But it's difficult to come after someone who has been at the club 25 years. Even if you are a great manager, the fans still feel the philosophy of Ferguson."

King Cantona didn't mince his words either about José. Wrong manager. Wrong club.

"I love José Mourinho, but in terms of the type of football he plays I don't think he is Manchester United. I love his personality, I love the passion he has for the game, his humour. He is very intelligent, he demands 100% of his players. And of course he wins things. But I don't think it's the type of football that the fans of Manchester United will love, even if they win. He can win with Manchester United. But do they expect that type of football, even if they win? I don't think so."

Cantona added, "Guardiola was the one to take. He is the spiritual son of Johan Cruyff. I would have loved to have seen Guardiola in Manchester (United). He is the only one to change Manchester. He is in Manchester, but at the wrong one."

Cantona would be open to an unlikely return to Old Trafford - but only as manager. "I do many things and I'm very happy. But if they asked me to become the manager of Manchester United, I would. Because Guardiola is in Manchester City and they want someone to win things with wonderful football? It's me."

Is he serious: "Yes, I'm serious. I say that just because it's like when you are in the pub or the club. When you say you don't care, all the girls want you. Maybe if I say I don't care about that job, they will ask me. If they asked me I'd work very hard, of course."

Conversely, Paul Scholes backed Mourinho to bring attacking football to Manchester United.

Former United midfielder Scholes, who was an outspoken critic of Louis van Gaal to the point where the former manager was riled by his comments, made a prediction about the type of football that the Red Devils will play under their new manager. "He will bring a style of play that will entertain," Scholes told BBC Sport, "He's done it before at Real Madrid and Chelsea."

Mourinho won three Premier League titles, two FA Cups and three League Cups during two spells at the west London club.

I made the point in my interviews that you never heard a peep out of Scholes when he was a player but couldn't shut him up now he turned pundit!

Scholes joked that Mourinho had now joined "a proper football club". Scholes, who played for Man United between 1991 and 2013, claimed that Mourinho's "track record of winning trophies" will restore a winning mentality to the Red Devils. "Who knows? We all thought Van Gaal was a good fit two years ago and it didn't quite happen for him. Mourinho has obviously managed big clubs before. Now he has come to a proper big club and there is expectation there," Scholes told talkSPORT. "He has messed around with these Mickey Mouse clubs - Real Madrid, Chelsea and Inter Milan - and now it looks like he is coming to a proper football club. I'm only joking, of course! He has managed big clubs and he has got a track record of winning trophies. United should be challenging for trophies but it is the style of football that has been the big problem for the last two years and if he can get players in that are likely to entertain then the fans will be happy."

David de Gea believes Mourinho can lead United back to the English summit. "I came to United to win trophies. It is true these last two years we have not been at the level the club deserves," De Gea told Spain's premier radio network, Cadena Ser. "We hope that Mourinho, with his will to win, will make sure United return to the top. I have not spoken with Mourinho and not asked team-mates about him. I think we already know him. At United we've missed a manager like Mourinho. With the personality and mindset of a winner. Getting him was right."

Mourinho was described as "really irritating" by former club captain Roy Keane, who admits he isn't a big fan of the 'Special One'. He told ITV: "He is not my cup of tea. I found him really irritating when I coached against him, but that is just a personal thing. Working at Manchester United is all about winning and his CV will tell you he is a winner. He was always going to be a good option when United didn't qualify for the Champions League. He was available, fantastic CV and it seems like a good fit, but maybe he is not for me."

Out-of-contract Paris Saint-Germain striker Zlatan Ibrahimović is a signing Keane would be in favour of. "I think he would be a good signing on a one-year deal. He is a big player, a big character. I have said that United have been lacking a few characters and he would be a good fit there."

Roy Keane gave a ringing endorsement of Mourinho's decision to want a player of such high profile as Ibrahimović, the player he was plotting to stop in the Euros. "Of course he is a good fit for United, he's a good player," said Keane, drawing a likeness to Cantona. "They're big characters, clearly, whatever you say about Cantona, he was a popular lad, and I get the impression Zlatan is the same. Whatever about his playing career you hear from his team-mates he seems to be a bit of a character, and you can see that in the way he plays. It's good to see that, because there's a lack of characters out there, and he certainly is that. On top of all that, he's a very, very good player."

In 2006, while working as a pundit at the World Cup in Germany, Martin O'Neill tried to quell the hype around the match-winning striker. "Good grief, he is the most overrated player on the planet," said O'Neill, who was recently reminded of that at Ireland's Versailles training base. "That was in 2006, wasn't it? That's how many years, 10, a decade, in which someone is likely to improve. He may well have been the most over-rated player in the game at the time but is certainly not now. Some players are allowed to improve in 10 years. I was put right (at the time), don't worry about that, because I spoke to Johan Mjällby and Henrik Larsson (his former Celtic players) who told me regardless that he was a very fine player - and I was prepared to believe them."

Ray Wilkins believes Mourinho will adapt his style to appease the club's supporters.

Wilkins is one of the few to have played for both Manchester United and Chelsea. He believed that if the supporters are to be kept onside at Old Trafford, then Mourinho must produce attacking football.

"He needs to change the way he thinks about his football a little bit. One of the criticisms levelled at Van Gaal was the fact that he was very defensive," Wilkins told Sky Sports Now. He went on: "Possession is fantastic, and Mourinho likes to play that way, but he likes to play with a progression as well. He likes his players to be aggressive, go forward and score. He will change a bit to the way a Manchester United supporter wants them to play and he will bring a winning mentality as well. Wherever he's been he's won. He won't settle for second best."

Wilkins believed Mourinho will prove a perfect fit for United, telling talkSPORT: "I think it is the right move. It is the only move for them. He will get them playing again and he will get them winning again. He is a winner, there are no two ways about it. When he goes to a club, normally he wins a big trophy within the first couple of years."

Bryan Robson thinks Mourinho can work wonders for Wayne Rooney, the forward he tried to sign for Chelsea. Perhaps the biggest question Mourinho will have to answer on his arrival concerns Rooney, uncertain of his place in the team, but also of his best position. Only one goal since February, only eight in the league last season is not the return that Mourinho would accept from his No. 1 striker. Fortunately for England's all-time leading goalscorer, the arrival of Mourinho might be the perfect tonic.

United legend Robbo certainly thinks so, and feels that Mourinho will change how and where Rooney plays to get the best out of him and extend his career and that the England captain could turn out becoming the next Scholes. He told The Sun: "Mourinho's influence will, I am certain, extend Wayne's career. It will definitely get him to the World Cup in Russia as captain. I think Mourinho will look to use Wayne in that deeper-lying Paul Scholes role that he played in towards the end of the season. I am sure that Mourinho will enjoy the way he gets on the ball, and the way he keeps possession. He is more of a creative passer than any of the other United lads and I think Mourinho will be good for Wayne as I think he will get the best out of him. Wayne can really develop in that deeper position, for England and for United, because Mourinho is such a good man-manager. You never see his players come out and criticise him and that's obviously because he tries to get the best out of them."

There are few managers who have been more enthusiastic about Rooney's talent. Mourinho's admiration for Rooney was made public when he moved to Real Madrid. In 2010, when he took over the Spanish side, Rooney was mentioned as a transfer target, and José, while playing down the possibility, expressed his interest. "I would like to coach Rooney but my friend Ferguson can rest easy - it is impossible," he said at the time.

It was the first of several attempts to sign him, the most famous was a public pursuit in 2013, as he made him not just Chelsea's No. 1 transfer target, but at one point their only target. "He is a player I like very much," Mourinho said three years ago. "Being fast and direct, I like that, but he's a Manchester United player." Mourinho was criticised for his repeated pronouncements to the press that he had made a formal bid for Rooney, who in the end decided to renew his contract at United, and on several occasions stressed that "we can't do more than we are doing" to sign the star. When it became clear that the deal was not going to go through, Mourinho claimed "it doesn't bother me at all."

So, José Mourinho now finally has the chance to work with Wayne Rooney, but at the most challenging time for both manager and United captain.

Carlo Ancelotti was promoting the release of his new book as he commented, "I think it is a good wedding (with United) because Mourinho really knows the Premier League well. He is one of the best coaches in the world and Manchester United at this moment need someone who can improve what they did in the last two years with Louis van Gaal. There are different opinions about the job of Van Gaal, no? My opinion is that he arrived in a moment when he needed to rebuild a team after Rio Ferdinand, after Scholes, after Giggs, after Ferguson and it takes time. The same thing happened to Milan. When Milan lost Maldini, Gattuso, Inzaghi it was difficult to rebuild the team quickly, they needed time. The last year they (United) showed they have really good young players. And maybe with Mourinho they could have a step forward."

He agreed that the expectation at United is high, Ancelotti observed, "The expectation at Manchester City is not high? It is high everywhere. The job is difficult but behind this you have the passion…I have a good relationship with Mourinho. (In the past) we had some discussion through newspapers. But I still have a good relationship. I'm not saying we talked every day but sometimes we sent regards through our mutual friends."

He went on: "I think he (Ibrahimović) is not young but still fit. He has a real winning mentality. Maybe Manchester United need this kind of player with experience. They are all young."

John Terry, long-serving Chelsea captain, expected him to make a big impact. "It's fantastic news for Man United," Terry told Sky Sports News. "I'm sure the Man United fans and players will be delighted with that. I've said many times before, he's the best manager I've worked under and a real delight. It's a shame the way he finished at Chelsea this year but I wish him well because he's a great manager and a great man as well, he'll be great for Manchester United I'm sure. I'm sure he'll settle in well with the likes of Ryan Giggs, hopefully he'll stay and support him along with the team. I've come up against José for previous teams before, he'll get a great reception when he comes back to (Stamford) Bridge, for sure, but first and foremost we have to really look at ourselves this year and start fighting for the title again."

Pep Guardiola and Antonio Conte were on their way to the Premier League as Terry said: "I think it's great for English football, not only what Leicester achieved last year with Claudio Ranieri coming in, José and Pep Guardiola up in Manchester, Conte coming to Chelsea as well, there's a real fight amongst the managers. I think it's going to be interesting, not only for football in general but also for the Premier League."

Chelsea icon Frank Lampard believes Mourinho will bring that special charisma Manchester United have been missing. United finished outside of the top four in two of the three seasons since Sir Alex retired, winning only the FA Cup and Lampard believes the Portuguese is exactly what United need. The 37-year-old told The Sun: "José gives them the X factor - he did that at Chelsea. I know it didn't end perfectly there but I can see him succeeding at United. Next season will be as competitive as it has been for a while because a lot of teams have something to prove. But he is a top manager and a team like United need a top manager. It's brilliant for the Premier League that José is back. I had a great experience with him, especially during his first spell at Chelsea because he really helped me take my career onto the next level. I know what he brings to English football." Lampard played 140 Premier League games under Mourinho at Chelsea, winning the Premier League on two occasions.

Cesc Fàbregas named Arsenal manager Arsene Wenger as having had the biggest influence on his career, but he also discussed Mourinho's impact on players, when he told: FourFourTwo: "Working with Mourinho was fantastic. His passion for football, his character, his ambition to always win every three days is not easy. The way he pushes his players to be better every day is what impresses me the most - it was a really fantastic experience."

Niall Quinn believed Mourinho will bring "rock and roll" back to Manchester United.

United were criticised for their unadventurous style under Van Gaal but Quinn felt that Mourinho's appointment will take Manchester United back to the big time. Speaking to Sky Sports News HQ, Quinn said: "There are two ways of looking at it: from a football point of view and the other from the commercial. I think it's rock 'n' roll from a commercial point of view. It will catapult Man United back onto the front stage. They have been quiet for the last few years. From a football decision there is always a doubt about a new manager no matter who it is. This is at the very top and one of the people who has done it for years. But he has to go and do it all again. The past is forgotten about and if he thinks he has been in goldfish bowls before he is really going to be in one now. Will he do it? It's not simple."

Jamie Carragher commented in his Daily Mail column: "Along with plenty of others, I have said for a long time that he doesn't tick every box for United, but there is only one box they want ticking now - the one that says 'trophies'. And they've got the best man for the job for that. In 14 attempts, he's won eight titles across Europe. That's more than a 50 per cent success rate! United had the chance to get him three years ago but went for David Moyes, believing they didn't need Mourinho and the baggage he brings. The argument then was that he was not the right fit for Old Trafford, but what the last three years have shown is that no manager can be what Sir Alex Ferguson was. He was a one-off in the modern game for promoting young players, playing with style and being able to stay out in front."

"The other man to do that was Sir Matt Busby. Both Busby and Ferguson lasted over two decades at the club but they are the only two men in United's history to be successful playing such attacking football. They also promoted youth, Busby with his Babes and Ferguson with his Class of '92. Busby and Ferguson are giants of the game and other United managers tried to bring success - including the likes of Tommy Docherty and Ron Atkinson - but couldn't pull it off. So for all the talk of the 'United way', the achievements were based around two extraordinary managers. Clubs like Barcelona and Ajax bring in managers to suit the club and have ideas of the way they want to play regardless of the manager's CV. Luis Enrique, for instance, was sacked at Roma but has thrived at Barcelona. United thought, when Ferguson left, that they could go down the same path, but it hasn't worked for them. Others have caught up and overtaken them. Moyes was very hard-working but he lacked the positivity and risk-taking that United fans had been used to. Louis van Gaal believed that a combination of a Dutch philosophy and his impressive CV would propel United forward, but it hasn't. Now they've finally turned to José: a man who won't please everyone but a man who won't change his way of playing. And why should he? At times he will strangle a game if he feels the opposition are superior. For prime examples, look at the games between his Real Madrid team and Guardiola's Barcelona. I'm sure José always felt his rival Guardiola had the strongest line-up in those titanic El Clasico battles, so he had an advantage. Pep won five of those 11 clashes, and José just two, but with United's spending power Mourinho will be able to go head to head with his great rival. They are playing on an even playing field - and he will relish that. Also, it is harsh to say Mourinho doesn't play good football. He broke plenty of Premier League records with Chelsea, while Real Madrid outscored Barcelona in two of his three La Liga seasons."

"As for not bringing young players through, if they are top class, he plays them. He played 19-year-old Carlos Alberto in the Champions League final at Porto, he gave a chance to Raphaël Varane at Real Madrid and picked Davide Santon at Inter when he was a teenager. So Marcus Rashford will be fine if he carries on as he is. One man who won't be fine, though, is Guardiola. He left Barcelona for a number of reasons but one of them, I'm sure, is the continual baiting to which he was subjected to by Mourinho in the media. It is inevitable, at some point, that theme will return. Guardiola must be thinking: 'Oh no, not him again.' Mourinho arrives at Old Trafford with a point to prove and, as a Liverpool supporter, it worries me! It should also worry the rest of the Premier League - he is coming back to win."

Fellow Portuguese football coach, José Morais, has been friends with Mourinho for 16 years and worked together for seven at Inter Milan, Real Madrid and Chelsea, collecting league titles in every country and the Champions League in a treble-winning season at Inter. In an interview with the Mail on Sunday, he said: "Mourinho is the kind of person that marks your life. I admired him before we worked together. After working with him, I admire him even more. He has influenced modern football with his vision. Like Rinus Michels and Johan Cruyff, he changed our sport as a coach and manager. And more than this, he is a friend, a special person."

Morais came close to getting the manager's job at Swansea after Mourinho and his back room staff were kicked out by Chelsea, before ending up in Turkey with Antalyaspor.

"If I was the owner of Manchester United, or Arsenal or anyone, I would call him and say these are the keys of my club, do what you have to do for us to be the best in England," says Morais. "And he will do it because he is the best. He can transform a club, the attitude of the players, the mentality. He is a specialist in building a winning organisation. I wouldn't think about hiring someone else."

Morais met Mourinho in 2000 at Benfica, where he was running the reserves when Mourinho was appointed manager. Morais then became inseparable from Mourinho after being appointed his coaching assistant at Inter Milan in 2009. He heard the theory that Mourinho doesn't give youngsters a chance. Morais explains: "I don't believe that Mourinho doesn't like young players. Age doesn't matter if you have the attitude. He looks for people who are willing to give more and more, be at the maximum every day. To be with Mourinho, you are one of these kinds of professionals or probably you are a little bit out because you consider his demands too much and are not able to respond. If you want to be the biggest professional, you will always have a place in his team. This is what he loves. It is what makes champions and he is winning and winning because of the character of the players he likes."

"At Real Madrid, we had Ronaldo, Benzema, Higuain but still Álvaro Morata played in the main team at 18. But in general younger players need more time to get mature than they used to. You can see someone of 20 and think he is a kid still because of his behaviour, and for the top level you need maturity. Some young players are mature though. If Anthony Martial has shown this season he can perform every week, why wouldn't José select him?"

Morais gives further insight into how Mourinho dealt with big-names, "Ronaldo was the most gifted one, a player who really made the difference. And he worked hard every day to take care of himself. He has this mindset, to be the best in the world. Eden Hazard was very, very skilful. The question was to combine effectivity with the fantasy of his game. Look at what Eden Hazard was and what he became one season after working with José at Chelsea, it is unbelievable. John Terry worked really hard. He could play against a striker from the under-19s in training and tackle like it was a Champions League final. There is a secret of managing big stars. You need to know how to communicate with them, to motivate them to do what you want the team to do. You don't have to laugh at all their jokes but sometimes you need to make them feel important, because they really are important."

After years of success, it all went horribly wrong at Chelsea, "I believe we were going to solve things, but if you ask me today do I understand the reasons why results fell away, I don't know. In the same way, do you understand how Leicester became champions? Football is just like that. It probably happens once in your lifetime. But big teams continue to be big teams if they don't win one year. In the same way, big coaches will continue to be big coaches."

As for myself, well, yours truly was much in media demand, billed as Mourinho's official unofficial biographer having written four books about the man. From Radio 5 live, to the Nick Ferrari LBC breakfast show, to Sky News twice, and also BBC World which has a 400 million audience.

Clearly I found him a fascinating character, otherwise I wouldn't have followed his career so intently. Not obsessively I might add, although four books might sound a lot I have actually written nearly 80!

On BBC World, I suggested that Mourinho faced the biggest challenge of his career as the new Manchester United manager which would tell us whether he was still the 'Special One'.

As I pointed out, certainly judging Mourinho on his second coming at Stamford Bridge, he was not as special as he once was when it came to his calamitous defence of the Premier League title.

Now he was been given the chance to manage the biggest club in English football - something he has long aspired to - if not the biggest in the world.

If his reign at Old Trafford should go pear-shaped, it will be his last job in English football.

Speaking on BBC Global News, I also suggested it could be the end of the Old Trafford line, for now at least, for Ryan Giggs. The Manchester United legend was assistant to Louis van Gaal and David Moyes, but will not be afforded that role under Mourinho who brings with him his own number two. "He has to take the decision to go into management and as that's not going to happen at United any time soon, he needs to move on."

I had a little dig at Paul Scholes, the 'Silent One' as a player, but you couldn't stop him now he had metamorphosed into a TV pundit. Scholes predicted Mourinho will bring more exciting football to United. Something lacking under Louis van Gaal. But in order for that to happen, I suggested live on air, they will need to bring in a number of young yet established players.

And one of the new additions I predicted was that the club would make every effort to land Cristiano Ronaldo. "There will be a concerted effort to bring Ronaldo back to Old Trafford. And given that he shares the same agent as Mourinho, there's every chance that will happen."

Chapter 4
THE CONSEQUENCES

The ramifications, the fall outs of the appointment were swift, intense, and headline-grabbing for days, and you knew it wouldn't subside until the day Mourinho leaves Old Trafford.

Louis van Gaal was Mourinho's mentor, they were friends, they text regularly, but now the Dutchman was convinced he had been stabbed in the back by his friend.

Van Gaal was so convinced he was seeing out his contract that he gave players and staff a programme outlining plans for the summer immediately following the FA Cup Final triumph, which emphasises that it was a split decision within the club's hierarchy about appointing José Mourinho.

United's players, however, had heard 'whispers' that Van Gaal was to be replaced by Mourinho as the team celebrated in their Wembley dressing room with the FA Cup on Saturday 21 May. As word filtered through there was a visible downturn in celebrations as players asked discreetly if there was official clarification.

The United party continued at the Corinthia Hotel where they were joined by Sir Alex and his brother Martin but the topic of conversation was dominated by Van Gaal's future rather than the celebration of a record-equalling 12th FA Cup win.

United's board members were conspicuous by their absence and as Van Gaal woke to headlines about Mourinho's pending arrival he gathered his staff together, as already planned, in a pre-breakfast meeting on the Sunday morning. He addressed them all, opening with the fact that as far as he was aware he was still their manager as no one had told him otherwise but expressed disappointment that, for the first time in his career, he was celebrating winning a title without any members of the board being present to share in the celebration.

Van Gaal thanked his staff, praising them for being the best backroom team he had known in his career, as he handed out an itinerary for the summer and said he would see them all soon.

Later on Sunday afternoon Van Gaal received a message from executive vice-chairman Ed Woodward asking to see him at his apartment in Bowdon where it became clear that the rumours were indeed true and he was to be sacked.

Van Gaal arrived at Carrington on the following Monday morning knowing his fate but still wishing to say his goodbyes to the office staff who hadn't travelled to London.

For all his troubles on the pitch, the dignity and warmth he showed to people off it had earned respect from staff and some had to turn away upset as he tearfully told them of his surprise that he was leaving, confirming he had fully expected to stay for another year.

As he cut a lonely figure patrolling Carrington's corridors for the final time, the manner in which he had learned of his demise left many staff, even those players who wished for him to go, feeling sympathy for their former boss. They all felt 'The Iron Tulip' deserved a better ending.

In the official releases, which usually hide a multitude of real emotions, Van Gaal admitted he was "very disappointed" after it was confirmed he had been sacked despite winning the FA Cup, as he ultimately paid the price for failing to secure Champions League football.

Van Gaal paid tribute to Sir Alex Ferguson and Sir Bobby Charlton in a 418-word statement. "It has been an honour to manage such a magnificent club as Manchester United FC, and in doing so, I have fulfilled a long held ambition. I am immensely proud to have helped Manchester United win the FA Cup for the 12th time in the club's history. I have been privileged during my management career to have won 20 trophies but winning the FA Cup, which is steeped in so much history, will always be one of the most special achievements of my career. I am very disappointed to be unable to complete our intended three year plan. I believe that the foundations are firmly in place to enable the club to move forward and achieve even greater success. I hope that winning the FA Cup will give the club a platform to build upon next season to restore the success that this passionate set of fans desire. Having managed in Holland, Spain and Germany, I had always hoped for the opportunity to manage in English football and be part of English culture. Both of these experiences have lived up to expectations and been fantastic. I thank my players and wish them well for next season. It has been a pleasure to work with them and it has been particularly rewarding to see so many young players take their chance to break into the first team and excel. I look forward to watching the continued development of these young players next season. Thank you to the owners and board of Manchester United for giving me the opportunity to manage this great club. I would also like to express my gratitude to the amazing United supporters. They are truly the best fans in the world. I am indebted to my support and coaching staff, who have given me their all during their time at the club. I am deeply grateful to each and every member of the club's staff - the sports science team, the medical team, the kit and laundry department, club administration, the press office, the manager's team, the academy team, ground staff and the catering team, both at Old Trafford stadium and Carrington training ground, all of whom have given me their unwavering support in my time at United. Never in my 25 years as a manager have I been so well supported in my role. Finally, my special thanks go to Sir Alex Ferguson and Sir Bobby Charlton for always making me and my family feel so welcome throughout my time as Manchester United manager."

Woodward thanked Van Gaal as he released official confirmation of the manager's departure via the New York Stock Exchange.

The statement read: "I would like to thank Louis and his staff for their excellent work in the past two years culminating in winning a record-equalling 12th FA Cup for the club (and securing him a title in four different countries). He has behaved with great professionalism and dignity throughout his time here. He leaves us with a legacy of having given several young players the confidence to show their ability on the highest stage. Everyone at the club wishes him all the best in the future."

Van Gaal long ago fell out with fellow Dutchman Ronald Koeman, but the then Saints boss was sure that United were sinners in the way they had treated his sworn enemy. The Dutchmen fell out when Van Gaal was Koeman's director of football at Ajax.

Koeman feels that the Old Trafford club should have kept LVG after being informed about their plan to replace him with Mourinho. He said: "I have watched the process around Louis and José Mourinho from a distance. For months we were all reading that Mourinho was busy with Manchester United. If Louis was not told about getting the sack until after the FA Cup Final, then Manchester United as a club don't deserve a medal for the way they treated him. If you know a little bit about the business at the highest level in football, then you know that these kind of deals are not done overnight. But Louis has been put under tremendous pressure for months. This is why I admire the way he kept his dignity. Of course, he had a number of run-ins with the media and there were moments when I thought 'Louis, you could have dealt with that in another way.' But Louis is Louis. But looking at the incredible pressure all around him, I think he did a great job winning a big trophy like the FA Cup."

Van Gaal escaped to his luxury villa in the Algarve after being told he was being sacked. Koeman has his own fabulous bolthole opposite his rival - but they never speak.

Having said all that Koeman knows that the treatment of managers generally is ruthless, just ask Manuel Pellegrini over at City - do we not think that a deal with Pep was done in pre-season when it was heavily speculated that a pre contract had already been signed?

Koeman also believes that the appointment of 'The Special One' increases the profile of the Premier League, and he cannot wait for the Pep v José show. He said: "The best managers in the world have now come to the Premier League. With Guardiola starting his work at City, with Leicester inspiring so many other clubs that winning the league is possible, and every club financially strong enough to buy top-class players, the Premier League will prove that it is the most fascinating competition on the globe. Nowhere in Europe can you find a league where so many clubs can attract top players. They might not be able to get Messi or Ronaldo, but apart from them the English clubs can buy any footballer. The fact that guys like Mourinho and Guardiola want to work nowhere else makes it all more beautiful. This is the reason why I think it is fantastic to be part of English football. I find the intensity and the fact that the Premier League is totally unpredictable now, amazing."

Koeman warned Mourinho that he faces a difficult job bringing title success back to Old Trafford. "It must have been a disappointment for Louis van Gaal that he was not able to guide United into to the top four. But Leicester have made the impossible possible and that is the biggest of wake up calls for the big clubs. They will all need to react - and we all know their budgets are almost unlimited. With Southampton, we beat every big club this season at least once. We only finished three points behind Man City and Man United and we finished 13 points ahead of Chelsea. So we performed above the maximum of what people thought was possible. It is only going to be more exciting and competitive. Next season will be the most spectacular fans have ever witnessed."

Mourinho headed to Carrington from his London home on the May Bank Holiday to have a look at United's training ground facilities and meet the staff he inherited. He met with Sir Bobby Charlton, who had, by all accounts, opposed his appointment in the past and again now. Charlton has previously been a harsh critic of Mourinho's toxic side and supported Giggs taking over, but spoke at length with the new boss as their new era began. Mourinho shared a warm embrace with him, while joking: "You killed my country's dream in 1966 but even so, all the best."

Charlton offered his congratulations. "I am very happy to see you," he said, before Mourinho told him to save the kind words until he starts winning matches.

Mourinho was shown the premises by executive vice-chairman Ed Woodward and met other members of staff, including managing director Richard Arnold and head of elite performance John Murtough.

He told those who work inside Carrington to continuously repeat their names to him as he aims to add a personal touch. He launched a charm offensive, making a point of shaking everybody's hand.

"Where do we go?" Mourinho laughed as Woodward formally welcomed him at reception before taking him upstairs for a tour of the offices.

By contrast Pep Guardiola did not officially start work at Manchester City until July 1, although he had sounded out transfer targets and was close to finalising a deal for Borussia Dortmund midfielder İlkay Gündoğan.

United made an enquiry about Roma defender Kostas Manolas and were ready to lodge a £54m bid for Atlético Madrid's Saúl Ñíguez. Mourinho remains an admirer of Nemanja Matić, with Zlatan Ibrahimović also on their radar. The future of Dortmund striker Pierre-Emerick Aubameyang was likely to involve United as well at Liverpool and Real Madrid.

Ryan Giggs's future at Old Trafford was on the agenda for days and his position looking precarious with Mourinho who was bringing in his own staff. Giggs will not be able to remain in his present role as assistant manager, and was very unhappy about the idea of a lesser role. Mourinho identified former United defender Rio Ferdinand as a potential member of his coaching staff. Giggs could possibly be given a position between the first team and the Under-21 side.

Giggs spent the quarter-finals onwards of the European Championship with ITV after agreeing to a punditry role. He had been in discussions with the broadcaster pre-tournament, but no deal could be reached then, with his Old Trafford future so much up in the air. Giggs travelled to France with his first assignment to be Poland's quarter-final clash with Cristiano Ronaldo's Portugal.

Having been linked with the Nottingham Forest and Bolton Wanderers positions Giggs now, arguably, wanted to go it alone as a No. 1 as his long association with United appeared to be at an end; and the deal with ITV indicated his situation at United was closer to the exit.

Rooney spoke about the appointment of Mourinho for the first time, while on England Euro duty, suggesting his new boss is "one of the best in the world".

Rooney was quizzed on the subject of the incoming United boss at a press conference ahead of England's clash with Portugal and he was quick to say how eagerly he is anticipating life under the former Chelsea chief. "It's exciting. He's one of the best managers in the world and knows the Premier League very well," said Rooney. "I'm looking forward to it."

He also praised Marcus Rashford following his inclusion in Roy Hodgson's final 23-man squad for the European Championship. "He's certainly showed what he can do in his first game for England, getting his first goal in the first couple of minutes. I think what's pleasing about him is his attitude. It's first class and that's shown around the hotel and on the training pitch and he deserves it."

Former Manchester United striker Dwight Yorke believed that only four players were safe from Mourinho's cull. Yorke, who was part of United's 1999 treble-winning side, felt that only David de Gea, Anthony Martial, Marcus Rashford and captain Wayne Rooney can feel safe. Speaking exclusively to *888sport*, Yorke said: "Everyone is jumping on the bandwagon but it's just rumours in the media. We obviously know about Mata and José and that hasn't changed. There will be a few players under the microscope who aren't Manchester United players who somehow got in there. They've underperformed and no-one is safe apart from De Gea, Martial, Rashford and Rooney. Everyone in between will be looking over their shoulders."

Of the four players, Yorke was impressed with Martial who finished as the club's top scorer in his debut season. "He came into this country relatively unknown and people were raising their eyebrows thinking 'Who is this guy?' But he certainly made an impact at Manchester United and has been one of the highlights of their season. He's only 20 so still at that junior stage of his career and he's just going to get better and better. There is no doubt he will be a big player for both club and country."

Yorke felt Giggs should have been given his first role in management. "When I look at the whole package out there my overall choice was Giggsy. Zidane, Enrique, Pep and Simeone and all those guys were given an opportunity at a big club and I thought there was a change of mentality with appointing managers due to players now being tuned in to what it takes. Giggs spent three years under two managers at Manchester United and at 42 it was a good time to hand it to him. The club decided against it and then when you look what is out there Mourinho was the best option after Giggsy. Mourinho is a big personality and successful manager so was the right choice. People may say about his boring style and how he approaches the game but that only happened at his second time around at Chelsea. With Duff and Robben and Lampard behind them they were quick and exciting and scored a lot of goals. He will bring a lot of success and is just who Manchester United needs."

Glenn Hoddle, writing in his Mail on Sunday column, said that Mourinho "rightly provoked discussion and interest on a global scale" and added: "I am also interested in what happens to Ryan Giggs, the club's major link to the glory years under Sir Alex Ferguson. Giggs appears now to have a choice between serving Mourinho on the coaching staff as he did Louis van Gaal, or to make a break from a club he's known as boy and man, and find his own way in management. I've got quite a clear view on this. If Ryan wants one day to be the manager of Manchester United, and we are led to believe that is his ambition, he will increase his prospects by going away to be a No. 1 at a Premier League or Championship club rather than stay and help José, no matter how instructive that would be."

As for the appointment of Mourinho, the former England, Chelsea and Spurs manager, commented: "Ideally, United would have liked to have gone against the trend and built over time, as they wanted to under David Moyes and Van Gaal. Mourinho wanted to do that at Chelsea. It didn't work out for either of them and they will hope to bring each other success now. I don't know José well, I've spoken to him a few times after matches, small chit-chat. He'll have learned more from last season than the rest of his career because something didn't go right at Chelsea. But we also have to remember what we're good at and José has shown at Porto, Inter Milan, Real Madrid and Chelsea that usually he is extremely good. He worked under Van Gaal early in his career and been like a sponge in taking the best information out of people he's worked with. But you feel that where Van Gaal was one kind of disciplinarian, Mourinho likes discipline but knows how to put an arm around a player's shoulder as well."

"It will be fascinating to see him and Pep Guardiola renew their well-documented rivalry. They may even have similar transfer targets in mind and City probably have the edge given they were in the semi-finals of the Champions League and have qualified again for the competition, in contrast to United. Mourinho has never shirked a challenge though. For Giggs, he should watch from afar, and gain his own managerial experience."

Juan Mata wondered what the future held for him after being sold by Mourinho to United when he was at Chelsea, and on the day of the new manager's arrival the Spaniard was linked with a move to Everton under new manager Ronald Koeman.

He was also linked with a move to Barcelona as his advisers sought assurances to make sure he still had a role just as they did two years ago at Chelsea. The 28-year-old scored in the FA Cup final win, but landing the trophy failed to save the manager, and might also fail to save the goalscorer.

Mata's camp had asked Mourinho about his plans for their client at Chelsea back in January 2014, whether Mourinho was planning to sell the player, and

Mata was told he had a future at Stamford Bridge. Three weeks later his advisers flew in from Spain and he was sold to United for £37.1m. Mata trained away from Chelsea's first team at Cobham in the days leading up to the transfer. He wanted to stay at Stamford Bridge but Mourinho supported the decision to sell Mata two years ago, despite him having twice been named Chelsea's Player of the Year, as well as being listed in the Premier League PFA Team of the Year in 2013 before being sold.

Mata hit back at Mourinho last October when he said: "If a luxury player is a player who scores and assists and has good stats, then I'm happy to be a luxury player. I want luxury players in my team. I've scored as many goals for Manchester United in the Premier League as for Chelsea, but in something like 30 games less. In terms of scoring and assisting, I'm quite happy with the stats, and stats don't lie. They are facts."

Marouane Fellaini was another in danger of being sold, while Michael Carrick was out of contract.

There was an anticipated revolving door at Old Trafford with a flurry of signings and exits.

Chelsea would block any attempts by their old boss to sign Willian after being linked with a £60 million bid for the Brazilian voted by Chelsea fans as their Player of the Year.

The 27-year-old had two years left on his contract and Chelsea had yet to agree an extension. Willian was signed by Mourinho for £30m from Russian side FC Anzhi Makhachkala in 2013 and thrived under him at Stamford Bridge. But Chelsea are determined to keep their best player of a poor season.

Chelsea's 'Special One' would be "eternally respected" by fans of the west London club, according to the Chairman of Chelsea Supporters Trust five months after he was sacked by Chelsea following the Blues' worst start to a season since 1979. Mourinho developed a strong bond with the fans due to his hugely successful two stints at the club and his charismatic personality. His first spell in charge of the Blues between 2004 and 2007 resulted in two Premier League titles, an FA Cup trophy, two League Cup titles and the Community Shield. His second spell produced two more pieces of silverware - the Premier League and Capital One Cup trophies last year.

Tim Rolls, chairman of the Chelsea Supporters Trust, believed Mourinho will always keep the respect he has from Chelsea fans, and his appointment will add "spice" to the fixture between the two clubs.

Speaking to Standard Sport, Mr. Rolls said: "The Chelsea supporters I have spoken to are focusing on Antonio Conte and the preparations for next season, particularly new signings. Bouncing back from this season's dismal showing is the priority. José Mourinho taking the United job is not of real concern, although he will obviously be eternally respected by Chelsea supporters for the job he did and the trophies he won. Having said that, it will certainly add further spice to the Chelsea vs United games next season."

However it remained to be seen how long that affection would survive given certain observations Mourinho made in his statement.

Zlatan Ibrahimović dropped a hint that a sensational move to Manchester United could be on, declaring Mourinho "is the man to win back the title".

Mourinho sounded out the 34-year-old via intermediaries and Ibrahimović was effusive in his praise of Mourinho, playing up to speculation that they could be poised for a stunning reunion. Asked if he was tempted to work with Mourinho one more time, Ibrahimović said: "I had a fantastic time with him, when I was working with him. Working again with him…when I left Inter I said, 'We had a short time together. I had a great time'. If we will work together again I don't know. Let's see how things play out." When pushed if he was close to joining United, Ibrahimović added: "I don't give guarantees. I said there are concrete offers from the Premier League so let us see what happens."

He apparently decided his next club "a long time ago". He told a press conference in Stockholm: "I know what I want. The future is already written. I made my decision a long time ago. There are concrete offers from England, Italy and other countries, including outside of Europe. Nothing is happening right now. It's the European Championship that's happening."

"I think it's a great move (for Manchester United to bring in Mourinho). I believe he is the man to bring them back to the top. If you want to win, you bring Mourinho. I have spoken to Mourinho every day since I left Inter, so there is no secret. I had a great relationship with Mourinho and a fantastic time when I was working with him. I don't know if I will work with him again. Let's see how it plays out."

Mourinho believed Ibrahimović could still make an impact at Old Trafford despite his age - 35 in October. In addition, Ibrahimović insisted he can cut it in the Premier League after he is finished having "fun" at Euro 2016 in France. "I am only warming up. I had a great season. I proved that age is just a number. Everything is in your head. If I want to do it, I will do it. I am looking forward to the games. Training is going good and I am not feeling my calf. We have the warm-up games, then to France, where the fun begins. It does not matter that (my future) is done before the Euros because it would already be done. I only need to push the button. There is time. I want to enjoy what you are writing. There is a lot being written. According to someone it would have been done in 48 hours, another said it was 90 per cent, another 10 per cent. It is fun finding out who the rat is; who is talking."

Should United sign Ibrahimović, the money they could expect to make in shirt sales and other marketing ventures would go some way to offsetting his sizable wage demands. He reportedly wanted €15m (£11.3m) per season as he is out-of-contract and leaving PSG after four years and four league titles. He had a very lucrative offer from LA Galaxy as well as clubs in the Middle East. Ibrahimović's preference was to join United. Ibrahimović's agent, Mino Raiola (who also represents Borussia Dortmund's 27-year-old Armenian star, Mkhitaryan), told United that Ibrahimović will want at least in the region of £220,000-a-week. Rooney is the club's highest earner at the moment on a weekly salary of £300,000.

The next day the striker's agent claimed it would be a "surprise" if he moved to Old Trafford. Mino Raiola told *Expressen*: "We have not decided anything yet. I think it will be a surprise in the end. Everyone is harping on about only United, United, United. There are some clubs in England, a few clubs in Europe, clubs outside Europe, but everyone assumes that he must go to Manchester United, but it is not true." He further added "Manchester United is a great club, with a great coach," said Raiola. "But Zlatan has not yet made his choice."

The Italian super-agent added: "The club that buys him do not have to pay a transfer fee. This means that Ibrahimović, who just finished a record season at PSG, can get an extra high salary. He is in a good bargaining position. It's about doing the right thing at the right time. The only thing we care about is quality. Let's see what happens. But we have a nice period ahead of us now."

MOURINHO ON IBRAHIMOVIĆ

Mourinho and Ibrahimović worked together at Internazionale during the 2008-09 season, and in April 2014 Mourinho recalled an episode at Inter Milan when he refused to substitute an angry Ibrahimović, who felt his team-mates weren't helping him to score the goals he needed to win the Serie A Golden Boot.

"He was very angry and upset as he came at me. He was shouting, 'We are champions, I helped a lot to make you champions, now nobody's helping me. I want to (come off) now'. But I pretended not to understand him. I said, 'What? What? Do you want a drink, do you want some water?' and I threw him a bottle. I told him, 'Here, take a drink and go'. A few minutes later he scored a beautiful goal." In the same interview, Mourinho admitted he had a special relationship with Ibrahimović, whose dedication was as valuable as his quality at Inter. "A player who gave me as much as Ibra will always be in my heart. He did a lot for Inter and Inter did a lot for him. I like seeing Ibra. I greet him whenever I get the chance to and I wish him all the best - except when he plays against me. He is very special, he is one of the best strikers in the world."

In the middle of that 2008-09 season, Mourinho described the Swede as a bigger talent than Cristiano Ronaldo. "Ronaldo is a good player but he is certainly not the best. He deserved the Golden Ball award because his team won the Champions League and the Premier League. But, for me, Ibrahimović is the best."

Mourinho was less complimentary when explaining the decision to allow Ibrahimović to join Barcelona a few months later. "Inter had two possibilities, tell Ibrahimović, 'We're not selling you', or take Samuel Eto'o, plus Alexander Hleb on loan for a year for free, plus 50m euros. To me that seems like an incredible deal, a deal worth 100m euros, the deal of the summer. Kaka 70m, Cristiano Ronaldo 96m. For me this is worth 100m because Eto'o is worth not even one euro less than Ibra."

Ahead of Chelsea's Champions League quarter-final with PSG in April 2014, Mourinho said it would be a shame if Ibrahimović did not get the chance to play in the Premier League. "I think he has to be where he is happy, and if he's happy in Paris then he has to stay. But at the same time I think it's a pity for him when he finishes his career and he played in the most important countries in the world of football, and won the most important championships in the world of football, but he didn't play in the best league in the world and never won the best league in the world. That's a pity."

IBRAHIMOVIĆ ON MOURINHO

In an interview with French media outlet *Telefoot* in March 2015, Ibrahimović hinted that he would like to work with Mourinho again. "We worked together for one year at Inter. The feeling was great between us and my only regret is that we were together for only one year."

Ibrahimović in his autobiography, *I am Zlatan Ibrahimović*, he said: "José Mourinho is a big star. The first time he met my partner Helena, he whispered to her, 'Helena, you have only one mission: feed Zlatan, let him sleep, keep him happy.'"

In that book he also compared Mourinho to Guardiola, "That guy says whatever he wants. I like him. He's the leader of his army. But he cares, too. He would text me all the time at Inter, wondering how I was doing. He's the exact opposite of Pep Guardiola. If Mourinho lights up a room, Guardiola draws the curtains. Mourinho would become a guy I was basically willing to die for."

On leaving Inter Milan to join Barcelona in 2009, Ibrahimović said: "No matter how happy I was going to Barça, it was sad to leave Mourinho. That guy is special."

Ibrahimović offered further insight into Mourinho's managerial techniques in Carlo Ancelotti's recently published autobiography, *Quiet Leadership*: "Mourinho is the disciplinarian. Everything with him is a mind game - he likes to manipulate. Such tricks were new for me - all the time doing one thing to get another thing, all the time triggering me. I like these games and it worked for me; I became top scorer under him and we won the league."

He revealed an insight into Mourinho's motivational techniques before Inter's games. "The way Mourinho prepared for games was also new to me. I would get pumped up, believing the story he would feed us. I went through a lot of adrenaline when I played for him. It was like nothing was ever good enough. He gave and he took. José Mourinho knows how to treat a footballer, but Carlo knows how to treat a person."

Ibrahimović showed more admiration for Mourinho ahead of last season's Champions League meeting with Chelsea - two months after his former manager's sacking. "I think everybody will miss Mourinho in the game. But I believe he will be back soon in football and if you are a little patient you will soon see him managing another club."

Mourinho wasted little time in getting to work revealing an extensive folder of plans on his official Instagram account with a section marked 'Summer with Euro 2016 and Copa America', sure to contain a list of targets, tactics and pre-season objectives.

Gary Lineker joked that Mourinho had already made a positive impact on Marcus Rashford and Wayne Rooney.

Rashford scored less than three minutes into his senior England debut, before Rooney also found the net in the Three Lions' 2-1 friendly win over Australia at the Stadium of Light and former England striker Lineker immediately took to Twitter.

Gary Lineker, @GaryLineker: "What a manager José Mourinho is. He's only been United boss for a few minutes and his players are scoring for fun."

Mourinho travelled to his native Portugal with assistant Rui Faria for a scheduled lecture at Lisbon University to address 'high performance football coaching' students in a post-graduation class at the Faculty of Human Kinetics at Lisbon University.

He had promising words for supporters of teams in his homeland, saying: "I am not taking any players from here," in his first public declaration on his transfer plans.

However Mourinho has already shown initial interest in Sporting Lisbon midfielder João Mário, the 23-year-old Portugal international. He was expected to hold talks with Giggs when he returned from Lisbon.

Mourinho pulled out of his first appearance at Old Trafford since becoming Manchester United manager after deciding not to take charge of an England team at Soccer Aid as he wanted to focus on his commitments to United. Mourinho still took training at Fulham on Thursday and Friday as an England side that included Jamie Carragher, Robbie Fowler and Phil Neville prepared to play Claudio Ranieri's Rest of the World team on Sunday.

However, he was expected to hand over the reins to Sunderland manager Sam Allardyce who was due to be his assistant for the day. United did not put their new manager under any pressure to stand aside, mindful that the match is in aid of UNICEF. But Mourinho was conscious that the charity event could be overshadowed by the inevitable focus on his presence in the home dugout at Old Trafford for the first time.

Mourinho took to his newly opened Instagram account to share a snap with Guy Ritchie. He captioned the image 'every top performance needs a top coach'. Mourinho seemed to form a friendship with the Snatch and Lock Stock and Two Smoking Barrels mastermind and was pictured leaving the home of Madonna's ex-husband in April.

Proving that he is certainly box-office, his brief existence on Instagram accumulated 500,000 followers in only five days.

His first image on Instagram was simply the picture of the front of his contract stamped with a Manchester United badge and topped with a red pen. Others included the car park at Carrington training ground and a picture outside the University of Lisbon where he'd given that lecture on football coaching.

Chapter 5
DR. EVA

The Eva Carneiro row. How events unfolded at Chelsea:

August 8: With Chelsea struggling late on in their Barclays Premier League opener at home to Swansea, Eden Hazard went to ground and the referee called for treatment, at which point Eva Carneiro and physio Jon Fearn went on to the pitch to treat him.

After the 2-2 draw, Mourinho branded his medical staff "impulsive and naive" as treating Hazard meant Chelsea would be temporarily down to nine men - Thibaut Courtois had already been sent off. "Whether you are a kit man, doctor or secretary on the bench you have to understand the game," Mourinho said.

August 11: It emerged that Carneiro's role at the club was to change with a downgrading of responsibilities, limiting her to the team's training base as she would no longer attend matches.

August 12: FIFA's chief medical officer Jiri Dvorak was among those to denounce Chelsea's treatment of Carneiro, with the medical community pointing out that she and Fearn had no choice but to respond to the referee's instruction to come on to the pitch.

August 14: Mourinho confirmed neither Carneiro nor Fearn would be on the bench for Chelsea's next match against Manchester City, but said they might return in the future.

September 11: FIFA said it would draw up a new code of practice for team doctors in the wake of the controversy.

September 22: After Carneiro parted company with Chelsea, Football Association board member Heather Rabbatts expressed her "sadness and anger" at the Portuguese's departure from the club.

September 23: The Football Medical Association (FMA) stated it would continue to support Carneiro "on a professional level".

September 24: Premier League Doctors' Group called for safeguards to be in place for team doctors.

September 30: The FA confirmed Mourinho would face no action over allegations he made discriminatory comments towards Carneiro during the August 8 confrontation. Women in Football questioned the verdict, while the FA said an "independent academic expert in Portuguese linguistics" had been called upon to analyse footage of the incident.

October 1: Rabbatts expressed "major concerns" over the FA's handling of the disciplinary process, with FMA chief executive Eamonn Salmon expressing surprise over the absence of Carneiro as a witness. FA chairman Greg Dyke, in a letter to council members, admitted Mourinho should have apologised amid "a failure of his personal judgement and public behaviour".

October 2: Carneiro issued a statement insisting she was not requested by the FA to make a statement about Mourinho's alleged remarks. She also said the FA did not ask her for a statement after she was the victim of sexist abuse at West Ham in March and criticised a lack of support from football authorities.

October 29: Carneiro's lawyers serve notice on the club that she intends to seek a claim for constructive dismissal.

January 6: First tribunal hearing takes place in Croydon, south London.

March 7: A further private hearing is held, also in Croydon.

About to be unveiled as Louis van Gaal's replacement, José Mourinho appeared to have other issues to deal with, as he was spotted carrying notes about the discrimination case brought by former Chelsea doctor Eva Carneiro.

On a piece of paper with a title referring to the employment tribunal, it was written "I have never heard this allegation before". Not much of the manager's writing was visible, but the phrases "not true" and "fantasy" were legible on the page lower down.

So, Mourinho's first appearance after the appointment at Manchester United could be in court, with the legal wrangle with Dr. Carneiro due to continue on June 6.

Embarrassing details surrounding Carneiro's exit were set to be made public, with text messages and emails sent and received by Mourinho likely to be used as evidence in a full tribunal.

Mourinho could be called to appear as a witness at the London South

Employment Tribunal in Croydon, and Dr. Carneiro still wants a public apology.

Carneiro left Chelsea in September after being dropped from first-team duties and was suing the club for constructive dismissal with a separate personal legal action against Mourinho for alleged victimisation and discrimination.

This posed a problem for Mourinho, as the Manchester United board were always concerned about his controversial history, and while a three-day hold up over talks were blamed on image rights and trademark issues, I speculated during my extensive round of TV and radio interviews that the club were more concerned about "reputational" issues, of which this was the chief one and clearly one I couldn't go into detail over in order to avoid being prejudicial to the cases in hand.

Carneiro spent five hours in a private hearing in Croydon in March, with the doctor seeking "substantial damages" from Chelsea. Asked if a settlement had been reached afterwards, she shook her head, while her legal team refused to comment. Cameramen and photographers had chased Carneiro when she left the court two months earlier and a full public tribunal would inevitably attract even more attention, particularly if Mourinho made an appearance. Whilst this was a problem for Chelsea to deal with, even though he'd been sacked by them, it now became an issue for Manchester United as he was now their manager.

So, for the first time with Mourinho as the Manchester United manager, the 'Dr. Eva' case that had been so eagerly anticipated was back in the courts on June 6. It was then disclosed in documents submitted to her employment tribunal that she had rejected a £1.2m settlement from the club (Chelsea).

Eva Carneiro claimed constructive dismissal against the club, plus a separate legal action against Mourinho for alleged victimisation and discrimination. Dr. Carneiro's lawyer said Mourinho would face at least one day of questions at the hearing, and that one day would not be enough time to cross-examine Mourinho about their falling out, so it could extend to two days. The case was anticipated to be heard over seven to 10 days at the London South Employment Tribunal in Croydon.

Dr. Carneiro's barrister Mary O'Rourke QC told the hearing she was likely to take at least a day to cross-examine Mourinho who did not attend the first day of the case. The tribunal was adjourned until the next day.

Legal papers submitted to the tribunal on behalf of Chelsea and Mourinho showed Dr. Carneiro had been "made an open offer of £1.2m to settle her claims", demanded a huge pay rise and was hungry for fame. The club's legal team said it would show the club had taken these steps only because it believed that it was "in no-one's interests that this dispute should be determined through litigation", arguing "They are conscious that, whatever the facts of the matter, it is likely to be widely and incorrectly assumed that they could have avoided this coming tribunal."

Chelsea's legal team had already argued that documents at the time showed Dr. Carneiro did not consider Mourinho's actions to be discriminatory. "The purpose of the discrimination claim was to lift the statutory cap, in order to justify the claimant's extravagant compensation claim," the clubs' legal team argued.

It seems the tribunal will largely hinge on whether Mourinho yelled: "Filha de puta (daughter of a whore)" or "filho de puta (son of a b***h)" when she ran on to the pitch to treat Hazard. QC Mary O'Rourke told the employment tribunal in Croydon: "He uses the word "filha" because he is abusing a woman." She added that Dr. Carneiro heard the term "clearly from behind her" as she ran on to the Stamford Bridge turf.

Mourinho employed a swearing expert from the University of Oxford to prove he said "son of a b***h" and has called it the Portuguese equivalent of "f*** off". Mourinho says he and other players, including Spaniard Cesc Fabregas, used the phrase throughout the match and denies it was sexist or aimed it specifically at the female doctor.

The tribunal panel was read an extract from Mourinho's statement in which he concedes that he used the Portuguese term "filho da puta", meaning 'son of of a b***h or whore', but that he had been using it throughout the match. He argued: "'Filho da puta' is a phrase I often use, all of the players know it. There is no sexist connotation in the use of the phrase - it is just like saying 'f*** off'. In the world of football, a lot of swear words are used." Referring to footage of earlier on in the August 8 match against Swansea, the former Chelsea manager highlighted that he had also been using the term then.

He added that Cesc Fabregas had also used the Spanish equivalent of the term when a Chelsea player was fouled during the game. In his statement, Mourinho said: "Cesc and I both speak English well, but in the heat of the game we both swear in our mother language. Eva was not on the pitch at that point in time."

Daniel Stilitz QC, representing Mourinho and Chelsea, told the tribunal the doctor had "made a series of scandalous, irrelevant and untrue allegations" in her witness statement, which was due to be made public today. He said: "She has been made an open offer of £1.2million to settle her claims, far more than the respondents (Mourinho and Chelsea) believe she could realistically recover even if she succeeded on all her claims." But she had rejected "all overtures", he said. He rejected the idea that Chelsea and Mourinho "were somehow hostile to the idea of women working in football".

Mr. Stilitz said it was Mourinho's style to "express himself bluntly", adding that the former Chelsea manager was "clearly angry and emotional" at the time. In the dressing room, Mourinho said to Dr. [Paco] Biosca, Chelsea's medical director, "If they don't know how to do their jobs and they don't understand the game, you get other ones. You have to understand the game."

Miss O'Rourke said: "Not 'understanding the game' is a common allegation put to women in the football world."

Dr. Carneiro allegedly also asked for a 40 per cent pay rise to £400,000 to return to work, plus bonuses and compensation for "distress" caused by the club and Mourinho. He accused her of making "extravagant" demands after the incident, to take her £286,000 salary to £400,000. She also demanded bonus payments to "properly reward" her for "my contribution to the club's success" and a "substantial payment" in compensation for distress, he alleged.

Chelsea also claimed she was "preoccupied with developing her profile" including nominating a Chelsea star for the Ice Bucket Challenge on YouTube and positioned herself behind Mourinho during TV matches and signing fans' autographs. Their lawyers also say Carneiro allegedly "secretly briefed against Chelsea to the media".

On the pivotal row over treating Hazard on the pitch Mourinho claims he had already warned her about it after treating Gary Cahill when he was "visibly unhurt".

The start of Dr. Carneiro's legal argument says: "This is a tale of two employees: one good (the claimant) and one bad (Mourinho). The bad employee forces the good employee out of the job of her dreams and the employer does nothing to stop it. The bad employee berates, sexually harasses and demotes the good employee for carrying out her professional duties, namely her health and safety duties as the first team doctor, pitch side. Rather than investigating and disciplining the bad employee, the employer allows the bad employee to confirm the demotion, both publicly and privately and to continue with his job. By comparison, the good employee's demotion is confirmed and she is instructed to work and to 'build bridges' with the bad employee."

The case could be settled at any time but all three parties must agree to a settlement for the tribunal, which would be accessible to the public and the media, to be averted. The Gibraltar-born British doctor is said to want a public apology from Mourinho as part of her demands - but she does not want to return to Chelsea.

The tribunal heard that Dr. Carneiro is expected to be questioned over two and a half days.

Private hearings in January and February took place without a resolution and it appears the case will proceed to the tribunal.

Witness statements and documents - including texts and emails - would likely be made public, while Carneiro, Mourinho and representatives from Chelsea could be called to appear as witnesses.

The club said they also had been concerned about Dr. Carneiro's "commitment to developing the skills required to progress to the role of medical director" and revealed she had been close to losing her job several years earlier, claiming she had been spared following the intervention of Roman Abramovich's right-hand woman, Marina Granovskaia, who also spearheaded negotiations aimed at avoiding the matter going to court."

Chelsea declined to comment on the case, but supported Mourinho even after his employment as manager was terminated. Whether or not Chelsea would continue to support Mourinho now he was employed by a rival club was unclear.

Mourinho was cleared of using discriminatory language towards Carneiro following an investigation by the Football Association. Afterwards, Carneiro and the Football Association's independent board member, Dame Heather Rabbatts, criticised the governing body for not interviewing the doctor as part of its investigation. Carneiro has also had backing from FIFA's medical chairman, Michel D'Hooghe, who contacted the doctor to offer his support and that of the world governing body. He has backed Carneiro's insistence that she was simply doing her job.

However, Mourinho faced an embarrassing dossier of witness statements and documents - including texts and emails - being made public. Given the acute embarrassment this would have caused had it all unfolded in court it was hardly surprisingly that the next morning it was settled on the steps of the court.

Mourinho and Chelsea agreed a huge pay-off for ex-club doctor minutes before she was due to give explosive evidence against them, and although the amount is confidential the majority of newspapers reported the payment to be £5m plus the enormous costs.

Chelsea also gave Dr. Carneiro an unreserved apology, but crucially Mourinho refused to say sorry and grinned as he was pictured as he left the tribunal pursued by the expected melee of media.

So, a deal was eventually concluded in a back corridor of the court and Chelsea then issued a statement saying it "regretted the circumstances" which led to former club doctor leaving and "apologises unreservedly to her and her family for the distress caused".

The statement added that Mourinho thanked Dr. Carneiro for the "excellent and dedicated support" she provided and wished her a "successful career".

But when asked "Why no apology from you José?" by MailOnline outside the court, he refused to comment and grinned as he was rushed away in a waiting car.

In a statement issued on their club website, Chelsea said: "Chelsea Football Club is pleased to announce that it has reached an agreement with Dr. Carneiro which brings her employment tribunal proceedings against the club and José Mourinho to an end. The club regrets the circumstances which led to Dr. Carneiro leaving the club and apologises unreservedly to her and her family for the distress caused. We wish to place on record that in running onto the pitch Dr. Carneiro was following both the rules of the game and fulfilling her responsibility to the players as a doctor, putting their safety first. Dr. Carneiro has always put the interests of the club's players first. Dr. Carneiro is a highly competent and professional sports doctor. She was a valued member of the club's medical team and we wish her every success in her future career. José Mourinho also thanks Dr. Carneiro for the excellent and dedicated support she provided as First Team Doctor and he wishes her a successful career."

In a closing statement Dr. Carneiro said: "I am relieved that today we have been able to conclude this tribunal case. It has been an extremely difficult and distressing time for me and my family and I now look forward to moving forward with my life. My priority has always been the health and safety of the players and fulfilling my duty of care as a doctor. In running onto the pitch to treat a player, who requested medical attention, I was following the rules of the game and fulfilling my medical responsibilities. I would like to thank everyone who has supported me including my husband, family and friends and members of the football community."

A spokesperson for Women in Football said: "Women in Football are delighted that Eva's name has been rightly cleared and her professional reputation as a doctor upheld. Eva has been courageous in her fight for a public apology from Chelsea and acknowledgement that on the day in question she was simply doing her job. We completely deplore and condemn her treatment by the club since and welcome their unreserved apology. We believe that every female employee in the football industry has the right to go about their working lives without being targeted for or subjected to discriminatory abuse. We hope that by working with football authorities and clubs we can bring about a greater understanding of the barriers in the industry that women routinely face and that more women will follow Eva's example by standing up for equality."

Chapter 6
JOSÉ VS PEP

Pep Guardiola will pick up the bill if he goes out for dinner with José Mourinho in Manchester. Really? New Manchester City assistant Domènec Torrent thinks so. But as we know, Pep has not always been able to keep his cool when confronted by his adversary.

Torrent has worked with Guardiola since he started his coaching career with Barcelona B in Spain's third tier and is always sat next to him on the bench. Guardiola's most trusted lieutenant is also the grandson of a former Barcelona player and the only member of the coaching staff that Pep allows to give team talks. In an in-depth interview in Spanish newspaper, *El Punt Avui*, Torrent insists Guardiola will adjust his style to suit the demands of English football in order to be successful in the Premier League as well as coming out on top over Mourinho.

Guardiola has a reputation for tiki-taka possession football but he will also make City hard to score against, not just pretty going forward.

Asked about the potential clash with Mourinho, Torrent says: "Asides from the famous press conference (before a Champions League semi-final in 2011) if there was anything between them it was from Mourinho towards Guardiola. Manchester is a small place and I'm sure we will coincide (with him) in restaurants. One day he can pay and another day Pep and I will pay. I think Pep is past being spooked by anything. You just get on with your work and control everything that is in your power to control. For our part we are very relaxed about it all."

Asked how Pep will deal with the demands of the Premier League, Torrent says: "I have said this many times that people sell this idea that Pep tried to change German football or will try to change English football. It is just not like that. We went to Germany and immediately we realised that we had to learn to deal with counter-attacks and that the football was much more physical. And we had to mix that with the desire to control games by having possession and playing out from the back and we came up with a combination. The Bayern that won the Treble was a much more end-to-end football style. With Pep they controlled the games more. He adjusted his ideas to the football there and in the Premier League he will do the same. There are many different styles in football and any one of them can be successful. He is not going there to give lessons to anybody."

Torrent promised City fans that Guardiola would work relentlessly to secure success. "There is no perfect coach but Pep comes close. There are people that just go into work every day and then there are people that actually work every day. He spends so many hours working and everyone that works alongside him has to do the same. Players who have had many other coaches come with the idea of what he will be like to work with but then they experience something different. He can lose games but it is never because of a lack of attention to detail. Luck always plays a part but you have to minimise its influence by making sure you leave no stone unturned in preparation - giving players options in attack and exploring the weaknesses of the rivals. Every training session is a tactical lesson and always based on the next rival, analysing them and looking to minimise their virtues. He has been seven years in the top flight in Spain and Germany and his teams have always conceded the least number of goals. Some people overlook that. He wants his teams to have the ball but he also wants to control the game when his team does not have the ball. He is not just an offensive coach; he knows you have to take care of everything."

Guardiola's workaholic approach makes it hard for him to relax. "We can take some time off in pre-season, but if we have a few beers the discussion always comes back around to if 4-3-3 is better than 3-4-3."

Asked about how that intensity might drain him, he says: "With the way he works it is impossible that he could stay at a club for 20 years. There is a lot of intensity, not just physically but also mentally. His day starts at eight in the morning and does not end until seven at night."

Guardiola has kept Brian Kidd and goalkeeping coach Xabier Mancisidor from

Manuel Pellegrini's regime, but added his Bayern Munich backroom team of Torrent, Lorenzo Buenaventura, Carles Planchart and Manuel Estiarte.

Buenaventura is the fitness coach and a rehabilitation expert, coaxing injured stars back to fitness swiftly, and has been part of the Pep set-up since the early days in 2008 - quickly transforming Barcelona's ability to press opponents high up the pitch, and playing a significant role in Barça becoming the best team on the continent. This, of course, is something Mourinho will be acutely aware of and will want his players to combat.

Planchart analyses all the data and videos, and is a vital part of Guardiola's attention to detail.

Estiarte is one of the most highly-regarded sportsmen in Spanish history, and for seven consecutive years was named as water polo's world player of the year. In 1996 he was awarded the Grand Cross of the Royal Order of Sporting Merit. Guardiola told Martí Perarnau for his book *Pep Confidential*: "Coaching a football team is a lonely job and that's why I value loyalty above all else. When you hit the inevitable rough patch, you need to know who you can trust. Manuel helps me enormously in a host of practical ways and is always happy to take on some of the more irksome parts of my job. All of that is vital to me, but more than anything it is his loyalty and emotional support I prize."

Guardiola was also keen to land Mikel Arteta for City's Football Academy.

The structure, with close friend, Manchester City sporting director, Txiki Begiristain running the football side of City, is designed to facilitate instant success for a single-minded coach focused solely on training.

Carles Puyol, captain throughout his time at the Nou Camp believed Pep's arrival at City will not only benefit City but everyone across English football. "I think he is going to do a great job," the former defender told Press Association Sport. "He has been a great coach for us. I appreciated working with him. I think he is going to be an asset for the Premier League, although I don't know the Premier League (as well). I think they play somewhat differently and therefore he might bring new techniques to them, which could be very beneficial for the Premier League."

Mourinho's team naturally included Rui Faria, the No. 2 who has followed him everywhere, and Silvino Louro - the goalkeeping coach who took on more responsibility at Chelsea. Additionally, Ricardo Formosinho, formerly of Real Madrid, joined the back room staff as the new club scout.

José Mourinho will not let "fights" with Pep Guardiola distract Manchester United from winning the title as he argued that their personal feud in Spain featured La Liga's two all-powerful clubs that so dominate the title race. That simply wouldn't work in the Premier League where even a Leicester City could win the league.

The former Real Madrid and Barcelona managers will now recommence their rivalry in England but Mourinho warned that focusing on the man that once called him "the f***ing boss" could allow an outsider to take the title.

City and United were ranked as Leicester City's most-likely successors by the bookmakers with both ready to invest heavily in their world-class managers' transfer targets. I was certainly expecting that the two clubs would splash a combined cool half a billion pounds on recruiting some of the best up and coming players in the world.

"My experience does not allow me to be naive," Mourinho said. "I was in Spain for two years, where the champion would be me or him. There, individual battles make more sense because they can affect the outcome (of the title race). If, in the Premier League, I were to focus on him and Manchester City and he were to focus on me and Manchester United, someone else would be champion."

"The level of the Premier League is going to get better with the players and coaches who will come. Four champions in four years shows how competitive it is, and also says a lot about the television rights and its distribution, which will allow the growth of the league and all its teams. It is different to other leagues where the sharks will always be sharks."

Despite Mourinho wishing to play down the conflict, it is one of the biggest side shows for the new season by far.

The reference to "the f***ing boss" reverts to their time in Spain in the great divide between Real and Barça.

Guardiola took his seat for what should have been a routine media conference at the Santiago Bernabéu on the eve of the 2011 Champions League semi-final, but the Barça boss shocked the assembled journalists when he looked up at the cameras pointing to the back of the room, and asked which one was José Mourinho's. In as bizarre an episode as Eric Cantona's "fish and trawlers" speech, the seemingly cool Pep concluded that they must all be Mourinho's spying on him.

Pep delivered his infamous long monologue aimed at his adversary, "In this room, he is the *puto jefe*, the *puto amo* - the f***ing boss, the f***ing master, and I don't want to compete with him for a moment."

The response: Barça won 2-0 at the Bernabéu, which left Mourinho whining "Why? Why? Why?", moaning bitterly about the dark forces of UNICEF and UEFA. "Josép Guardiola is a fantastic coach," Mourinho said, "but I have won two Champions Leagues. He has won (only) one Champions League and that is one that would embarrass me. I would be ashamed to have won it with the scandal of Stamford Bridge and if he wins it this year it will be with the scandal of the Bernabéu. I hope that one day he can win a proper Champions League. Deep down, if they are good people, it cannot taste right for them. I hope one day Guardiola has the chance of winning a brilliant, clean championship with no scandal." Guardiola did win it that year.

José versus Pep has now clearly moved to Manchester. Wonderful! Talk about Sir Alex's mind games for best part of two decades, it would be nothing compared to this.

"I know him and he knows me," Guardiola had said in justification of his personal rant at Mourinho, when the pressure finally cracked the man who seemed to be immune from it, and from the Mourinho antics.

Clearly familiarity bred contempt. They had worked together at Barcelona, captain and assistant coach, faced each other as managers in El Clásico, and also when Chelsea played Bayern Munich in the 2013 European Super Cup. Well, perhaps not contempt, more a loathing of each other's footballing philosophies, the fact that Mourinho was overlooked for the Barça job twice, and irrespective of how many trophies he won, there seemed more respect for Guardiola's style. Mourinho once declared that Barcelona would be "for ever" in his heart, so you can imagine how passionately he wanted the job there where he had been Bobby Robson's assistant as well as worked with Louis van Gaal. Guardiola actually told Barcelona's president, Joan Laporta, that it would be easier to appoint Mourinho as manager in 2008, but he had been chosen instead. Resentment burns deep with Mourinho over the Barça snub.

Maybe Manchester United felt that they were the Barça of English football and City the Real Madrid. Reputation and tradition at Old Trafford runs deep, and therefore not everyone would think the abrasive Mourinho was the right fit. Yet Sir Alex was not always politically correct himself, mostly with the media, and kicking a boot at David Beckham was not the best PR for the club, but he was rarely as outrageous as Mourinho.

However, Mourinho is a serial winner, a hoarder of trophies, and despite what happened at the Bridge, the break usually refreshes his appetite for more silverware and a new challenge. Needs must, and for Manchester United there was an urgent need to wind back to the Sir Alex days of domination of domestic and European football as with each year that prospect seemed to grow ever more remote.

Once City got Guardiola, United had to get Mourinho.

The hype of over Guardiola's arrival in the blue half of Manchester would have left United in the shade of their own City, lagging behind in the Premier League and, as it turned out, cut adrift in the Champions League.

It has a familiar ring to it as when Madrid signed Mourinho in the summer of 2010 his mission was to defeat Guardiola.

A life-sized cardboard cut-out used to be propped up in Mourinho's office at Valdebebas, Madrid, depicting him sprinting across the Camp Nou turf, finger in the air, celebrating at the end of the 2010 Champions League semi-final when his Internazionale reached the final, at Barcelona's expense.

Mourinho had saved Real Madrid from the ultimate humiliation; watching the Catalan club lift the trophy at the Bernabéu.

To complete the job of regaining domination over Barça, it was not so easy and Mourinho's pursuit of supremacy was becoming increasingly personal with Guardiola.

Guardiola had won the treble in 2009 and the league in 2010 but Mourinho got his foot in the door by preventing Barça reaching a second successive European Cup final.

One of the big issues in Spain was how Mourinho went about breaking up the powerful bond between Madrid and Barcelona players that became so influential within the national team that won the 2010 World Cup having spent so much time together bonding for that tournament. He told his Madrid players that he knew that their Catalan team-mates hated Spain and would never truly be their friends.

Mourinho also set about a campaign that might seem all too familiar from his days at Chelsea, criticising referees and the football authorities for conspiring against him and his team, positioning Madrid as the victims, the hard done by.

Mourinho rarely referred to Barça by name, instead he constantly talked about the "other club" and bemoaned the advantages they were afforded, for example, by referees or by the fixtures providing them with a leeway that Madrid were denied.

Top of Mourinho's agenda was to embrace and enhance Real Madrid's status as sacrosanct as he saw it; their whiter than their white shirts image as the game's good guys, their esteemed worthiness as the sole defenders of "football" that their playing philosophy was the one that mattered and should prevail as it was the 'real' beautiful game.

Mourinho accused the "other club" of diving, therefore of cheating, and pressuring officials, in a successful strategy to gain favourable decisions. He viewed it as a form of manipulation, if not another of cheating. But in reality he and Guardiola were not so different, they both wanted to win at all costs and nothing else much mattered.

At one stage Guardiola promised he would revise his behaviour!

The clashes between the two clubs were littered with red cards, but red hot derbies are passionate, emotional and highly charged even without the touchline issues, and it certainly will be no different now in Manchester derbies.

However, one would not expect such an incident that marred not just a passionate derby, but also scarred the whole relationship between the two clubs and their managers. It occurred during a Spanish Supercopa encounter, in August 2011, when Mourinho gouged the eyes of Barcelona's and Pep Guardiola's assistant coach, Tito Vilanova.

Asked about it after the game, Mourinho claimed not to know "this Pito Vilanova or whatever his name is". He knew Pito is Spanish slang for "penis". Mourinho knew he had over-stepped the mark, regretted his action and later apologised for them.

It didn't help Mourinho's cause that the unsavoury episode was captured on film and clearly showed him walking over to Barcelona's assistant manager during a melee in the closing stages of the Supercopa, and gouging him in one eye. The fracas followed a particularly bad foul by Marcelo Vieira on Barcelona's Cesc Fabregas.

When he walked away, Vilanova reacted by pushing Mourinho, causing outrage from the Madrid team which had not seen their manager's actions and referee David Fernández Borbalán did not note it in his match report.

The shocking incident actually came at the end of a wonderful game which saw

Barça twice take the lead through Iniesta and Messi with Cristiano Ronaldo and Benzema replying. But, with extra-time looming, Barça won it when Messi volleyed home Adriano's right-wing cross. Madrid's frustration then spilled over with Marcelo sent-off for that crude tackle on debutant Fabregas. It sparked a bust-up which saw Mourinho's clash with Vilanova and red cards for substituted players David Villa and Mesut Özil. Barça central defender Gerard Pique commented at the time, "It's a shame, it is not the first time and it's always the same. Someone has to take action on the matter. Mourinho is destroying Spanish football. There is talk about the Catalans, but the problem is with Madrid."

In addition, Mourinho was already due to serve a touchline ban in Champions League fixtures after comments he made about Barcelona the previous season.

There was even a monumental row over the ball boys. Yes the ball boys! Mourinho was particularly unhappy that the ball boys appeared to disappear after half-time with the home side 2-1 up on the night and 4-3 ahead on aggregate. Mourinho stated: "Real Madrid gave a spectacular performance from the first to the last minute. We came here to play. What I'm about to say is not a criticism, I'm just stating a fact: there were no ball-boys in the second half, which is something typical of small teams when experiencing difficulties. I'm not going to say we're happy because we didn't win the Spanish Super Cup, that would be hypocritical of me. But we intended to play like men and not fall on the ground at the slightest touch."

Mourinho was given a two-match ban by the Spanish Football Federation. Both men were fined 600 euros with the bans only being served in future Supercopa matches - the pre-season competition that pits the reigning Primera Division champions against the Copa del Rey holders. The Football Federation's president, Ángel María Villar, exonerated them as part of a general amnesty so they could take their places on the bench for the first leg of the traditional season opener at Barça's Nou Camp stadium and the return game at Real's Santiago Bernabéu Stadium. Mourinho eventually, almost a year after the event, admitted he was wrong to poke Vilanova in the eye. "I should not have done what I did, obviously not. The person who messed up there was me."

Mourinho, whose Real side ended Barcelona's three-year grip on the Spanish title, said shortly after one of the most ugly incidents in Spanish football that his relationship with Vilanova had since been repaired. "I work a lot with my players precisely on this, control the emotions, only think about playing and work well. The key thing is the negative image. As Tito said a few weeks ago, the footage will be there forever. There are no problems between him and me. The story is over and what needs to be done now is to make sure nothing similar happens again."

Tito Vilanova sadly passed away in April 2014, aged 45, after losing his battle with throat cancer, which had been diagnosed in November 2011.

The two coaches had made their peace, and Mourinho (whilst back at Chelsea) stated at the start of the 2013-14 season that if he had three wishes, he would use one of them to cure the health problems of the ex-Barcelona boss, who won the La Liga title last season in his one and only campaign in charge of the Catalan giants.

On learning of the sad news Mourinho declared "Tito Vilanova's passing is a sad day for football, for Barcelona and most importantly for his family and friends," the Blues' boss said in a statement issued via Chelsea's official website. "On behalf of everybody at Chelsea Football Club I send my deepest condolences at this most difficult time."

For Mourinho, the constant discussion of his off-the-field behaviour and his 'dark-arts' mind games, is vastly overstated; at least according to the man himself if not necessarily the media who follow his every move, his every nuance. "In football, the only game I know is the 90-minutes game. It's not mind games; I don't try to do that. The period before the game can be important to influence opinions, characters, personalities, feelings and, of course, I use that to touch my players, to touch opponents, to touch supporters. But for me, the only game in football is the 90-minutes game."

Do the exchanges become personal? "No, I never have that," he insisted in the past. Surely there are personal clashes. With Guardiola? Wenger? "I prefer to play against the best players and the best teams and the best coaches. Never personal."

In his first season with Madrid and aiming to become the first coach to lead three different clubs to European titles after guiding Porto to the 2004 crown, and Inter the previous season in 2010, it was suggested he would stop at nothing to break that personal record that would elevate him to true greatness.

UEFA charged Mourinho and four players with unsporting conduct after Xabi Alonso and Sergio Ramos appeared to get themselves deliberately sent off in the Champions League, both dismissed after second bookable offenses for time wasting towards the end of Madrid's 4-0 win at Ajax. The result ensured the Spanish giants qualified in first place from Group G and the dismissals, perhaps conveniently, meant Alonso and Ramos would miss the final round robin match against Auxerre rather than carry the threat of suspensions into the knockout stage. TV cameras caught Jerzy Dudek talking to Mourinho on the sidelines before the substitute keeper went to talk to Iker Casillas, who in turn had a word with Ramos. All denied they were transmitting instructions for the players to coax red cards from Scottish referee Craig Thomson.

UEFA, nonetheless, charged Mourinho, Alonso, Ramos, Casillas and Dudek with unsporting conduct.

After the match, Mourinho insisted: "I spoke with many players throughout the game, not only with Ramos and Alonso. Stories sell, but the important thing is the 4-0 win and the fantastic game we had. Let's talk about that and not other things." Ramos, who was dismissed for having taken an age to take a goal kick, maintained: "We didn't go looking for the cards. Seeing what the score was, the referee could have saved them. But he sent me off and that's that."

Mourinho had plenty of 'previous' with the European football authorities as well as the FA. He clashed with UEFA when manager of Chelsea. UEFA banned Mourinho from the touchline for two matches in 2005 after he accused Barcelona coach Frank Rijkaard of visiting Swedish referee Anders Frisk at half-time in the first leg of a last 16 clash.

However, deliberate bookings are not new, it's as old as diving, but none the less abhorrent to the ethos of the game. As I said in a recent interview about Pele, the players still retain the passion for playing, but no longer the passion for the game itself or its morals and virtues.

So, it's hardly surprisingly in this new world that there are a number of previous cases of players deliberately seeking cautions to manipulate the timing of suspensions. David Beckham was England captain when he intentionally committed a yellow-card foul against Wales in a World Cup qualifier, explaining he'd sustained a rib injury which he knew would sideline him for the next match, so wanted his second caution of the qualifying campaign to serve a one-match ban. Australia skipper Lucas Neill admitted getting a yellow card against Qatar in a World Cup qualifier so he could serve a ban immediately and not risk carrying it into the finals in South Africa. Lyon players Cris and Juninho were both fined by UEFA for deliberately incurring a second Champions League yellow card against Fiorentina to miss the meaningless group tie with Bayern and be clear of suspension ahead of the knockout stage.

Mourinho, though, was never going to be the Real Madrid manager for too long. He bemoaned the "worst season of my career" after seeing his Madrid side slip to a 2-1 extra time defeat to capital rivals Atlético in the final of the Copa del Rey. Widely tipped to return to Chelsea, he made his feelings clear to the media after seeing his last chance of silverware that season slip away as Real lost the semi-finals of the Champions League to Borussia Dortmund and Barcelona clinched La Liga title. A season which started with such promise after beating Barça to win the Spanish Super Cup petered out. "This is the worst season of my career with a title that is not sufficient to satisfy Real Madrid and therefore it is a bad season."

His swansong in the Santiago Bernabéu wasn't the best of nights for Ronaldo, either, as he saw red in the dying minutes. Mourinho was ordered to leave the touchline by the referee for protesting a decision late in the second half as Atlético won their first Copa del Rey in 17 years.

Mourinho was teased by the *Atleti* fans. "Mourinho, stay!" they implored with heavy sarcasm. The scrappy contest that featured more than a dozen yellow cards and two reds was settled by Miranda's header in the eighth minute of extra time on a night when it seemed Atlético, who hadn't beaten their city rivals since 1999, were destined to lift the trophy. After Ronaldo opened the scoring in the 14th minute with a typically impressive header, Diego Costa leveled on a counter attack in the 35th after superb work by striking partner Radamel Falcao.

Real struck the post three times prior to the game entering extra time and Atlético keeper Thibaut Courtois made two stunning saves to preserve the victory and help end his team's three-match losing streak in Copa finals.

The affair turned ugly in the dying minutes, with Ronaldo given a straight red card for kicking out at Gabi and players from both benches having to be separated. Courtois fell to the ground when struck by an item thrown from the stands.

Mourinho believed his team should have lifted the cup and had been plain unlucky, a familiar gripe. "The result is 1-1 and it is not normal to hit the post three times. You don't have to be a magician of football to think that the result is not fair, that Atlético are not the deserved winners of the final. The refereeing is forgotten, the shots off the post are forgotten, all that remains is that the winner is Atlético."

Several of his players cared more about their public appearance than about winning trophies, according to Mourinho, who after three years in charge at the

Santiago Bernabéu, was not impressed by their attitude. "Lots of times at Real Madrid, the players would be queuing in front of the mirror before the game while the referee waited for them in the tunnel, but that's how society is now. Young people care a lot about this: they are twentysomething and I am 51 and if I want to work with kids I have to understand their world. How can I stop my players on the bus doing, er, what do you call?... Twitters and these things? How can I stop them if my daughter and my son do the same? So, I have to adapt to the moment. I'm a manager since 2000 so I'm in my second generation of players. What I feel is that, before, players were trying to make money during their career, be rich at the end of their career but, in this moment, the people who surround them try to make them rich before they start their career. They try to make them rich when they sign their first contract, when they didn't play one single match in the Premier League, when they don't know what it is to play in the Champions League. This puts the clubs in difficult conditions sometimes. You have to find the right boy: the boy who wants to succeed, has pride and passion for the game. His dream is not one more million or one less million, his dream is to play at the highest level, to win titles, because if you do these things you'll be rich the same at the end of your career. So we are working hard to give the best orientation to young players, to follow examples of guys from the past - the Lampards, the Terrys - who were always fanatical for victories."

For the first time in a decade, since he took the reins at Porto, he endured a term without a trophy (bar the Spanish Super Cup). Mourinho said, "But I don't know any manager who always has a fantastic season. For others this might be a great season: second in the league, a cup final, a European semi. But for me it is the worst. This season I have failed."

Mourinho fell out publicly with two of the *Galácticos*: Iker Casillas and Sergio Ramos, globally revered goalkeeper and defender respectively. In a bust-up leaked to the papers after a defeat to Barcelona, Ramos sniped at Mourinho: "Because you've never been a player, you don't know that that sometimes happens." Additionally, it was suggested that Mourinho and Ronaldo barely spoke to each other at the end of his time in Spain.

Mourinho can be viewed as a 'Marmite Manager', some seem to loathe him, while many, perhaps the vast majority, have a completely different story to tell. Zlatan Ibrahimović felt his manager made him "feel like a lion". Dutch playmaker Wesley Sneijder went even further: "I was prepared to kill and die for him." When Frank Lampard's mother died in 2008, Mourinho phoned him every day, commiserating and offering advice. Mourinho wasn't even his manager then. "He's the most loyal, the most caring manager I've ever worked with," Lampard said. "I might be biased, because I love the man, but he does it instantly. He brings instant success."

Mourinho has commented about the way he tries to improve players. "It's impossible to make every player better. With some I don't succeed and with some I cannot improve. But - if I go player by player - my percentage of players who reach the best years and the best moments of their career with me is huge. Of course, there are a few where the connection was not good, because the personalities couldn't find each other, or because I don't enjoy working with them. But that percentage is minimal."

José Mourinho was overlooked not only for the Barça job, but it seemed he would never manage Manchester United either. Mourinho was interviewed for the Barcelona job in 2008, but they opted for Guardiola. It was generally felt that Manchester United should have pursued Mourinho to replace Sir Alex, but they preferred David Moyes for the long term and he was undoubtedly someone far less controversial. Mourinho denies that he cried when he learned he'd been passed over at Old Trafford, but he also denies that he was ever approached. Johan Cruyff didn't like his style of football and was therefore not deemed conducive to the Barça philosophy, others find him arrogant, while many found him to be the best manager they had ever worked with.

Does he find the job of being a football manager stressful, he was once asked? "No. I find life stressful sometimes. Not in London, but in Madrid, in Italy, it was stressful."

What keeps him awake at night? "Nothing. Nothing! I sleep seven, eight hours every night. I cannot compare my job with the doctor who is doing heart surgery. The difference is that I have millions of people know the result of my work and the only people who know the result of his work are the family of the person who is on the operating table. But there is much more responsibility for him than for me. That's why I sometimes feel that we earn too much money compared to people who do much more than us to benefit humanity."

"What is football?" Mourinho continues. "Football is emotion. No more than that."

Equally Mourinho had no fears being pitched against the world's best managers too, including his old foe Guardiola; in fact he relishes the challenge. As for those personal spats with the City manager, he has had plenty of skirmishes with many of the best. He said: "It was never a problem for me, so to meet Pep at City or Pellegrini or Mancini or whatever, it is no difference. I was in Milan coaching Inter and Carlo Ancelotti was there coaching AC Milan. I was in Madrid coaching Real and Diego Simeone was coaching at Atletico. I was in London, Arsene Wenger was at Arsenal and there were other top managers at West Ham and Tottenham."

So who would have thought it, certainly not Pep or José, that they would be locking horns again but this time in Manchester?

Mourinho and Guardiola left Spain a year apart, neither of them totally fulfilled. When Guardiola departed, he was asked about his memories of the *Clásicos;* famous victories 6-2, 5-0, and a 2-0 in the European Cup semi-final. His reply was quite astonishing: "I don't have good memories of them."

On the other side of the great divide, Real Madrid justified some of Mourinho's remarkable antics. "We didn't bring Mourinho here to make friends," said Emilio Butragueño, Madrid's institutional director.

At Barça, he was detested. "I don't fancy talking about him," Andrés Iniesta told Spanish newspaper, El País. "But it's clear that Mourinho did more harm than good; he damaged Spanish football." Mourinho responded by saying that Spanish football had been "damaged" in their eyes only because he had "ended Barcelona's hegemony".

The dislike stemmed mostly from how, in 2012, Madrid all but claimed the league with a 2-1 win in the Camp Nou, beginning a run of just one defeat in seven *Clásicos*. And, in his first season his team took the Copa del Rey from Barça, enough to get the blood boiling in Catalonia. Guardiola failed to win just four trophies out of 18 when at the Camp Nou, but three of the four were lost to Mourinho's sides.

Yet, in two years of Pep versus José, the score was pretty much even; Guardiola had won three major trophies, Mourinho two. A league title and a cup for Mourinho versus a league title, a cup and a European Cup for Guardiola; the latter tipping the balance in Pep's favour.

When Guardiola went at the end of the 2011-12 season, it heralded a miserable end for Mourinho as he finished the season empty-handed and 15 points behind Barcelona, under coach Tito Vilanova.

They headed in different directions: to Germany, where Guardiola won three league titles and two cups; and to England, where Mourinho won one league title and the League Cup.

Departing Manchester City manager Manuel Pellegrini regrets his decision to announce, mid 2015-16 season, he was leaving. The club revealed in February 2016 he would be replaced by Guardiola. Pellegrini decided to go public he was to leave just minutes before City officially confirmed a new man would take over in the summer but it had a detrimental effect on his players. At the time City were second, just three points behind Leicester, but they immediately lost three matches in a row in all competitions and eventually finished fourth, 15 adrift of the champions. "After Guardiola said he was coming to England it was my decision (to go public) because all the media was talking about Guardiola here, Guardiola in Arsenal, Guardiola in Manchester United," he told The Guardian. "It was not fair for all managers - when everyone knew he was coming here. If I ask if I would do that again, I have some doubts. Yes. I am very self-critical about what I do. Always. I don't want to use (this) as an excuse but it was so difficult to work after that - not for me, for the players. It's impossible to know if it was the right decision but when you see the consequence of losing immediately three games in a row, when you are winning the last five or something. The most difficult thing in a group is when you break something. Something was broken in that moment."

Guardiola will take City "to a new level", according to club chairman Khaldoon Al Mubarak. "I'm absolutely excited about Pep joining our team," said Al Mubarak. "I consider Pep to be one of, if not the best manager, in football today. We are getting a manager that epitomises passion and commitment. He is a proven winner."

Guardiola won Champions League twice at Barcelona, including their treble-winning campaign in 2008-09. He won the German title with Bayern for three successive seasons, although he failed to win the Champions League there. Speaking to the club's website, Al Mubarak added: "I have no doubt that he will transform our team to a new level."

City finished fourth, failing miserably to mount much of a challenge to win the title they claimed under Pellegrini in 2014. They won the League Cup and reached the Champions League semi-finals, losing to eventual winners Real Madrid. Al Mubarak praised the efforts of Pellegrini but admitted this season had been a disappointment, adding: "We had high expectations."

Mourinho thrives when he invents enemies for himself, says former Inter Milan striker Diego Milito.

The Argentine was a key figure in Mourinho's treble-winning Inter side of 2009-10, scoring both goals in the 2-0 Champions League final win over Bayern

Munich. "Sometimes he invents (enemies) himself on purpose," the 37-year-old is quoted in the Italian newspaper *Gazzetta dello Sport*, "Guardiola included, just go and ask Pep. Mourinho is a great leader of groups, we are talking about a coach of the highest level in the world. He makes sure that every player gives 100 per cent, has the right word at the right moment and can be punishing when necessary. He knows how to protect his team and always needs an enemy to be able to attack or defend his squad."

Ricardo Carvalho was convinced Mourinho will take the title back to Old Trafford. The Portugal central defender knows Mourinho better than most after three spells with him at Porto, Chelsea and Real Madrid. The 38-year-old Carvalho commented: "He's a great coach, the best. I have no doubt that he's going to be a champion with Manchester United again. I hope that things go well. Chelsea is a special club for me and for him as well but overall he's a professional coach and he will do well there."

However, ex-Barcelona captain Xavi didn't think Mourinho would represent Guardiola's closest rivals. "Manchester City and Manchester United has always been a big game - and with Pep and José now coaching I am sure it will be even more intense. If I am honest I don't think United will be their main competition for the league. They are a big club, but they have rebuilding to do."

Guardiola's desire to coach in England had been an open secret at the Nou Camp. "With Pep it was never if he would manage in England, just a case of when," added Xavi. "We used to talk about the Premier League a lot - we are both very passionate about it. I am sure he will sign players, but the most important thing for Pep will be getting Manchester City playing his style of football. He has not compromised his style of football at any time - and if you don't buy into his philosophy - then there won't be a place for you at the club. He will be a success at Manchester City just like he has been at Barcelona and Bayern. I know that Manchester City want the Champions League - and I am sure that he will deliver it for them."

Chelsea and Spain forward Pedro is one of a few players to have played under both Pep and José and he was far more confident that Mourinho will be a success at Old Trafford, than Guardiola at City. The winger won La Liga, the Champions League, and the Copa del Rey with the former Barcelona boss, while only seeing Chelsea struggle in the bottom half under Mourinho when he was parachuted in at a desperate time for the Blues.

"It's a tricky and complicated league where it will be difficult for him to deploy his style of play, although we know he is a great coach but it's not going to be easy for him," Pedro told Spanish, Marca.com, of the Catalan's chances. "He is true to his ideals and can convince players to change their philosophy of direct play for a more elaborate style. We'll see how it goes this first year."

The 28-year-old then sang Mourinho's praises. "One thing is certain and that's he'll bring a lot of intensity. It will be a very strong team and consistent in defence because has bags of character and very clear ideas."

Arjen Robben, another to have played under both, can't decide who his favourite manager, José or Pep, was. The Dutch winger won two Premier League titles under Mourinho at The Bridge and three Bundesliga crowns with Guardiola at Bayern Munich.

When asked who he preferred working for, the 32-year-old told Goal magazine: "No, I cannot say that. They were two completely different periods in my career. When I worked with Mourinho I was still young and it was my first club abroad. With Pep, I was already older and it was different. Both have been interesting and suited me in my career."

Mourinho and Guardiola, of course, had a legendary rivalry, and he added: "They are both big coaches, I worked with each of them for three years. They are top professionals and they will bring their own style of play and mentality to the team. I'm convinced of that. It will be interesting to follow. But it's not only about Pep vs Mourinho, but also about the players on the pitch in the end."

Former Liverpool midfielder Xabi Alonso (now with Bayern Munich) also gave his thoughts on Mourinho vs Guardiola, having worked under both managers. He was excited about what will unfold next season. "On the football side, they have different approaches and style. What you get with both is huge charisma and leadership. It is going to be very exciting to watch them, especially in the same city now. It is a challenge for both to be against each other. I am definitely going to be watching it from here and keeping my eye on what is happening.

Chapter 7

A SUMMER OF EUROS, RUMOURS, SCANDALS, SIGNINGS & CONTRACTS

The media were simply salivating at the prospect of José vs Pep, and while the Euros were on and there was a lull before the storm, The Daily Star whipped up some hype around both managers chasing the same players. In this case, the day of the Premier League fixtures being announced, it was a £50m tug of war for England central defender John stones.

Mourinho tried to sign Stones the previous summer, whilst at Chelsea, with an eye to a long term replacement for the ageing skipper John Terry, and the club's failure to pay the going rate was one of the symptoms of the manager's eventual inability to mount a proper defence of the title. It was clearly an obvious assumption to make that he would renew his interest in Stones with a far bigger budget and transfer ambition at Old Trafford than there was a year ago at the Bridge where the appetite to pay inflated prices had waned many years ago.

Guardiola had now also targeted the Everton defender as well after missing out on Athletic Bilbao's Aymeric Laporte, even though he had been out of action with a broken leg and dislocated ankle. Laporte decided to sign a new deal with Bilbao instead.

Guardiola believed Stones can be the long-term successor to Vincent Kompany, who continued to struggle with serious injury problems, and was a BBC TV pundit at the Euros having missed the tournament through injury.

Mourinho had three bids of up to £40m rejected by the Toffees last summer, who held firm to keep hold of one of their prize assets, and there was clearly friction behind the scenes as Roman Abramovich refused to sanction any more £50m transfers after the signing of Fernando Torres. Mourinho remained a huge admirer of the 22-year-old as he needed to strengthen his defence as he looks to rebuild a title-winning side at Old Trafford.

Mourinho had a £200m plus budget to spend on new signings and is on a mission to bring in some marquee names, but equally new Everton manager Ronald Koeman would not want to part with Stones at any price. But, Mourinho won't want to miss out on getting Stones again - let alone to Guardiola - and could offer him a contract worth a basic £150,000-a-week.

Looking to the future, two bright young stars both signed new contracts.

18-year-old striker Marcus Rashford and defender Cameron Borthwick-Jackson, 19, signed new deals which will keep them at Old Trafford until June 2020.

Rashford scored twice on his first-team debut against Midtjylland in February and finished the season with eight goals in 18 appearances.

"I am grateful for having the chance to prove myself," Rashford said. "To be able to play football at the biggest club in the world means everything to me and my family."

Rashford's new contract is thought to be worth £20,000 a week.

José Mourinho's first signing arrived pretty quickly and was confirmed when the club issued this statement which popped into my email in box... "United sign Eric Bailly"

"Manchester United is delighted to announce that Eric Bertrand Bailly has completed his transfer from Villarreal CF, subject to successfully obtaining a work permit. Eric joins on a four year contract with the option to extend for a further two years."

Bailly, 22, has made 47 appearances for Villarreal CF since joining on 29 January 2015. The Ivorian central defender has made 15 appearances for his country and was part of the 2015 Africa Cup of Nations winning team, having appeared in all six matches during the competition.

Eric Bailly said: "It is a dream come true to be joining Manchester United. To play football at the highest level is all I have ever wanted to do. I want to progress to be the best that I can be and I believe working with José Mourinho will help me develop in the right way and at the right club. I am looking forward to meeting my new team mates and to starting this new chapter of my life."

Eric Bailly joined United even though Yaya Touré had tried to persuade him to team up at City. A phone call with Mourinho and chat with Didier Drogba, though, convinced him to switch to Old Trafford.

He spoke to fellow Ivory Coast players before making the decision and Drogba, who was an integral part of Mourinho's success at Chelsea, offered a glowing reference on Mourinho.

"Mourinho called me as well and he told me to come and play for him. I prefer Mourinho, in part because of Didier Drogba, who worked with him. Didier is a friend and he told me José did a lot for him. Yaya also called me and wanted me to come to City, but once José spoke to me and Didier gave me advice, I knew straight away I wanted to play for him."

José Mourinho added: "Eric is a young central defender with great natural talent. He has progressed well to date and has the potential to become one of the best around. We look forward to working with him to help nurture that raw talent and fulfil his potential. Eric is at the right club to continue his development."

Manchester United had confirmed the signing of Eric Bailly from Villarreal for £30m just 24 hours after the news first broke that he had the first stage of his medical and on the same day Manchester City were ready to make a significant statement of intent in the transfer market with talks over the signing of Borussia Dortmund striker Pierre-Emerick Aubameyang.

José and Pep were going head-to-head in the big money stakes to recruit new teams for the forthcoming season and were not about to hang around with eye-watering sums being paid in transfer fees and salaries.

Both Manchester clubs were rushing through their transfer business in early June in order to have the important stars ready for training in plenty of time to formulate pre-season plans.

Bailly's journey to Manchester United was quite unusual. The young Ivory Coast international has been watched by Manchester City, Bayern Munich, Barcelona and Borussia Dortmund over the past two seasons after he joined Villarreal from Espanyol in January 2015 for £4.4m. He was also on Barcelona's list of possible signings this summer so United had to act fast.

He could not make his Espanyol debut until he was 18 because he did not have the correct paperwork. He trained and played friendlies until finally he could play with the club's youth side. He made just 21 appearances for them before then Espanyol manager Sergio Gonzalez gave him his first-team debut in January 2015 in a 1-1 draw against Villarreal, who then signed him five games later.

His rise has been quite phenomenal; Ivory Coast made him an ever-present starter in their 2015 Africa Cup of Nations campaign after he had played only two friendlies. Villarreal signed him from Espanyol after he had played a mere five games in La Liga. But Villarreal only owned 50 per cent of his rights and as they did not have the money to buy him outright.

After only 35 matches Mourinho wanted him at Manchester United, but his emergence is a consequence from last January when Villarreal sold Gabriel Paulista to Arsenal for £11.2m and found an immediate replacement in the £4.4m two-footed centre-back, who can also play as a full back. He had to compete with experienced pair Mateo Musacchio and Victor Ruiz but he became first choice in less than a year.

He was away on international duty playing in the African Cup of Nations that Ivory Coast won when he signed. He had had been a late call-up to the squad having just played two friendlies but he started all six games and scored a penalty as Ghana were beaten on spot-kicks in the final.

Quick, powerful and agile, Bailly was still raw but in keeping with the clubs policy to invest heavily in emerging young talent, and Mourinho believed he could grow into a strong presence at the back with the new manager seeking a physical dimension to the squad.

Bailly's former coach at Espanyol, Manolo Marquez, said: "I'm absolutely convinced that he'd be a success in England. He's similar to Sergio Ramos and while he's not as good technically, he's much stronger. Mourinho would be good for Eric because Mourinho always has his defences very well organised. He's also the type of very strong defender he likes to work with."

Former Manchester United winger Quinton Fortune believes Bailly has all the attributes.

Fortune, the first of four previous African internationals to play for United, watched Bailly while commentating on *La Liga* games. "He's a very good signing," the South African told MUTV. "The first thing I realised when watching him was that he's very young - he's only 22 but the way he was playing, I thought he was more experienced. He's an out-and-out defender who can play across the back four. He's quick, good in the air and, when he gets the ball down on the floor, he can pass it. Not a lot of people will know about him but he's a good defender. People will need to have some patience at the beginning but he has all the attributes to play in the Premier League."

Quinton made the transition from Spanish to English football when he joined the Reds from Atlético Madrid in 1999, and says: "He'll definitely feel the pace! In Spain, the play is a little slower and more tactical, whereas the majority of games in the Premier League are high-tempo and you need to be on your toes all the time as a defender. He's played against Real Madrid and Barcelona, and he's an Africa Cup of Nations winner, so he's had that exposure and has been put under some pressure. But it's a completely different situation playing for

Manchester United. The only way to find out is to throw him in."

United also made enquiries about Chelsea midfielder Nemanja Matić and remained interested in Zlatan Ibrahimović…

Mourinho was widely reportedly plotting to raid his old club for Azpilicueta, Willian and Nemanja Matić. Mourinho recruited Azpilicueta at the Bridge to play left-back ahead of Ashley Cole, and reports in Spain claimed new Chelsea boss, Antonio Conte, was ready to let him leave for just under £12million.

La Liga side Athletic Bilbao were also interested, but Azpilicueta insisted he was focused on his future at Stamford Bridge and not a move elsewhere, and denied contact with his old boss Mourinho. He told radio station, *Cadena Cope*: "[Mourinho?] No. If you believe me or don't believe me. It's always a compliment that you are wanted. I've heard highly about (Bilbao boss) Ernesto Valverde but I'm focused on the national team and Chelsea. I've been there for four years, I am very happy and I feel highly valued."

Azpilicueta was hoping to get a chance ahead of either Jordi Alba or Juanfran in the Spain side at Euro 2016.

The former Marseille defender's versatility means he can play on either flank, but Azpilicueta added: "At the World Cup in Brazil and the Confederations Cup I was playing on the right-side of defence. While at Chelsea this season I've mostly been playing on the left and even in the centre, but I feel comfortable in any defensive position. I just want to play for my country."

But the rumour mill went into overdrive during the Euros as Mourinho was linked in The Sun with a shock bid for Aaron Ramsey if he failed to land Borussia Dortmund star Henrikh Mkhitaryan.

The 25-year-old Welshman was taking the Euros by storm along with his countrymen in reaching the last 16, and Mourinho wanted him to be Manchester United's Frank Lampard, according to the eye-catching report.

Raiding Prem rivals Arsenal for Ramsey would be one of Mourinho's boldest ever transfer moves, The Sun suggested, knowing he would face fierce resistance from old adversary Wenger.

Wenger, however, had just spent £30million on Borussia Mönchengladbach playmaker Granit Xhaka, leaving Arsenal in midfield 'overload' with Mesut Özil, Santi Cazorla, Jack Wilshere, Francis Coquelin and Mohamed Elneny all vying with Ramsey for a midfield role. Wenger also remained in the hunt to sign Leicester's N'Golo Kante.

Ramsey was growing increasingly frustrated at his failure to nail down a central midfield role at the Emirates, so all the signs were that a move to Manchester United wouldn't be as daft as it might sound.

Mourinho was ready to tempt Ramsey by offering a similar role to the one he gave Lampard at Chelsea, knowing he has a similar capacity to strike from midfield.

Mkhitaryan, however, remained his top summer target, but Borussia Dortmund were playing hardball over a fee as United tabled an improved bid of £28m for the Armenia captain, after an initial offer of £19.3m was rejected. The Dortmund winger, however, made it plain that he wanted to leave the German side and join Mourinho. He informed Dortmund he won't be extending his contract beyond next June, when it is scheduled to expire, and remained determined to force through a move to United.

Dortmund saw key defender Mats Hummels and influential midfielder İlkay Gündoğan already move to Bayern Munich and Manchester City respectively this summer while star striker Pierre-Emerick Aubameyang has also been linked with a big money move to City. "We have discussed the question of an early transfer in all club bodies and came to the conclusion that Mkhitaryan will stay in Dortmund next season," Hans-Joachim Watzke, the Borussia Dortmund chief executive steadfastly confirmed.

The Armenian international's agent Mino Raiola confirmed his player wants to head to the Premier League, despite Dortmund previously saying they would block any move. "It would be a sin to stop talking," said Raiola. "I am a positive guy. If I wasn't confident of reaching some kind of conclusion, I wouldn't try. I am very proud Manchester United want him and the talks are being held in a good atmosphere, but at the moment Dortmund are still saying no."

"He wants to go to Manchester United and we are still trying to resolve the situation," Raiola added. "We are still talking to Dortmund. We are trying to be reasonable. They are aware that Micki wants to leave now."

Raiola was the man who brought Mario Balotelli to the Premier League and also represents Romelu Lukaku and was sure to be someone at the end of the phone virtually all summer long to Mourinho. Raiola masterminded the Pogba's move to Juventus, which so incensed Sir Alex in 2012. Pogba was just 19 at the time and was a free agent, and despite Sir Alex's best efforts to keep him, United only received minimal compensation of £800,000 for a player who is now valued at £78m. And now Mourinho would love him back at Old Trafford.

Plus, he represented not only Ibrahimović but also Henrikh Mkhitaryan, another of Mourinho's prime transfer targets. Speaking to GQ magazine, Raiola gave his thoughts about his high profile clients, saying: "Pogba to Chelsea? Not now." Raiola was winding up the market: "Ibrahimović could return to Italy, to Milan." He later let it slip that Bayern wanted him, upping the ante with United. Balotelli was fighting to convince Milan to keep him at the San Siro with Liverpool desperate to sell in the summer. Raiola: "Balotelli? If he had the head of Ibrahimović, Messi would have less Ballon d'Ors." Mourinho would know, as 'Not-so-super Mario' was one player not even José's silky skills could tame.

Mkhitaryan, 27, impressed for Dortmund last season, helping them to second place in the Bundesliga and the German Cup final, scoring 23 goals and adding 32 assists along the way. He would certainly add width and significant attacking quality to United.

Dortmund chief, Hans-Joachim Watzke, was clearly fearful that losing Mkhitaryan would send out the wrong message to Marco Reus and Pierre-Emerick Aubameyang, talking of whom...

Manchester City were about to smash their transfer record, with Pierre-Emerick Aubameyang, valued at £58m, which would top the £54m spent on Kevin De Bruyne last summer. Guardiola had keenly watched the player's progress at first hand during his time at Bayern Munich.

Aubameyang scored 40 goals for Dortmund last season, naturally interesting every top club in Europe. But Barcelona and Real Madrid planned to keep their main strikers, leaving City as the outstanding favourites to sign the 26-year-old Gabon international.

United also wanted Aubameyang but could not offer Champions League football. Guardiola told City sporting director Txiki Begiristain that the Gabon international, French-born but with 49 caps for the African nation, was high on his list of priorities to bring in another proven goalscorer to support Sergio Agüero. Chairman Khaldoon Al Mubarak said City "will provide the necessary resources for Pep to build a team that has the ambition and the capability to go and win back this Premier League".

City had already sanctioned the £21m capture of Dortmund midfielder İlkay Gündoğan and were in talks for Ukrainian teenager Oleksandr Zinchenko from Russian side FC Ufa.

Their third summer signing was Spain forward Nolito from Celta Vigo after meeting his £13.8m release clause. The 29-year-old signed a four-year contract.

Nolito started all four of Spain's matches at Euro 2016 before they were knocked out in the last 16 by Italy. "I think that Pep Guardiola is one of the best managers in the world," said Nolito, whose name is Manuel Agudo Durán. "He knows a lot about the game and he's going to help me progress as a player. I'm sure he'll get the best out of me."

United, though, had their biggest gun already lined up, but they allowed Zlatan Ibrahimović's Paris Saint-Germain contract to expire on June 30 before securing the striker on a free transfer.

Ibrahimović, 34, was initially due to become José Mourinho's first signing at Old Trafford after positive talks between United and the player's representative, Mino Raiola. But, with both Ibrahimović and Raiola due to receive a lucrative loyalty bonus from PSG should he see out his contract at the Parc des Princes, United waited until the player officially became a free agent before formalising a one-year deal, with the option of a further 12 months, worth £250,000 -a-week.

LEADING SCORERS IN 2015-16:

Luis Suarez: 40

Zlatan Ibrahimović: 38

Gonzalo Higuain: 36

Cristiano Ronaldo: 35

Robert Lewandowski: 30

Pierre-Emerick Aubameyang: 25

Harry Kane: 25

(Stats from the top five European leagues)

Ibrahimović scored 50 goals in 51 appearances for PSG last season and is the proven and experienced goalscorer Mourinho was to pin his hopes on having worked with him before.

Mourinho identified the need for exceptional players through the entire spine of his team, with Ibrahimović's experience deemed vital with Anthony Martial and Marcus Rashford still developing.

It's #ZlatanTime

It was Ibrahimović himself who finally confirmed he would sign for Manchester United on social media.

The 34-year-old, capped 116 times for his country, was out of contract after four years at the French champions and wanted to link up again with his former Inter Milan boss at Old Trafford.

"Time to let the world know. My next destination is Manchester United," he wrote on his Instagram account before United actually confirmed the move and Ibrahimović had yet to complete a medical and sign a contract with the Old Trafford club.

Ibrahimović signed on a one-year deal at Old Trafford worth £200,000-a-week, and said he was relishing the opportunity. He was "ready to create more special memories in England" after his move to United was officially confirmed as Mourinho's second signing of the summer and admitted he was "delighted" to join United. On announcing he was leaving the Ligue 1 club, he tweeted in his usual modest way: "I came like a king, left like a legend."

"I am absolutely delighted to be joining Manchester United and am looking forward to playing in the Premier League. It goes without saying that I cannot wait to work with José Mourinho once again. He is a fantastic manager and I am ready for this new and exciting challenge. I have thoroughly enjoyed my career so far and have some great memories. I am now ready to create more special memories in England."

Speaking to *MUTV* (United's official TV channel):

How does it feel?

"I'm super excited, super, super happy. Finally it's done. There's been a lot of talks but it came to the moment where everything is done, and now we start. Now the hard work starts, so I'm super happy. I'm just waiting to get to know the guys, the first training and I'm here in the training facility. It looks like it is a big club, a huge club, so I'm excited."

Are you glad the speculation is over?

"I'm happy, now I can focus on one thing and that's the United shirt, and leave everything behind me. Because I played the European Championship and there was more talk about my future than the Euros. Finally now everything is over and I can focus on my new club and go back to hard work and doing as good as possible."

Did José Mourinho influence your decision?

"I think my decision was pretty easy. (The difficulty) was more to make it possible, everything. I compare it with the Mayweather and Pacquiao fight - they said it would never happen but it happened. I want to say thanks to my team, United and José Mourinho, obviously, because they made it possible. Now I'm at United, so I'm super happy. So my decision was the easiest part. The rest was a puzzle, but the puzzle came together and we are happy, all of us."

Are you excited to be working with José again?

"I have great memories. The only regret I had with José was that I had a short time with him. I had one season. We won together, we enjoyed it together and had a great time together. I learned a lot, and I got to know him as a person, not only as a coach, and only positive things. He's a winner, I'm a winner and we know both what we want. We want to win. Wherever we go, we win. And we will win."

Is the Premier League the only missing piece in your career?

"I think it's a big challenge for me. Wherever I came I won, and I'm looking forward to this new adventure, a new chapter in my career, in my life. If I could win here, I don't know how many players have had the possibility to play in different competitions like I have and at the same time be winning. So I will work hard. I know my mentality, I know what I want, I come to win. I want to win, but behind everything is hard work. That is what we have been doing so far, and that is what we come to do here also."

In his book, *I Am Zlatan Ibrahimović*, he described Mourinho as a manager he was "willing to die for".

Speaking when Mourinho was appointed at United, he said: "He is the man to bring them back to the top. I had a fantastic time working with him. If we will work again I don't know."

Ibrahimović is unquestionably not so complimentary of the new Manchester City boss, whom he played under for two seasons at Barcelona.

He referred to Guardiola as a "spineless coward" in his autobiography, and Barcelona president Josép Maria Bartomeu revealed Ibrahimović said he "might punch Pep" during his time at the Nou Camp. He fiercely dislikes the footballing mantra of Guardiola, his coach for one unhappy season at Barcelona. "Guardiola started his philosopher thing. I was barely listening," the Swede said, reflecting on a team talk at the Nou Camp. "Why would I? It was advanced bull**** about blood, sweat and tears, that kind of stuff."

Mourinho, naturally, was confident that Ibrahimović can propel United to great things and hailed him as one of the best. "Zlatan needs no introduction. The statistics speak for themselves. Ibra is one of the best strikers in the world and a player who always gives 100 per cent. He has won the most important league championships in the world of football, now he has the opportunity to play in the best league in the world and I know he will grasp this opportunity and will work hard to help the team win titles. I am certain that his talent will delight fans at Old Trafford next season and that his experience will be invaluable in helping to develop the younger players in the squad."

Ibrahimović made his debut for hometown club Malmo in 1999 and played for Ajax, Juventus, Inter Milan, Barcelona and AC Milan before joining PSG, scoring 392 goals in 677 games and last season was his most prolific, with 50 goals in 51 matches - a record for the French club. His 38 league goals was also a club record. He has won a trophy every season of his career since 2001, including 13 league titles. In his four seasons at PSG, Ibrahimović won 12 trophies, including the domestic quadruple twice.

He announced his retirement from international football after Sweden's exit from Euro 2016.

Ibrahimović's League Career:

Years	Team	Apps	(Goals)
1999-2001	Malmö FF	40	(16)
2001-2004	Ajax	74	(35)
2004-2006	Juventus	70	(23)
2006-2009	Internazionale	88	(57)
2009-2011	Barcelona	29	(16)
2010-2011	Milan (loan)	29	(14)
2011-2012	Milan	32	(28)
2012-2016	PSG	122	(113)

United chose to publicise the move on their Twitter account with a video, which was captioned "Are you ready? It's #ZlatanTime." The footage featured the striker in darkness before walking forward into the light where he is clearly visible and smiling.

Ibrahimović confirmed the move on his Instagram page a day earlier than expected. Delaying officially signing meant he secured a bonus payment from his former employers in the region of £1million.

"Time to let the world know," he posted alongside a picture of United's crest on the day his PSG deal expired, before adding: '#iamcoming.'

Ibrahimović attempted to keep supporters guessing for over a month, his agent Mino Raiola even suggesting earlier in the day that no decision had been made on his future. In reality, he checked out properties in Cheshire in readiness for the switch, with his personal chef, Frenchman, Joël Robuchon moving too.

Ibrahimović had earlier said he had "many options" for next season, including a return to Italy, but the lure of working with Mourinho was a key factor. He played for him at Inter in 2008-09, helping them win the Serie A title, before joining Barcelona.

Ibrahimović joined Eric Bailly as new men alongside Mourinho, with Borussia Dortmund midfielder Henrikh Mkhitaryan set to follow. A fortnight earlier United officials were privately conceding they would struggle to land the Armenia captain with Dortmund in no mood to sell but an increased offer of nearly £30m sealed a deal.

It didn't take too long before Ibrahimović was making Twitter headlines. He created a record before he even kicked a ball by breaking new ground during their routine medical tests.

"Making history already," United's official Twitter account tweeted. "We can confirm Zlatan broke #mufc power records in tests during his medical. #ZlatanTime."

Ibrahimović will be a success at United and could help further develop Marcus Rashford, according to Ryan Giggs, commenting in his new role as TV pundit. He said: "I think it's a terrific signing. At United we were short of goals last season and he's a proven goal-scorer. As a player, you see a winner. You see character and a bit of class. You want to learn first-hand from more experienced players (if you are Rashford), and Marcus can only learn from someone like that."

Sir Alex would have rejected this sort of transfer "nine times out of 10" according to former number two René Meulensteen.

Dutchman Meulensteen told The Sun: "Maybe nine times out of ten he would not have made a decision like this. That is because of everything that Alex

Ferguson wanted to do with youngsters; bring them through and improve them as players. But if he felt the situation was there for the one time out of ten, he would do it. Like bringing in Laurent Blanc, a player in his 30s, after Jaap Stam left. It's a similar scenario."

United legend Paul Parker suggested Mourinho and Ibrahimović would struggle. He was also worried that the manager's confrontational style, as once again illustrated with his recent dig at Arsene Wenger, would eventually manifest itself with Pep Guardiola.

On Mourinho, the former England and United defender told talkSPORT: "He suggested when he came back to Chelsea that he'd learnt from his time at Inter Milan and Real Madrid but then went back to his old ways at that press conference again where he mentioned Arsene Wenger. As manager of Manchester United the only thing that should matter is Manchester United. It shouldn't concern him. Why is he concerned about any other manager? Mourinho has got a style of play and, regardless how good or bad his squad is, that hasn't changed from any of the clubs he's been to. I don't think it can or will change. If the priority of United fans is to win games by any means then they haven't really been United fans for very long - I'd have gone for Laurent Blanc."

Parker, at Old Trafford from 1991 to 1996, explained why Ibrahimović had a long way to go before he can be compared to Eric Cantona. "I'm sceptical about Ibrahimović. He's going to have to prove himself and has age against him. Mourinho likes a focal point up front. He likes an aggressive centre-forward. Ibrahimović playing the same way as he did at PSG won't work in the Premier League because teams down the bottom are far too competitive."

Paul Scholes also had reservations, believing Ibrahimović will struggle at Old Trafford, as United's squad are nowhere near as creative as the PSG team. "We don't know about Zlatan. He is 34 and probably going to play only for a year," Scholes told website Sport Witness. "Okay, he is a fit lad... but he has been playing in a team of PSG and they created a lot of chances. It was easy for him to score goals in that league. This Manchester United team isn't as good as the PSG team. It might be in time to come. He is going to have to do more for himself in the Manchester United team. More than he did at PSG."

Writing in his Daily Mail column, Jamie Redknapp commented: "Am I excited to see Zlatan Ibrahimović in the Premier League next season? Absolutely - but I can't help but wish he had come here five years earlier. I am sure United will get a good year or two out of him, but it's a sad indication of the pulling power of our league that we won't see him at his prime. Instead of signing a world-class 24-year-old like Neymar, they are bringing in someone 10 years older. Having said that, there's no doubt he will be box office - particularly alongside José Mourinho. There won't be enough column inches for the pair of them! With an enormous personality and a physique to match, Ibrahimović won't be bullied the way some players have been over here. He's also got sublime technique and an absolutely booming shot. I can see him scoring plenty of screamers from distance. There is concern among United fans about Mourinho's apparent disregard for bringing through the next generation from youth teams, and that may be exacerbated by a signing like this. What does it mean for someone like Marcus Rashford, for example? However, if there's one thing the Old Trafford faithful do love it's a big character - a talisman. Just look how popular Eric Cantona was. United fans are desperate to get back to the top at the moment and Ibrahimović has the broad shoulders to carry that burden. He was never really appreciated by us before netting four against England in 2012. 'He never scores against English teams,' we said. He certainly will next season."

Paul Ince believes United have got exactly the right man in Mourinho, and Zlatan Ibrahimović is the right man to lead the new attack.

"Eric Cantona was a lot younger when he arrived at Old Trafford but Zlatan can still do it at 34," Ince told the *Manchester Evening News*. "He's got the stature like Cantona, the flicks and tricks. He'll puff out his chest and take the whole stage on board like Eric did if he signs. I don't want it to become about him though. You don't want team-mates to be over-awed."

Mourinho's appointment had Ince purring. "When you looked down our line up as we marched out and there were figures and characters like Cantona, Roy Keane, Bryan Robson and Peter Schmeichel - you had players who made up a man's team. A team of winners," Ince added. "Then you had Fergie walking down the touchline as well. I think we beat a lot of teams before we even kicked off. There was a winning mentality and an aura that frightened opponents. That aura has gone in recent seasons. Teams could easily take three points at Old Trafford. Nobody was scared when United went to their grounds any more. There won't be another Sir Alex again but José is the nearest you'll get. There is nobody better than him. He's what United have needed."

I was provided with this interesting observation from a big Manchester United fan - Oli Winton, Senior Director, Public Affairs, FTI Consulting - and someone well-connected: "Ibrahimović is a great player at the tail end his career. He could well be the short term catalyst to some success, just as Robin van Persie walked into Old Trafford and was absolutely key in delivering a league title. The comparisons to Eric Cantona seem slightly less direct. Ibrahimović's impact will be one of possible two seasons, whereas Eric oversaw five seasons all of which he was able to significantly influence. And not only were Eric's own performances so astonishing, but he also influenced those around him. The likes of David Beckham, Paul Scholes, the Nevilles and Nicky Butt have all spoken about how much Eric did to teach them, stay behind with them after training and give them confidence to succeed. We will have to wait to see whether Ibrahimović will help develop the younger players rather than being a threat to their place in the team. Is there room for him as well as Rashford, Martial and Lingard?"

In 1992, when the likes of Aston Villa, Blackburn, Norwich and QPR were all ahead of Manchester United, the club needed a new leader, someone to ignite the ailing team. The 'Man from Marseille' turned it all around when Eric Cantona arrived from Leeds United and would set United on the road to domination. Yet, Sir Alex paid a modest £1.2million for Cantona, when United hadn't been champions since 1967 and were in danger of missing out again in 1992-93, as they had a year previously. In the Cantona era, four Premier League titles were won in five seasons. Like Cantona, the Swedish striker could be the catalyst, certainly in the short term. They speak their minds and there are similarities in substance and style: Cantona's upturned collar to Ibrahimović's distinctive tash. "Whatever you say about Cantona, he was a popular lad, and I get the impression Zlatan is the same," said Roy Keane. "Of course he is a good fit for United."

Cantona was 26 when he arrived at Old Trafford, almost a decade younger than Ibrahimović. His career had largely been spent in Ligue 1, where he made his debut in 1983 at Auxerre and played for five other sides before moving to Leeds. Punching an Auxerre team-mate and throwing a ball at a referee during a match at Nimes, and a TV interview calling French national coach Henri Michel a "bag of s***" should have been an indicator of the 'baggage' that accompanied the genius. Cantona was highly derogatory about the playing ability of former France captain Didier Deschamps in 1996 when he described him as a "water carrier".

Ibrahimović was far more established as a global superstar when he arrived at Old Trafford. He played at the highest level on the international stage, something King Eric never managed, and is widely regarded as one of the globe's elite players, whereas Cantona was still establishing a reputation in the game.

Football finance expert Rob Wilson, of Sheffield Hallam University, was interviewed on the BBC sports web site where he suggested Ibrahimović would be United's most marketable player since Cristiano Ronaldo, with shirt sales alone topping £50m - enough to cover the cost of failing to qualify for this season's Champions League. "Zlatan has a global profile and global appeal," Wilson was quoted as saying. "Fans will buy shirts with Ibrahimović on the back in Africa, South East Asia - markets United had a foothold in but not the leverage. Only a few select few players can do that: Gareth Bale, Neymar, Lionel Messi and Ronaldo."

Ibrahimović, with an ego to match his footballing talents, is infamous for outrageous statements. When Arsene Wenger wanted the then teenager to have a trial for Arsenal in 2000, he instead chose to join Ajax saying: "Zlatan doesn't do auditions." After Sweden missed out on the World Cup finals in Brazil in 2014, he said: "One thing is for sure, a World Cup without me is nothing to watch."

Memorable of all the Frenchman's unpalatable traits came in 1995 with his Kung-Fu kick on Crystal Palace fan Matthew Simmons at Selhurst Park, for which he received an eight-month ban and was told to undertake community service. Ibrahimović also has a temper. In his book, *I Am Zlatan Ibrahimović*, he reveals an altercation with Milan team-mate Oguchi Onyewu in 2010 in which he deliberately targeted the American with "the worst kind of tackle" in training as retribution for "trash talk". "I head-butted him, and we flew at each other. We wanted to tear each other limb from limb. It was brutal," he wrote. "We were rolling around, punching and kneeing each other. We were crazy and furious - it was like life and death." Rafael van der Vaart and Saint-Etienne goalkeeper Stephane Ruffier were both victims of Zlatan's excesses on the field, with a crude tackle and a stamp on the chest respectively.

Cantona now has 29 movie and TV credits, according to online database IMDB. His most recent appearance was in the French film 'Marie and the Misfits', in which he played 'Antoine'. The 50-year-old won 42 caps for his country in the beach football arena.

The word Zlatan was trademarked at the Swedish Patent and Registration Office in 2003. A song written entirely in tribute to Ibrahimović and sung in his home dialect, entitled 'Who's Da Man', stayed at the top of the Swedish charts for 10 weeks in 2006. A keen fisherman with a newly-released clothing brand to his name, he's found his face on stamps in his native Sweden and helped fund a footballing facility in his hometown of Malmo, named 'Zlatan Court'.

Cantona played himself in 2009's 'Looking For Eric', in which he delivers the line "I am not a man, I am Cantona" with the same, third person approach that Ibrahimović brought to Twitter with the "Dare to Zlatan" phenomenon.

Cantona and Ibrahimović have both provided some of the most compelling football quotes ever:

"My best moment? I have a lot of good moments but the one I prefer is when I kicked the hooligan." - Cantona refuses to show remorse for kicking Matthew Simmons back in '95.

"We're looking for an apartment in Paris. If we don't find anything, then I'll probably just buy the hotel." - Ibrahimović on his quest to find a new house in Paris.

On what birthday gift to buy his wife: "Nothing. She already has Zlatan."

Cantona also uttered, arguably, a footballer's greatest ever quote:

"When the seagulls follow the trawler, it is because they think sardines will be thrown into the sea." - Cantona on the media circus around his eight-month ban from football.

BBC Sport's Simon Stone said at the time: "The imminent arrival of Ibrahimović looks to be perfect for Manchester United. Their history is littered with temperamental big-name players: George Best, Eric Cantona and Cristiano Ronaldo to name but three. The big question is whether, at 34, the striker can adapt to the physical demands of the Premier League. Delve into the past of this contradictory forward and it seems he is at his best when questions are at their fiercest. But, as every stockbroker will tell you, past performance is no guarantee of what will happen in the future."

So, two extraordinary talents. Two extraordinary minds. One very lucky fanbase. Manchester United has something special to look forward to all over again.

Their respective honours:

Eric Cantona:

Date of birth: May 24, 1966

Age: 50

Clubs: Auxerre, Martigues (loan), Marseille, Bordeaux (loan), Montpellier (loan), Nimes, Leeds United, Manchester United

Appearances: 410

Goals: 157

International caps (France): 45

Goals: 20

Honours: Division 1 (1989, 1991), Coupe de France (1990), First Division (1992), Charity Shield (1992, 1993, 1994, 1996), Premier League (1993, 1994, 1996, 1997), FA Cup (1994, 1996)

Zlatan Ibrahimović:

Date of birth: October 3, 1981

Age: 34

Clubs: Malmo, Ajax, Juventus, Inter Milan, Barcelona, AC Milan (loan), AC Milan, PSG

Appearances: 620

Goals: 368

International caps (Sweden): 116

Goals: 62

Honours: Eredivisie (2002, 2004), KNVB Cup (2002), Serie A (2007, 2008, 2009, 2011), Italian Super Cup (2006, 2008, 2011), La Liga (2010), Spanish Super Cup (2009, 2010), UEFA Super Cup (2009), FIFA World Club Cup (2009), Ligue 1 (2013, 2014, 2015, 2016), Coupe de France (2015, 2016), Coupe de la Ligue (2014, 2015, 2016), Trophée des Champions (2013, 2014, 2015)

Ibrahimović was soon in Las Vegas and Los Angeles, on his extended break before linking up with his new Manchester United team-mates, and posed for a picture with Phil Neville's son Harvey. He took time out of his holiday in America to speak to the former United star and his family. Neville described Ibrahimović as "the main man" after uploading the snap of Harvey and Ibrahimović on to his Instagram account. Harvey Neville is a member of Valencia's Under-15 side. He recently signed a new one-year deal to remain with the Spanish giants despite his uncle, Gary, and his dad both recently leaving the club.

Mourinho was also determined to sign Juventus midfielder Paul Pogba, twelve months after failing to engineer a deal to take him to Chelsea when, had Roman Abramovich sanctioned a world record splurge and also signed John Stones, then Mourinho might still be at the Bridge.

Manchester United opened discussions with Juventus over Paul Pogba, according to French publication, *L'Equipe*. Pogba, now 23, left United to join Juventus on a free transfer in 2012 after refusing the offer of a new contract from Sir Alex due to a lack of first-team opportunities at Old Trafford after making seven first-team appearances.

L'Equipe suggested Mourinho wanted to implement a 4-3-3 formation at Old Trafford with Rooney in central midfield, Ibrahimović the focal point of the attack, with Anthony Martial and Henrikh Mkhitaryan on either side. The publication also hinted that Pogba had always intended to return to United as part of his career plan but the club's lack of involvement in the Champions League could affect his decision.

Real Madrid were also interested in Pogba with reports in Spain suggesting 'Los Blancos' asked Pogba for more time as they assessed their approach. Madrid boss Zinedine Zidane is a fan of his compatriot but also said it was difficult to improve the squad at his disposal. "I like Pogba. At the moment, he's a Juventus player. I'm happy with the squad I have and it's difficult to improve it," Zidane said at Madrid's pre-season training camp in Canada. "But after saying that, I like Pogba - yes. He is a good player. He is not the only one, because there're many good players, and every club wants to have good players. But he is playing for Juventus."

It should be noted that both Barcelona and Real Madrid were ordered to repay millions of pounds in illegal state aid by the European Commission following an investigation into the financial help they have received from the Spanish government; something which could affect their transfer kitties.

At the time of Pogba's departure from United, Ferguson said: "It's disappointing. I don't think he showed us any respect at all, to be honest." Pogba then revealed to ESPN: "He's a coach I respect a lot. But he's a human. I'm someone who says what he thinks. Whether it's Ferguson or (United States of America President, Barack) Obama, I'll tell him. Ferguson came to my place. We talked. It did make me think. He wanted to keep me, but I'd made my decision to leave."

On his relationship with Raiola, Ferguson admitted in his recent book *Leading*, with Sir Michael Moritz: "There are one or two football agents I simply do not like, and Mino Raiola, Paul Pogba's agent is one of them. I distrusted him from the moment I met him. He became Zlatan Ibrahimović's agent while he was playing for Ajax, and eventually he would end up representing Pogba, who was only 18 years old at the time. We had Paul under a three-year contract, and it had a one-year renewal option which we were eager to sign. But Raiola suddenly appeared on the scene and our first meeting was a fiasco. He and I were like oil and water. From then on, our goose was cooked because Raiola had been able to ingratiate himself with Paul and his family and the player signed with Juventus."

In each of the four seasons at Juve, Pogba lifted the Serie A title, as well as playing a key role in winning the Italian Cup in the past two seasons, and Italian Super Cup twice. He scored 10 goals in 49 games in all competitions for Juve last term.

Michael Carrick agreed a new contract at Manchester United, according to Perth Glory CEO Peter Filopoulos. The veteran midfielder's current contract expired in the summer and he had been approached by Perth over a move to the Australian A-League. Carrick has a close relationship with Perth captain and former West Ham team-mate Richard Garcia, who was the best man at his wedding, but Filopoulos has conceded the club will not be signing the 34-year-old.

Instead, Carrick will sign a new one-year deal at Old Trafford and form part of Mourinho's first-team squad with the new manager personally letting him know he wanted him to stay on despite all the uncertainty over his future and the delay in the offer of a one-year extension.

"It was a long shot opportunity due to Richard Garcia's relationship with Michael," Filopoulos told FourFourTwo magazine. "Perth was an option for Michael Carrick as he was going through what he was going to do in his career had he not landed a new signature with Manchester United. We understand he's now secured an extension with Manchester United so that's off the table. It certainly was an option to him and his family for lifestyle reasons."

Press Release:

Michael Carrick to extend contract.

Manchester United is delighted to announce that Michael Carrick has agreed terms to extend his contract for a further year to June 2017. Carrick, 34, signed for United in July 2006. During his time at the club he has won five Premier

League titles, an FA Cup, one League Cup, a FIFA Club World Cup, and a UEFA Champions League.

Michael Carrick said: "This great club has been a part of my life for the past ten years so I am delighted that this incredible journey is continuing. It's great to have the opportunity to work under José Mourinho, who has achieved so much during his managerial career. I would like to thank the fans for their unwavering support. Winning the FA Cup was a special moment and hopefully we can go on to win more trophies in the future."

José Mourinho said: "Michael is a very intelligent midfielder and a great reader of the game. I am pleased that he will be extending his contract. His form this year shows his ability and his enjoyment of the game are as strong as ever. Michael has a wealth of experience from his many years at the club and that knowledge will be invaluable to me. I am really looking forward to working with him."

Carrick took to Twitter minutes after the announcement to show his happiness at agreeing a new deal:

Michael Carrick, @carras16 - Can't wait to get back to work. 1 more year for this great club and hopefully more of this!!! (holding the FA Cup trophy)

Marouane Fellaini was linked with a move away from United but he wanted to play under Mourinho too. The Belgium international was in contact with the new manager as Mourinho texted his players involved at the Euro. Fellaini said: "As far as my future is concerned, I'm under contract with Manchester United. In addition, a great manager, José Mourinho, is arriving. He likes to win titles and I would be honoured and proud to work with him. Now it's up to me to show he can trust me. Mourinho contacted me by text to say welcome to United and to wish me a good Euro," Fellaini told reporters after Belgium's training when he expecting to start in Belgium's opening game against Italy in Lyon.

Mourinho, in fact, texted all his United players to wish them luck ahead of the Euros.

Paddy McNair was in the Northern Ireland squad to face Poland in Nice, and received a message from Mourinho at the squad's camp outside Lyon.

The 21-year-old knew that the tournament gave him a chance to impress the new manager after making four starts last season under Louis van Gaal.

"Of course, I'm sure he'll be watching," he said. "I'll be trying my best and I hope he likes what he sees. He sent me a text message wishing me good luck for the tournament so that was nice of him."

Sir Alex was going to the game in Nice after McNair bumped into him after last month's FA Cup final at Wembley. He added: "I got into the hotel lift and he was in it. He said good luck for France and told me he's going to the Poland game in Nice."

McNair was ready to face Robert Lewandowski after a fortnight of training in Austria and France. He added: "When you go on the pitch, you know your job, and make sure you're ready to go. On set-pieces, you need to know where you are. Even away from the pitch getting treatment, the massages, make sure your body is right. I actually quite enjoy looking at the video clips and seeing what I'm doing right, what I'm doing wrong; seeing what the opposition's strengths and weaknesses are. With Van Gaal we did a lot of video analysis and a lot of stuff on opposition so it's not really something new to me. Poland are favourites but we'll be going into the game with a game plan. We've watched videos and I think there are areas to exploit. Lewandowski scores a lot of goals but I don't think he's their only threat. Milik and Grosicki too. We need to keep an eye on all three of them."

McNair backed Marcus Rashford to make an impact for England. "He came in at the end of season and it was breath-taking in a way, how well he adapted and the goals he scored. You see him in training, he's got a lot of ability and I think he will be a top player."

Pep Guardiola chose Ibiza for a family summer break, pictured on a yacht with his long-term partner Cristina Serra and their three children Marius, Maria and Valentina, while José Mourinho travelled further afield, spending time in the Maldives, documenting it on his new Instagram page.

But Mourinho also took to Instagram to remind fans that his focus was on the job as the Premier League fixtures were announced. While most of the pictures were of the 'Great One' relaxing, we all knew he was also in touch with just about everyone connected with a host of potential transfers, as well as busy revamping his back room staff. And, during a spell in his native Portugal, he uploaded a photo of himself by the sea with his phone to his ear with the caption "always working".

He also posted an image of himself with his son shortly before England's European Championship opener with Russia. With such a busy period of reconstruction of his new team, United new boss didn't have the time to go to the match, but having already having watched a third successive match had left the sofa over-used. Practising being back on the bench! Maybe. More likely it was far easier to see so many more games by staying at home and watching the wall to wall coverage on ITV and BBC.

Mourinho said on his account: '3 matches in a row, the sofa is getting tired of us.'

Mourinho would have been watching with enormous interest how Wayne Rooney played his first England game in midfield, while Chris Smalling was in the heart of the defence, and long standing United target Harry Kane lead the line.

Luke Shaw also took to social media. The left-back hadn't played for United since breaking his leg in a Champions League match against PSV in September, an injury which robbed the full-back of any chance of making it into the England squad.

Shaw posted a picture of his TV at the start of the match and showed his support for England with a message reading 'Come on Boys!!!'

Bastian Schweinsteiger came off the bench for the final few moments of Germany's opening game win at Euro 2016 over Ukraine, scoring the second, having not played since United's win over Manchester City on March 20.

André Schürrle, also a late substitute against Ukraine, said that Schweinsteiger could yet make Mourinho sit up and take notice in his 'veteran' stage. "The goal was amazing. When you see the criticism he got: is he fit, is he old, is he too slow, or whatever, and then to score like this in an important game is amazing. It's good for the team because he's our captain and he's so important for us, and it's good for him to have this confidence. He's a great person. Mentally, he's so strong. He knows what to do on the pitch and he's so calm. We've seen it in the training sessions. He's been one and a half weeks with the team and class is permanent, you know. It's not that easy to come from the Bundesliga into the Premier League. It's something different. It's not an easy way to play football and it was not easy for him when he came with the injuries. It was a hard year for him. When he's fit, when he's the leader he wants to be, he makes every team better."

Could Schweinsteiger impress Mourinho, Schürrle said: "I think so, I hope so. I don't know what Mourinho's plans are at Man United but I hope so because he's a great player."

Schürrle was sold by Mourinho in January 2015 midway through his second Premier League title-winning season of his second spell at Chelsea. He made the mistake of being one of a group who got on the wrong side of Mourinho by attending Arsenal's Christmas party in 2013.

Feyenoord attacker Tahith Chong confirmed he was joining Manchester United on Twitter.

Tahith Chong, @TahithChong_: Future player of Manchester United

The 16-year-old impressed playing for Feyenoord's U17s at a tournament held at United's Carrington training ground last summer.

Manchester City and Arsenal were among a number of Premier League clubs that had shown an interest in the attacking midfielder but he's opted to move to Old Trafford.

Chong took to Twitter and uploaded a photo of himself in a Manchester United shirt

Chong also updated his Instagram bio to read: "Future player of Manchester United".

But, United might regret missing out on the teenage wonderkid, Renato Sanches. United lost out to Bayern Munich in the race to sign Sanches from Benfica for £27m that could rise beyond £60m with add-ons. Fellow Portuguese international, Nani, said Mourinho will now live to regret the day the teenager chose Munich over Manchester. "Renato would have been a great signing for Manchester United, I have no doubts. He had a choice, and the choice he made was Bayern Munich. I hope he has made a good choice and will be happy in his career, but United will now know what a big player they have missed."

Sanches could not resist the lure of the German giants, and fellow Portugal star José Fonte said it is a shame for the Premier League that Sanches will not be at Old Trafford. "They missed out on a very good talent. And being a Premier League player myself, it's a shame - he's a great talent and Bayern Munich are very lucky," said Fonte. "He has no fear, no fear at all. He just doesn't care. He asks for the ball all the time, every second. He has power, strength, and energy to run all day and great ability." Fonte added that the teenager, who only made his international debut three months ago, has the perfect attitude to get better and better. "He is a nice quiet kid, he listens to the old guys and wants to learn, which is good. It's great to have him around and he will be the future of the national team for sure."

Goalkeeper Victor Valdes and midfielder Nick Powell were released.

Valdes, signed as a free agent in January 2015 as back-up to David de Gea, made only two appearances 13 months ago and was farmed out to Belgian side Standard Liege on loan in January after falling out of favour with Louis van Gaal.

Powell, who scored on his senior debut after joining from Crewe in 2012, played 10 matches, the last two coming in December before going to Hull on loan in February where he managed five substitute appearances.

Another goalkeeper, George Dorrington, and midfielder Oliver Rathbone, were also released.

Talking of goalkeepers, text messages, which allegedly show David de Gea trying to arrange a prostitute for five Manchester United teammates, emerged at the start of Euro 2016.

The goalkeeper denied any wrongdoing after he was reportedly implicated in a police probe into a porn director accused of running a child prostitution ring.

Reports said a protected witness in the case against pornographer Ignacio Allende Fernández - better known as 'Torbe' - claimed de Gea set up a date between her, one other girl, and two Spanish Under-21 players in 2012. It has also been claimed that the keeper tried to arrange a prostitute for five Man United players.

However de Gea denied any wrongdoing, describing the accusations as "lies".

At a Spanish Euro 2016 press conference, de Gea said: "I'm the first to be surprised by the news. I want to refute these allegations. These are lies and mistruths. This gives me more strength to play with the Spanish national team, with the support of my team-mates. The matter remains in the hands of my lawyers. It is all false. I am very calm. I want to go out to train and continue doing what I enjoy. I have no idea where this has come from. I know that it is false. I just have to keep going. I found out in my room. I let me family know of the situation. They are calm because they know me."

Sources close to de Gea said he remained relatively calm and intended to stay with the Spain national team for the duration of Euro 2016.

The protected witness is understood to have made the statements on May 6 last year in Madrid and another on June 3 last year in Murcia.

Police sources close to the case confirmed the reports are genuine, adding "we can't confirm anything else at this stage".

She claimed the hotel meeting was set up by de Gea. There is no suggestions he was involved in the sex session.

It is understood that the matter is now in the hands of de Gea's lawyers and the player was expecting to remain with the Spain squad for the duration of the European Championship in France.

When asked about de Gea at a press conference, team-mate Aritz Aduriz replied: "We're not going to talk about this. That's the last question on that."

Sources close to the Manchester United goalkeeper admitted that the player is aware his image, honour and reputation have been "gravely affected" by the allegations. However, they also insisted the player remains relatively calm despite the legal case and is focused on the task at hand with the Spanish national team.

END OF AN ERA

Ryan Giggs' confirmation that he had, indeed, left his role as assistant manager, ending a 29-year association with the club, came amid a flurry of official announcements and his departure statement contained a reminder to Mourinho that the club's DNA is to give youth a chance and play attacking football.

The 42-year-old made a record 963 appearances for United and had a year left on his contract at Old Trafford. Giggs, who gained his UEFA Pro Licence in 2014, hoped to manage in the future. "The time feels right and, although I have no immediate plans to step into management, it is where I want to be. It's time for a new chapter and a new challenge. I'm excited about the future - I've had the best apprenticeship into management anyone could ever ask for."

Cardiff-born Giggs joined the United academy on his 14th birthday, turning professional aged 17 in November 1990 and making his first-team debut against Everton on 2 March, 1991. Giggs won a record 13 league titles, two European Cups, four FA Cups and four League Cups before retiring in 2014. He became a player-coach following the arrival of David Moyes as manager in 2013, and had a brief spell as caretaker-manager following the Scot's dismissal in April 2014, taking charge of the final four games of the season.

Had Van Gaal seen out his three-year contract, Giggs would have taken over in a seamless transition. In December, it was the future envisaged by senior figures in the United hierarchy. Giggs retained influential backers at Old Trafford, but the club targeted Mourinho as a potential replacement for Van Gaal as results and performances suffered in mid-season and United eventually failed to make it into the Champions League. So, Giggs was leaving United after almost three glorious decades, but he hoped to return one day.

The former Wales international paid tribute to both Sir Alex, his manager for all but one season of his 24-year professional career, and Van Gaal as "great managerial mentors", and said it was a difficult decision to leave the club he joined as a 14-year-old in 1987. Giggs had hoped to take over as manager following Van Gaal's sacking, but he magnanimously backed Mourinho to be a success.

In a full statement on the club's website, Giggs published this open letter:

"After twenty-nine seasons at Manchester United as a player and assistant manager, I know winning is in the DNA of this club - giving youth a chance, and playing attacking and exciting football. It's healthy to have high expectations, it's right to expect to win. Manchester United expects, deserves, nothing less. This is why it is a huge decision for me to step away from the club that has been my life since the age of 14. It has not been a decision that I have made lightly. I'll take away so many special memories as well as a lifetime of experiences that will, I hope, serve me well in the future.

However, the time feels right and although I have no immediate plans to step into management, it is where I want to be. I've been extremely fortunate in having two great managerial mentors, firstly in Sir Alex who I've spent the majority of my life working with and learning from, and who I believe will remain as football's greatest ever manager, and in more recent times, Louis van Gaal, whose CV speaks for itself. The knowledge I have gleaned from them has been invaluable. I want to reiterate my thanks to the backroom staff and support teams at Manchester United I've worked with over the years. The results on the pitch are a reflection of the hard work off it, I would not have achieved the success I have without the dedication, sacrifice and commitment of these people in creating the best environment for the team to succeed.

I want to congratulate José Mourinho on his appointment as manager of the world's biggest club. There are only a handful of proven winners at the very highest level and José is unquestionably one of them. I know the fans will welcome him. My final thank you is to the fans. I cannot begin to tell you how much I will miss walking out at Old Trafford in front of you. It's extremely difficult to say goodbye after 29 years. I have loved every minute both as a player and assistant manager. The support you have always shown me has been phenomenal, thank you. It's time for a new chapter and a new challenge.

I'm excited about the future - I've had the best apprenticeship into management anyone could ever ask for.

Best Wishes

Ryan"

Not surprisingly, the accolades were swift and plentiful.

Executive vice-chairman Ed Woodward said Giggs' "rigour and diligence" will help him become a successful manager in the future. "The experiences and discipline he developed at United will undoubtedly be a big help as he continues to learn his trade. He has all the attributes to be a terrific manager in the future."

Sir Alex Ferguson was quick to comment on Giggsy: "His place in history is assured. I doubt we'll ever see a career like his again."

Sir Alex later said it was time for Ryan to leave and that he has the "steel" to succeed in management. Fergie, though, also said that his long-time rival Mourinho was right to go with "his own man", long-time assistant Rui Faria.

Mourinho worked with Faria in his six previous managerial jobs. "You have got to have, in your assistant, someone you have trusted all your life," said Ferguson. "When I came to United, I brought Archie Knox because he was a valuable person for me. I trusted him 100%. José Mourinho has had his assistant for years and, quite rightly, has stuck by his own man. If José hadn't had an assistant, I know he would have taken Ryan."

The 74-year-old told BBC Sport: "It is time Ryan stood on his own feet, got out there and accept the challenge."

Ferguson thinks Giggs has the qualities to make it on his own. "I talk about his poker face," said the Old Trafford legend, who stepped down as manager in 2013. "He has a bit of steel about him. It is such a highly intense results industry, you need people who go into it to have a bit of steel about them, a bit of character and personality."

Giggs left United after failing to reach an agreement with the club over an alternative role. He has passed all of his coaching badges, had a four-game spell as caretaker boss when Moyes was sacked at the end of the 2013-14 season. Ferguson wants Giggs to "be himself" and make sure he picks the right club. "I think he is ready to manage and he has a lot of quality. He doesn't want to spoil that quality by going to a club where it is sacking a manager every two minutes."

Ferguson nurtured Giggs before the player joined United, spending so much time at his house persuading the then 13-year-old to leave Manchester City that the winger's mother Lynne started offering to make his tea.

Ferguson was confident Giggs would be a great player the moment he saw him. "You knew right away... the way he ran over the ground," said Ferguson, who was responsible for all but 22 of Giggs' club-record 963 appearances. "I referred to it like a cocker spaniel chasing a piece of silver paper in the wind. His feet never seemed to touch the ground."

Twitter was red hot with the news:

Manchester United, @ManUtd: Ryan Giggs, Manchester United legend. Always and forever. #GiggsLegend

Manchester United, @ManUtd: Sir Alex on Giggsy: "His place in history is assured. I doubt we'll ever see a career like his again." #GiggsLegend

Ander Herrera, @AnderHerrera: It has been a great honor to learn from such a football legend like you. I wish you all the best #Giggs #Legend

Rio Ferdinand, @rioferdy5: Ryan Giggs 963 apps 168 goals 34 trophies#MUFC Legend

David De Gea, @D_DeGea: Ryan Giggs, Ryan Giggs, Running down the wing... #GiggsLegend

Michael Carrick, @carras16: Gonna miss this fella. All great things come to an end I suppose. He's gonna make a top manager. Good luck mate

Memphis, @Memphis: It was a huge honour to have worked with you. I wish you all the best for the future! #GiggsLegend

MKHITARYAN SIGNS

United jumped the gun after showing their new away kit on the club's website with Mkhitaryan on the back. He had agreed personal terms and was all set for a medical, but before he had actually signed, the United website were showing pictures of the away kit for the new season with the letters "Mkhitaryan" on the reverse side of the blue shirt. The photos were swiftly removed from the website later the same evening.

Finally, though, it was announced that the club had an offer for Mkhitaryan accepted by Borussia Dortmund.

The Armenia captain, who cost the German club £23.5m in 2013, was signing for a fee close to £30million "Had we refused it, the player would be available for free in 2017," Dortmund chief executive Hans-Joachim Watzke told the club's official website.

The player only required a work permit to become United's third major signing of the summer.

Interestingly, Jürgen Klopp recruited Mkhitaryan from Ukrainian side Shakhtar Donetsk when he was in charge at Westfalenstadion. He was named Bundesliga Players' Player of the Season in 2015-16 after scoring 18 goals in all competitions, including one against Liverpool in the Europa League defeat at Anfield.

Mkhitaryan is the son of one of Armenia's most famous footballers, Hamlet Mkhitaryan, winning the first of his 59 caps a week before his 18th birthday

Press Release: United sign Henrikh Mkhitaryan:

"Manchester United is delighted to announce that Henrikh Mkhitaryan has completed his transfer from Borussia Dortmund. Henrikh joins on a four-year contract with the option to extend for a further year.

Mkhitaryan, 27, made 140 appearances and scored 41 goals for Borussia Dortmund after joining them in 2013. Last season he scored 23 goals and registered an impressive 32 assists across all competitions. Henrikh was voted Bundesliga Player of the Season for 2015/16 in a poll of his fellow professionals, and he was named in the Team of the Season following votes by the players' union in Germany, VDV.

The midfielder is Armenia's all-time top scorer, with 19 goals in 59 appearances since his international debut in January 2007. Henrikh captains his national team and has received the Armenian Footballer of the Year award on five occasions."

Henrikh Mkhitaryan said: "I am very proud to join Manchester United, this move is a dream come true for me. I am excited to play for a club with such an illustrious history and hope to be part of it for a long time. I thank the trust the club and José Mourinho have put in me. Finally, I believe playing for such a great club honours my father's memory, and the inspiration and drive he gave to me when I was young."

José Mourinho confirmed: "Henrikh is a very talented footballer who has been in such prolific form for both his club and his country. He is a real team player with great skill, vision and also has a good eye for goal. I am delighted he has chosen to sign for United. I believe he will make an impact on the team very quickly as his style of play is suited to the Premier League. We are all looking forward to working with him."

The new manager had a clear vision how he wanted his new United to take shape, and added "We want to play differently than last season. My philosophy is different (to Van Gaal's). It's not better, it's different. I am more vertical, I am more intense and I like the ball possession as a way to create a chance to be vertical. I don't like ball possession as a way to just keep statistically possession of the ball and be afraid to play a game with transitions. Transitions always come during a game. I'm not afraid to lose the ball. I'm not afraid of risk."

While his arrival was greeted well with the new manager, Dortmund players were shocked that he was leaving. "I was surprised that Micki decided to make the move after all," said, now former team-mate, Marcel Schmelzer. "Many players after the season talked to him about his plans. In the end, all you can do is to accept the decision. It's a major upheaval when your captain leaves and also a player like 'Micki', who's had a hand in 55 goals last season. The key now will be to offset it as a team. We have signed a lot of talented players, who will have to grow into their role. It will be difficult in any case because you can't replace Mats and Micki like-for-like."

José Mourinho took a break from his United revolution to watch Andy Murray at the Wimbledon Final. Mourinho admitting he cried when the Scot won Wimbledon in 2013. Mourinho was just one of a number of famous faces spotted at SW19. British actors Benedict Cumberbatch and Hugh Grant both watched on from the Royal Box. Hollywood actor Bradley Cooper, a regular Wimbledon spectator, was joined in the stands by Cristiano Ronaldo's former girlfriend, Russian model Irina Shayk. Former Prime Minister David Cameron also took to the Royal Box alongside his mother, Mary, to watch the tennis alongside the Duke and Duchess of Cambridge. Andy Murray beat Milos Raonic to win his second Wimbledon men's singles title.

Only a few hours later Mourinho then celebrated Portugal's Euro 2016 final victory in his pyjamas. Mourinho held a Portugal scarf up as his country lifted their first international trophy. Clearly now getting the hang of it, he soon posted a picture of himself holding the scarf on his Instagram account with a caption, which proudly read "if you want to visit the country of the European champions visit Portugal." Fernando Santos' side secured Portugal their first piece of silverware with a 1-0 victory in extra-time against France in the Stade de France despite Cristiano Ronaldo forced off with injury in the first 45 minutes. Eder, who replaced Renato Sanches in the 78th-minute, shrugged off Arsenal's

Laurent Koscielny before firing past Hugo Lloris from 30 yards.

A story then emerged that a burglar broke into Mourinho's London home while he was watching the Euro 2016 Final. The 25 year old intruder tried to force the basement door to the £25million house. A Portuguese maid came face-to-face with Gabor Roman who screamed at him: "What are you doing here?" Her scream alerted Mourinho and the police were called and the thief subsequently arrested. The maid was doing the ironing when she spotted the intruder trying to get in through the basement door. The thief tried to escape, but a security guard who had been tracking him blocked his path. A private security guard hired by residents first spotted Roman wandering from house to house trying doors to see if they were unlocked. The guard watched him disappear into Mourinho's basement and alerted police. Roman made threats to punch the guard who stood his ground - and then coolly smoked a cigarette until police officers arrived. Eight police officers dashed to the central London house and led the intruder away in handcuffs while Mourinho and wife Matilde Faria watched from a window. Roman, from Eastern Europe, of no fixed address, was jailed for four weeks by Westminster magistrates after admitting attempted burglary.

Chris Smalling was rushed to hospital suffering from food poisoning while on holiday in Bali. A picture emerged of the 26-year-old lying on a gurney (a wheeled stretcher) with his head, neck and left hand bandaged amid claims he had been stung by a jellyfish. He was seen to be penning an autograph on a replica Manchester United shirt while being seen to by doctors.

The club clarified that Smalling had food poisoning during his holiday which resulted in him fainting. Smalling was given the all-clear after being checked over by medical staff on the Indonesian island.

A statement released on the club's official website read: "Manchester United can clarify Chris Smalling has had food poisoning during his holiday which resulted in him fainting on Sunday. The 26-year-old defender was taken to the hospital and is now feeling fine. Smalling is currently on vacation following his time with England at Euro 2016 before reporting back for pre-season training later this month."

The central defender travelled to Asia after England were dumped out of the European Championship by Iceland. He was given time off by Mourinho before joining the United squad for pre-season training at Carrington.   Smalling often spends time relaxing in Bali with partner Sam Cooke. Claims that he was surfing when the accident happened are understood not to be correct.

Chapter 8

THE MANCHESTER UNVEILINGS

Gary Lineker, @GaryLineker: You know football is getting the better of you when managers' press conferences become exciting. #guardiola

FIRST PEP...

Pep Guardiola's arrival in Manchester was superbly stage managed by City. First there was a well manipulated and controlled unveiling before a selected audience, prior to Mourinho's first press conference, then Guardiola had his own media conference, and as Gary Lineker tweeted to his massive social media audience, the managers' utterings before the media were becoming as fascinating as the matches themselves.

A picture of Noel Gallagher and Guardiola was posted on the City manager's Twitter page with the caption: "Cool selfie from Pep with @NoelGallagher!"

City's Twitter account shortly afterwards tweeted a picture of their own showing Pep taking the picture.

Guardiola arrived in a black cab to find in his office PG Tips, a guide to Manchester, an Oasis vinyl, a Coronation Street box set, and a personalised club umbrella. He will live in a Salford apartment with fashion designer wife Cristina Serra and their three children - daughters Valentina and Maria, and son Marius.

Guardiola's unveiling as Manchester City's new manager in front of 5,800 supporters at the City Football Academy was a declaration of intent and an attempt to defuse his feud with old foe and Mourinho.

He remarked "the past is the past." But there was little chance of that!

He took questions from the crowd as well as Twitter and Facebook as the fans clapped nearly every answer and chanted his name. He spoke on stage for half an hour and was coerced into joining in with a rendition of *Blue Moon*. It was a very relaxed Sunday including a selfie with Noel Gallagher and an interview with the club's No.1 celebrity fan.

When he was asked about coming to the Premier League he appeared to take a swipe at Mourinho, when he said: "In England, the people don't come to see who the manager is, they come to see how good our players are. I don't think

9/3/2004.
Porto manager
Jose Mourinho jumps
in the air as he celebrates
knocking Manchester
United out of the
Champions League,
3-2 on aggregate.

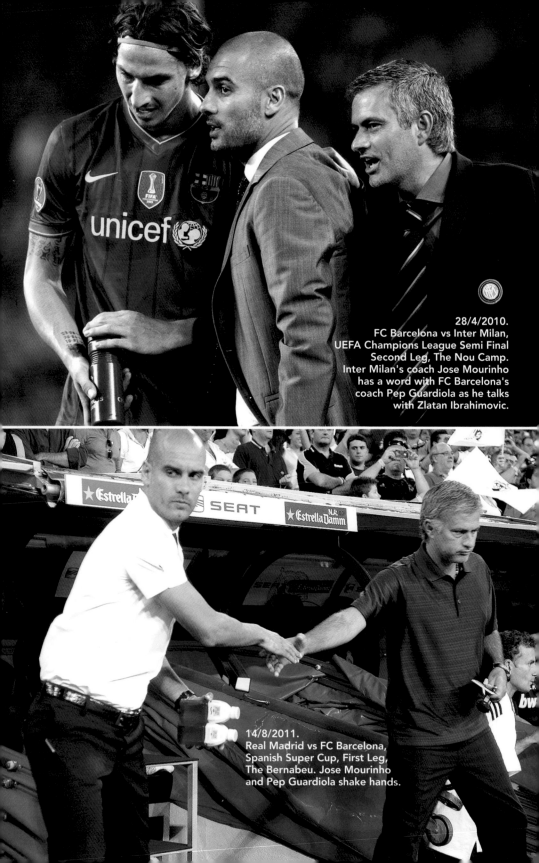

28/4/2010.
FC Barcelona vs Inter Milan,
UEFA Champions League Semi Final
Second Leg, The Nou Camp.
Inter Milan's coach Jose Mourinho
has a word with FC Barcelona's
coach Pep Guardiola as he talks
with Zlatan Ibrahimovic.

14/8/2011.
Real Madrid vs FC Barcelona,
Spanish Super Cup, First Leg,
The Bernabeu. Jose Mourinho
and Pep Guardiola shake hands.

11/3/2012.
Paul Pogba in action
for Manchester United
in the Premier League.

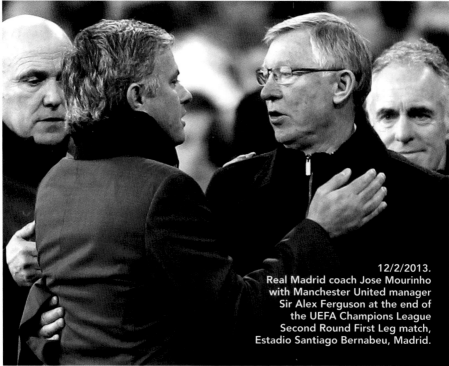

12/2/2013.
Real Madrid coach Jose Mourinho
with Manchester United manager
Sir Alex Ferguson at the end of
the UEFA Champions League
Second Round First Leg match,
Estadio Santiago Bernabeu, Madrid.

26/8/2013.
Ryan Giggs listens to, then, Chelsea manager Jose Mourinho
ahead of their Premier League match at Old Trafford.
After a 29-year association with the club Giggs announced
his departure in July 2016.

5/7/2016.
Jose Mourinho poses on the Old Trafford pitch
ahead of his unveiling press conference.

16/7/2016.
New signing Eric Bailly in action at the DW Stadium in the pre-season friendly vs Wigan.

22/7/2016.
Manchester United vs Borussia Dortmund,
International Champions Cup,
Shanghai Stadium, Shanghai, China.
Recent signing Henrikh Mkhitaryan
in action.

30/7/2016.
Zlatan Ibrahimovic
opens the scoring
on his debut in
the pre-season friendly
against Galatasaray,
in the Ullevi Stadium,
Gothenburg, Sweden.

30/7/2016.
Zlatan Ibrahimovic celebrates with team mates after scoring their first goal in the friendly vs Galatasaray in his home country of Sweden.

3/8/16.
Jose signs autographs for his new adoring fans at Wayne Rooney's testimonial against Everton at Old Trafford.

just this year, in the past as well, with Mourinho, with Klopp, with Conte, with Ranieri, Pochettino, Koeman, but the reason I work here is just to help the players. I've come here to learn, learn the way the people live here, for my family, for my kids. That is why I was curious to move in Europe."

Guardiola added: "The first target is team spirit and play good," he said. "The past is the past. We are here to try again. My tactic is to develop the players."

He explained that he arrived with a simple aim - to make City supporters "proud".

"I proved myself in Barcelona and after I prove myself in Germany in Bayern and after I want to prove myself and my staff here in Manchester City," declared Guardiola, in front of the City supporters. "(The aim) is to try to win every game, every weekend and for Manchester City people to be proud of the way we play, and at the end we will see what is out level to achieve. But at the end, after all the games, I want our supporters to be proud of what we did. If the people are not proud there is no point. We need our fans, without that it's impossible."

Guardiola was famed for his style of high-pressing and 'tiki-taka', as well as the development and promotion of young players, but he's open to changing his ideals. "I have no preconceptions at all about coming to England or the football in the Premier League. I want to learn as much as possible. I have an idea of how we will play, but when I arrived in Germany with Bayern Munich, I had some ideas of how the team would play but changed them as I went along. I know how hard the Premier League is and some people have said that I will find it hard to play the football I like to play in England so I said to myself 'Why not?' That's why I'm here - because I want to try. We have to find a way to win and if we win one game, the next week we will say 'OK, let's try and do the same things this week' - and if we win again, we'll say, 'let's do the things that won us those two games' and so on. I've been told that it will be hard to do that in the Premier League but we did it at Barcelona and Bayern Munich and people may say, 'Yes, that's because it was Barcelona and Bayern - it won't be possible to do that in England'. I just say OK, let's try."

Guardiola promised to give City a kick up the backside on a day he labelled his appointment "a dream come true". He will not accept passive attitudes within his squad.

Guardiola revealed a pursuit of signing of Lionel Messi from Barcelona is not on his agenda after a cheeky heckle from the crowd during a Q&A session.

"You will see when we are going to play the first game. First I have to meet my players and know them. I know them from TV. I have to hug them, kick their a**** and after I need time to know them. I have an idea but I need time. I like the players who think not about himself but think about City. We are all the people who are working here. The reason we are here is thinking what can we do to make this club a better club in the next three, four, five years. I don't want the guys to think about what the club can do for them. Now my dream came true. Of course the atmosphere here is 'wow'. We have one of the best facilities in the world."

Guardiola will live in the city centre with his family, keen to immerse himself into Manchester culture despite the enormous attention expected during a three-year contract worth up to £45million.

He looked relaxed, wearing skinny jeans, blazer and Converses while perched on a stool answering questions as City paraded their new badge and kit. He was given a slight fright by a burst of confetti at the climax of his presentation.

Guardiola has already been working alongside Manchester City sporting director Txiki Begiristain to make more signings happen, and said his close friend has fully briefed him on the squad.

"I know them, I play against City in the last two or three years many times," Guardiola said. "I spoke many times with Txiki. I know them, I know their quality but they have to show me, show the fans again. The past is the past. The people don't come here to remember what we did. Every manager in the world wants to improve their players. I have my point of view, my way to do my job. I need time but as soon as possible we are going to try and create team spirit. That is the most important thing. After you can create tactics but we have to create something special ourselves."

He welcomed Mikel Arteta to the backroom staff. The former Arsenal midfielder announced the news himself just before midday, saying: "I am now looking forward to the challenge ahead at Manchester City. The opportunity to join Pep Guardiola and his team was an amazing opportunity for me and I am incredibly excited for the future. Throughout my career I have always been interested in more than just the playing side and have had a passion for helping progress and develop the team outside of just my own role as a player. Coaching has always been something I've been keen to go in to and over the past few years I've worked hard off the pitch as well as on it to develop my skills in order to put me in a position to be able to pursue a coaching role once I finished playing."

Arteta will coach Kelechi Iheanacho throughout the pre-season after the striker was told he would not be allowed to travel with Nigeria to the Rio Olympics. Iheanacho had been named in the provisional 35-man squad, but Guardiola wants the teenager to stay close to 'home'.

İlkay Gündoğan insisted City will achieve with Pep because he is one of the best managers in football history. The Germany international, also speaking at the unveiling of Guardiola, stood on the stage in front of the thousands of City supporters. He spoke about playing outside Germany for the first time and working with the former Barcelona and Bayern Munich boss. "I'm really excited, to be honest. I am very happy and glad to be here. It's an honour and I'm looking forward to the new season. It's a great club. An incredible club and a big honour. It is my first time outside Germany so it will be a big adventure for me. I am really happy and cannot wait to play my first match in the stadium. I know him (Pep) from Germany. I was lucky to play against him. He's incredible. He's one of the biggest managers in the world and history and we are all very lucky to have him here. We will have big achievements in the future."

Guardiola told Manchester City fans to fasten their seatbelts, suggesting that the challenge from managers of the highest calibre, such as Mourinho, only served to enhance his own game.

His response to the questions about Mourinho and their rivalry were answered in a similar approach to which Mourinho answered the inevitable questions about Guardiola. "It's not about him or about me," he said. "We are focused between each other. The other one is going (to try) to win. What I saw from a distance it's no matter the team, it's so tough win the games here. I will improve myself, I'm pretty sure of that. The big coaches, José is one of them, help me reach another level. My experience against him, against Jürgen Klopp at Dortmund, Thomas Tuchel and a lot of managers in Spain and England, they've made me better. It's going to be interesting. Conte is a master tactician, I think he's a great signing for Chelsea. It's going to be very interesting competing against him. Claudio Ranieri (at Leicester City) too. (Ronald) Koeman (at Everton) as well. It's hard to say how it's going to pan out. Of course all the managers in the world want to win and here we are going to try to win as well. I don't know why the other coaches came here. I came as a player two or three times and was taken by the atmosphere, we said 'wow, it's pretty good'. I never went to stadiums when it's freezing and windy. Not on Boxing Day. That's why it's a personal ambition to prove myself. Maybe with the others it was the same."

And, asked if he was worried about the presence of Mourinho across the road at Manchester United, Guardiola said: "I don't see it as a question. He wants to win, I want to win, we know each other pretty well from before at Barcelona. I think it's great that top managers are here, big managers take me as a manager to another level. Competing with them takes me to another level, they push you to win things like the Champions League. And then you find out if you're big enough of capable enough of running teams like Barça, Madrid, Bayern, like Manchester City, but I've only just started here. I think at every stage I've had a big challenge. It could be the biggest because City haven't won as many titles as Barça or Bayern, but I can't answer. The challenge is trying your best to prove yourself."

He confessed to being "nervous" before his first media appearance but confidently addressed the big issues. He is here in England to show that his style can conquer in the Premier League. Asked whether he can earn results playing in a similar tactics to that of Barcelona and Bayern Munich, Guardiola said: "That's why I'm here, to prove myself. I was in Barcelona where I had absolutely everything, the best player ever, and a team where most of the players grew up from the academy so I knew them. Bayern Munich, a club who have a lot of experience as well for many, many things. Here is another test for my career. It would've been comfortable to stay where I was, I feel that it is the right moment to come here and prove myself. If I'm able to convince these players the way we want, and show a level at the end then we'll see. Fasten your seat belt for the other side of the car."

Guardiola took advice from Mikel Arteta and Brian Kidd during his first week at the City Football Academy and as a result was ready for aggression in the Premier League, and even seemed to warm to the prospect of the festive period - twice referencing the Boxing Day schedule!

"I think (in) my career, always the people are going to demand of my teams," Guardiola added. "The way we are going to train to try to win as much as possible. At the end that is good. It's better to live with that pressure than to live 'okay, if we win it's okay, if we don't win it's okay as well'. I think it's going to be more physical. Some say it's not as attractive but I can't say that. Kidd knows the club perfectly. He's getting me to know the players. Arteta knows English football. I need to learn and understand. I've brought people from Barça and Bayern - I know their abilities. Every stage has been a big challenge. We depend on the players and they depend on us as well. You've got to adapt to the country in which you're in, it was the same in Germany. These players have played all over the place. They've got to qualify for the Champions League. It's a case of trying to maintain the level that's been set at this club and try that every match they go into they make it difficult for the opposition and play for the shirt."

Guardiola was desperate for "magnificent" captain Vincent Kompany to get over his injury problems. He also backed Raheem Sterling after the winger had faced fierce criticism following England's Euro 2016 exit at the hands of Iceland. Guardiola - who sent Sterling a text message of encouragement during the European Championship - added: "They were criticised when they lost. Sterling, I hear the last 10 days what happened with, especially with Sterling of course he has a little problem with the money they paid and that is in the mind of the people. But I am encouraged and I am looking forward to work with him and show him how good a player he is and not just him, Joe Hart and the other English players. In Barcelona the basis was Catalan players, in Bayern the basis was German and I would like to work with English players here but they are so, so expensive."

More detail from the Q&A session:

What do you think of the reception so far?

Not bad! Thank you for coming here in, of course, your house. It is my new house. I am so, so glad to be here so thank you for Manchester City for giving me this amazing opportunity to live in England, in Manchester and to be part of my job in the Premier League and I am pretty sure we are going to enjoy.

You have known great success in the jobs you have done before. How much are you looking forward to the challenge of doing the same thing with Manchester City? Because it is a challenge, isn't it?

Yeah, that's why I am here. That is the reason why I am here. I prove myself in the place where I was born, in Barcelona, Catalonia, and after I prove myself in Germany. And after I want to prove myself here, I am able and with my people, with my staff and of course with amazing players Manchester City have and the new players that is coming too, to try every game, every weekend, that Manchester City play so that people can be proud and can enjoy our way to play. And at the end, we will see how is our level to achieve our titles. In the end, after the game and the season, I want our supporters and maybe the people who love football to enjoy and be proud of what we did. It is, in the end, the most important thing. After that, maybe we'll achieve the titles. Of course, we need our fans. Alone, we cannot do that. I cannot do that alone.

We need the players, the staff and we need our fans. Without that, it is impossible.

You have a reputation as a man who works on and knows how to improve players, improving the way they play and the way they train. What do you hope to achieve before the start of next season?

Every manager in the world wants to improve their players. That's why, if he is able to improve his players, he improves the team. I work like all managers in the world. I have my point of view, the way to see my job, the way I want my team to play and of course, I need time. In the world, we don't have time but as soon as possible we are going to try to create a team spirit. That is the most important thing. After, we can talk about the tactics, about many, many things. But you have to create something special between each other. Our body language, in that moment in the beginning, is the most important thing and after, the rest, it's coming along.

We are here in a training centre dedicated to youth and to excellence. Is a long term goal to use that youth that's coming through this academy as much as possible?

I grew up in one of the most important academies in the world in Barcelona, where the academy and the young, talented players are so, so important, to double up and maybe in the end, play in the first team. So one of the reasons, there are many reasons, but one of the reasons I decide to come here to Manchester City is because I knew, from Txiki Begiristain, from Rodolfo, from many people working here for a long time, how good they are working in the academy and with the young players. For me it is amazing as a coach to see the young players, 13, 14, 15, 16, 17 and growing and growing and imagining and maybe in one year or two years can join us and can play in the first team. And I think it is the...the fans, Manchester City needs the people who grow up from the academy because from that moment, they feel something special about the player. Of course, it depends on the players. Now, we have maybe one of the best facilities in the world training, good trainers, so after, it depends on the quality of the young players.

What is the biggest challenge you face? What is top of your 'to-do' list?

Play good. And after, try to win one game. And try to win the second game, and another one. But the first target is team spirit and play good as much as possible and after, try to win one game. And after, the second one.

How well do you know the existing players?

I know them, I play against Manchester City in the last two or three years many, many times. I spoke many times with Txiki, with the people involved. I know them. I know their quality but they have to show me and show our fans and the team again. So what they did, these players, in the past is the past. People don't come here to remember what we did. So we are here to try again.

Will you adapt your style/tactics for the Premier League or try and impose methods used previously?

My tactics are the quality of my players, the players they have, so I cannot demand something that the players are not able to give me or give us, so it is impossible. But another point, I cannot talk about my players or the way we are going to play if I don't feel it. I love football, I love the way I feel and that's going to convince. We meet each other and day by day, know the players and of course they have to know me as well.

What are the most important qualities you want from a player?

Be a good team-mate. I like the players that think about himself but a little bit about Manchester City. At the end, we are all the people working here, the reason why we are here is thinking about what we can do to make this club a better club. That is the only reason why. So I don't like the guys to think about what the club can do for them. We are here to help Manchester City's next period. Two, three, four, five years, a better club. That is the reason all the people are here.

How would you describe the kind of football you want? What attracted you to the club and to English football?

My friend from Jakarta, you see (the kind of football) when we go to play the first game. Definitely. First I have to meet my players. I have to know them. I know them from TV but I have to know them, speak with them, hug them, kick their a*** and after, I need time to know then. I have an idea but I need time.

One of my dreams, it would have been playing here, like a football player. It was not possible. Now, my dream has come true so I came here like a coach. The atmosphere here, wow, it is amazing. I want to live that in life. Of course, prove myself, if I am able to be a good manager here in England. That is the reason why. And of course, come here to learn, to learn the way the people live here for my family, my kids. That's why I am always curious to move across Europe and learn about what it means to live in England.

Many top managers have come to the north of England, what's the main attraction you've brought to City?

In England, of course... I think the most important thing in football, the people don't come to the Etihad Stadium to see how good the manager is. They come for our players, that is the thing. We are here just to help them. But that is true. I don't think that just this year, in the past as well but this year, José (Mourinho), Jürgen Klopp, Antonio Conte, Claudio Ranieri, Pochettino, Ronald Koeman, there are many, many, many good managers. But I think that in Spain as well, in Germany as well, in Italy as well. But the reason we are here is just to help. To help the players.

Are you looking forward to living in Manchester and getting to know the fans?

Yeah. At the end, maybe it looks easy, but we so we make our job for the people. Our job with nobody in the stadium is no reason why we are here. What we do here, the players, the trainers, it is for the people. When we try, the most valued prize is for us when you realise, wow, these people, we made happy. That is most valued thing for us. In the end it is a game, we spend two hours together and enjoy our time together. When that has happened and they are at home and say 'OK, I spent two hours, I was happy, it was fun' - it is enough. Of course, if you win, it is better.

Are you going to buy Messi? (from a heckler)

What I said before...I think he is not a bad player, this guy. Definitely not. But I am sorry, Messi has to stay in Barcelona for the rest of his career. Sorry.

Arguably the club's most influential and iconic fan, Oasis star Noel Gallagher, discussed the motivation behind his move to England, his expectations and his desire to work with the club's young players:

So, El Senor: The Man. Welcome to Manchester... I see you brought the weather with you?

The reason I came here was for the weather. I'll have to wear my coat.

A new era at the club. Back to the old badge, a new manager. Why did you choose to come to City now and how tough is the task going to be?

I chose Man City because they wanted me a long time ago, because Txiki and Ferran are here. I've know them for a long time - I played with Txiki and Ferran was on the board during my first period in Barcelona.

The challenge is to play as well as possible. We always want to win titles, how successful we will be will be a consequence of how we are going to play. I want to convince these guys to play as well as possible and try to make the fans across the world to be proud of how we play.

All football fans will be excited to see you and if you weren't to come to City we'd be fascinated to see how it was going to play out. Thank God you are here, it's going to be amazing. How have you prepared for the Premier League from afar? Have you any preconceptions about how it's going to be?

I don't want any preconceptions before, no. I have to learn as much as possible. I have an idea how we are going to play but I learned in Germany - I arrived there with an idea and after I (found) I should change.

Did you speak to any of the other managers who have been to England? When they come from other countries they quickly become obsessed with the place. They become addicted to the place...

They told me it was so hard, so tough. All the people say 'Pep is not going to adapt good in that way' so that is why I'm here - to try and do it. Some of the people are confident it's going to go well but some of them - in Germany as well - say the way I play is not possible here in the Premier League.

So I said to myself 'why not travel there to try it?' It's a big challenge, not just for me, but always in my teams I was able to involve the players and it's going to happen here as well. When that happens everything will be easy.

Are you ready for the intensity of the league? It's relentless, seven days a week... the games come thick and fast. How do you prepare for the workload?

That is true, when you look at the statistics over the last two, three, four, five years in the Premier League every team wins and then loses the other ones. It's difficult to find one team with five, six victories in a row. It's so difficult to find it. It happened in one season, when Leicester won and was an amazing surprise for everybody.

That is amazing. What I have to do to control that - to avoid that, not to lose more often - I don't know. I've never been here before, I've never experienced here.

That's why I am here. If we are able to win one game and then say 'why can't we win again?' and then another one week later why can't we try again to win like we did in the last two games. That is the reason I am here. In Barcelona and Bayern - in Spain, in Germany - we were able to do that and people say 'ah, because we were in Barcelona and Bayern'. Yes, that's true. People say 'you will not be able to do that in England'. Ok, let's do it. We're going to try.

So, we're at the City Football Academy. An amazing place. Some of our younger teams have won their respective leagues in three different age groups. How are you going to get involved in the academy side?

I grew up at maybe the best academy in the world at Barcelona. When I arrived (as manager) in the first team I knew most of the players - (Sergio) Busquets for example, Pedro and others.

If you have the talent, quality and enough passion to become something in the world of football...if they show me something they will be in my hands. It depends on the quality of the players.

I'm a good trainer but not good enough for the players who don't have quality to convince them to play.

Would you like to see it (the academy) with your own eyes or rely on your coaching team to look at the younger players?

First of all I have to know them. In the pre-season all the big talents are going to join us - all of them. After they have to show me how good they are.

After my intuition (taps nose)... maybe sometimes I'll be right, maybe sometimes I make a mistake. But it depends on them. I'm not a genius to come here and say 'oh you are not good and now you are good'. But people tell me the academy at Manchester City compared to other places they have very, very good talents.

There are seven top managers in the world, only two don't work in the Premier League now - Carlo Ancelotti and Diego Simeone. Are you looking forward to locking horns with Jürgen Klopp, Claudio Ranieri, Antonio Conte... another guy across the road?

Of course we know each other and the way they play. We're going to start to play and afterwards we're going to meet each other better. You have an idea but it depends on the quality of players you have. Normally I have a very good relationship with my colleagues so it is not a problem.

Manchester is to become the centre of the football universe with two new coaches. The press are relentless...how do you plan to deal with that?

The managers when we win and happy in the press conference we are funny guys, comfortable with the media. When you lose and people say b******* you are angry and don't speak properly so that is how it is. But I lived in Barcelona - the people in Madrid are absolutely crazy. I've never had a press conference with the English media here and I'm looking forward to what's going on. I can survive, no problem.

You say you only really stay anywhere for three or four years, so do you intend to build a legacy here or at least put the foundations in place?

I have come to learn - that's why I move on. If I was building legacies then I would have stayed in Barcelona.

Is it true that Stuart Pearce turned you down when you were a player?

I came here at when the club was at the other training ground. I have to say that Stuart Pearce was right because I came here at 33, 34 years old and at that age for a player it was a disaster. It was intelligent not to pick me up. My dream was to play in the Premier League. He offered me six months but I would have had to move my family and so in the end we decided not but if you analyse my physical condition at the time I think it was the right decision.

Were you looking at Manchester City last season and worrying we wouldn't get in the Champions League? We were worried you weren't going to bother coming!

I wasn't worried. I was coming to Manchester, I was never going to stay at home. But we are not in the Champions League, we have to be clear. That situation is now in this moment better than Manchester United's though.

We like to think you went out of your way to avoid City in the Champions League last season. What would it have been like to play us?

I don't know the players from Manchester City so it wasn't a problem. I know some to say hello to but not personally to have a coffee with or anything. It's better like this because you can make decisions easier but we are going to meet each other. I have spoken to Vincent Kompany and we have had a little brief.

You have a reputation of being a very intense coach, but when you left Bayern Munich the players only had great things to say about you. How do you balance driving the players on but still maintaining their respect?

It's difficult to think about what people think about you. I think they know I am here 24 hours a day thinking about them. I love my job and what I do. They have to know and they will realise that I am here just thinking and working for them. That is maybe the reason why some of them - because people who don't play hate me! - but those who try to understand the game and why we do some things and not the other situation we have a good relationship.

At the end our job is to convince the other guy that this is the best way to cross the road. Tactics are important, as are training and facilities but in the end it is what I have to do to convince them. Maybe with you, we take a beer in the bar and this will convince you and with other ones maybe we talk tactics, or with others maybe we don't talk football. It depends on the player.

How would you sum up your time in Bayern Munich now, looking back on it?

It was amazing. I know for some people it was a big failure because we didn't win the Champions League but for the other side it was one of the best decisions in my life to go there. When I went to America after my time at Barcelona I went there to improve my level of English but after two months I signed the contract at Bayern Munich.

At Bayern it is so demanding. You have to win and win and win or they sack you. But it is a fantastic club and especially during my time there we had amazing players with a huge mentality. That is the big difference.

Three years from now when you threaten to leave and we tie you to a chair, because we won't let you leave, what does success look like for Manchester City?

For the media it is how many titles you are going to win. That is success or not. But while titles are amazing, two days after you lift it people say what's next? The process here is being comfortable working with these guys. At the end my life depends on that. I'll be happy when we decide to play in a way and it works. I am sure the club will be fantastic and the people I am working with are going to help me. I am sure that will happen. It happened at Barcelona and it happened at Bayern Munich.

It will happen here. We are going to fight every day to lift the titles but especially for the people when the game finishes and they think '90 minutes that was not bad, I would have preferred to be here than in the bar' that will be a good signal. Finally, the relationship with the people. Maybe because I am a Latin guy I have to be close with the guys, to say 'I'm going to kill you' and five minutes later to love each other. I need that to be happy and I hope that in three years that is going to happen.

The stadiums are always full in England so what are you expecting from the fans and the atmosphere?

When I came to England to play in the Champions League with Barcelona and Bayern Munich the atmosphere was the big difference compared to the rest of the world. There is no doubt about that. I hope they are going to help me to please our fans. We need their help. Our fans are going to be proud of our players. They are going to fight and they are going to be proud to be Manchester City fans. I am sure of that.

Guardiola went on to warn City supporters that he is "not good enough" to work miracles overnight despite winning 21 trophies during seven years at Barcelona and Bayern but he sought to temper expectations among those City fans who believe the club have appointed the Messiah.

"To come to the country who created football and believe you have to change something would be a little bit presumptuous," he said. "I'm not good enough to change everything. To change the mentality of a club of 120 years would be presumptuous. I trust a lot in myself. I think I am able to do the job but I don't come here to think I can change the mentality or the culture of England. I think at every stage I've had a big challenge. It could be the biggest because City haven't won as many titles as Barça or Bayern. I am here to try to think in the same way (as at Barcelona and Bayern). We are going to play that way because we were able to convince them that is the best way. It won't be easy. We need time but we don't have time. People don't expect to see in January and February how good we are, they expect to see in the first friendly game against Bayern Munich (this month) how good Pep is. I was lucky to train Barcelona and Bayern Munich with these amazing players and we won a lot of titles in a short time. The expectations now are the same. We will try. I don't need two months to know here will be completely different. When I see a guy who played here, like Xabi Alonso, I'm like, 'Tell me about England, tell me about the Premier League'. I never found one person who said, 'Oh, it will be easy for you'. They all said it's tough. I don't know why. That's what I want to discover. The big clubs go wherever, they're soft (in a game) and they are able to lose. I have to discover that for myself."

Guardiola's relationship with Mourinho turned toxic in Spain but he would have dinner with his United counterpart down the line. "He (Mourinho) wants to win, I want to win, we know each other pretty well from before at Barcelona," Guardiola said. "I think it (going out for dinner with Mourinho) will happen naturally. One day I will arrive and he will be there. It will be, 'Hi, how are you?'

He will say 'hi' as well."

Asked if he could rebuild Sterling's confidence after a troubled past 12 months, Guardiola said: "We're going to learn. The problem is recovering confidence when a player has no quality. That is a big problem. Then I cannot help him. But Sterling has the quality. He just has to focus on his life, his profession and I'm pretty sure he will play good."

Guardiola has been in the hunt for another goalkeeper but told Hart that he remained his first choice - for now. "At the moment, there's no doubt about that," he said. "He's No. 1. We're always looking for the best option to create a better team. But in that moment I don't worry about that - the performance of Joe Hart in the Euros. It's important to analyse their quality and to decide what we are going to do with him. It's similar with Sterling. Last season, expectation was high and, OK, he didn't play regularly and his confidence went down. It's so important to create good body language and after there is the quality. And I think he (Sterling) is a good talent."

Kompany had more cause for concern. "My dream for Vincent Kompany is to be fit," Guardiola said. "He's a magnificent central defender but he has to be fit."

Asked how many offers from England there had been he said: "Seriously, it was this one, so always I will be grateful to the people who trusted me to join the country and the Premier League. A coach, sooner or later, has to prove what it means to play in the Premier League. Manchester City gave me this chance and I will always be grateful. I will do my best until the last day to achieve what we want."

PEP'S BACKROOM STAFF:

Domènec Torrent - Been there, seen it. Won just as many trophies as Guardiola after being his assistant everywhere since 2007.

Lorenzo Buenaventura - An expert in rehabilitation, which may come as a boost to some of City's stars, including captain Vincent Kompany.

Carles Planchart - The video man. Attention to minute detail absolutely vital to Guardiola with the way he plays and Planchart is also heavily involved in recruitment.

Manuel Estiarte - Pep's lifelong friend, his confidante. An ex-Olympic water polo champion and used as a sounding board should problems arises.

Mikel Arteta - The former Arsenal and Everton midfielder joins his former Barcelona colleague at the Etihad Stadium as a coach.

Rodolfo Borrell - Guardiola's compatriot joins him as an assistant coach and was technical director and head of coaching at Liverpool following Rafa Benitez's appointment in 2009.

...THEN JOSÉ

José Mourinho pulled into Manchester Piccadilly station in the early hours of Monday morning ahead of his Tuesday unveiling at Old Trafford. He announced his arrival on Instagram telling followers: "I am here/UNITED we can" alongside a video of him disembarking the 21.25 London Euston-Manchester Piccadilly service. He took the two-hour 47-minute journey from his home in London in first class, with tickets priced at £237.50, arriving at Manchester's main transport hub at 00.12 on Monday morning.

He stayed at the Lowry Hotel in Manchester city centre and was pictured leaving with his entourage at 7.50am on Monday morning.

I received this official notification from Old Trafford just 24 hours before Mourinho's unveiling: "Due to a high volume of responses for tomorrow's press conference. We are only allowing two people from each organisation into the press conference."

Interestingly Mourinho never mentioned the name of Pep Guardiola, and enigmatically when asked if his greatest challenge came from the new boss at City, he talked about the legacy of Leicester City.

But he admitted the last few months of his Chelsea spell were "a disaster" and he had a thinly-veiled dig at long-term rival Arsene Wenger.

He was relieved of his duties at Stamford Bridge last December after enduring a disastrous start to the defence of their Premier League title and he talked about the closing months of his second spell at Stamford Bridge, conceding they were a far cry from his glory days with Chelsea. He said: "I was in trouble for the last five months: the first month was fine, the second month was not so good and after the second month it was a disaster."

Mourinho then appeared to have aim that dig at the Arsenal manager, who has clashed with him often enough in the past, when insisting he has nothing to prove. Arsenal last won the Premier League during the 2003-04 season and Mourinho insisted there is no pressure on him to win the title this campaign.

He added: "There are some managers who last won a title 10 years ago, some of them the last time was never. The last time I won a title was one year ago," he said. "I have a lot to prove, imagine the others.'

The only manger he named was the one time Laird of Old Trafford. Mourinho relished the "many opportunities to be together" he will now have with Sir Alex. When asked if he had received any advice from the retired 74-year-old Scot he jokingly replied: "Yes, bring the umbrella."

But he was deadly serious when it came to a question about whether his captain Wayne Rooney would be playing in his deep midfield role. No way José, was the definitive answer. Mourinho comprehensively dismissed the possibility of Rooney midfield position. "Maybe he is not a striker, not a No. 9 anymore but for me he will never be a No. 6, playing 50 metres from the goal. For me he will be a 9, a 10, a nine-and-a-half but never a 6 or an 8."

There you go Wayne. No messing about there, then. Mourinho had put the brakes on Rooney's conversion into a midfielder, which was started by Van Gaal and taken up by Roy Hodgson with England. With 245 club goals to Rooney's name, only four shy of Sir Bobby Charlton's record, Mourinho wanted him to play where he could still get goals. "It is normal that a player of this age changes a little bit," said Mourinho, who then continued, "But you will never change the natural appetite of putting the ball in the net."

Mourinho added: "I am more a manager that likes specialists and not so much the multi-functional players because I am very clear in my approach. Multifunctional players are like one or two, when you are in trouble you need someone who can fill but basically I want specialists."

He began his United reign by claiming that the club have been too limp with low expectations since Sir Alex's retirement, aiming to win the Premier League in his first campaign in charge and took a swipe at Van Gaal in the process, claiming he would not hide "behind words or philosophies."

Apart from his dig at old foe Wenger he also suggested that United's promotion of youth over the last 12 months, under Van Gaal, was purely down to injuries.

He all but announced the signing of Borussia Dortmund midfielder Henrikh Mkhitaryan. The Armenian forward is expected to be confirmed for a fee in the region of £26million. Mourinho announced that a third "priority" signing - known to be Mkhitaryan but not yet confirmed by the club - had already been ratified. That slip was met with laughter and a chuckle from the press officer sat beside him.

His ambition and aggression came across loud and clear. "I was never very good at hiding behind words and philosophies," Mourinho stated inside Old Trafford's Europa Suite. "Finish fourth is not the aim. I would never be able to work without success. That is my nature and I have always to find the reasons why I have always many questions towards myself and the people working with me. That is my nature." References to finishing fourth as a measure of success were clearly aimed at Van Gaal and Wenger.

A return for Ryan Giggs was not ruled out as Mourinho stressed it was not his fault that Giggs had left the club after 29 years. Giggs was not pushed out as was commonly perceived and he wanted to make the point that Giggs left only because he was not offered the manager's job instead of Mourinho himself.

Mourinho bristled with indignation and seemed to have a ready-made list on which to rely when challenged over his record of bringing young players through into the first team at other clubs, and the suggestion that his style would not fit with United's desire to promote youth.

Overtly waving his notes, he said: "You know how many players I promoted to the first team? Forty-nine. Forty-nine!"

Mourinho also insisted that managing United was not his "dream job" but a reality.

It all began with Benfica 16 years ago in his native Portugal, Mourinho then moved to União de Leiria and Porto, before joining Chelsea in 2004. He then coached Inter Milan and Real Madrid, and returned to Stamford Bridge in 2013, where he won his third Premier League title before parting company "by mutual consent" on 17 December, after losing nine out of sixteen league games. Mourinho lifted six trophies with Porto, eight with Chelsea during his two spells, five with Inter and three with Real. In that collection of 22 items of silverware, he has collected eight league titles, and two Champions Leagues. It was clear that the ego had landed at Old Trafford. Although he said the club was far more important than the manager passing through, he used the word 'I' 91 times during his introductory press conference where he was questioned on his standing in world football, his transfer plans and whether he has anything to prove following his departure from Stamford Bridge.

Someone even kept record of the buzz words:

'I' - 91 times

'We' - 27 times

'Club' - 8 times

'Manchester United' - 6 times

'Champions League' - 6 times

'Manager' - 6 times

'Title' - 6 times

The Q&A in more detail:

José, now you're at Manchester United are you the Special One, or the Happy One?

I don't know, really.

The other two times, I was arriving at the country, this is a different one.

I was sacked by Chelsea and then I stayed in the same country, the same competition with the same faces in front of me so it is nothing new for me really it is just to arrive into a club which is difficult to describe, to find the right words to describe this club.

I don't like the denomination people use like 'dream job', it is not a dream job, it is reality as I'm the Manchester United manager but the reality is I think it is a job everyone wants and not many have a chance to have and I have it and I know obviously the responsibility, the expectation.

At the same time I know the legacy, the history of this club, I know what the fans expect from me and I expect this challenge doesn't make me nervous because my history in the last 10 years or more was always to leave with big clubs; expectation and I think it comes in the right moment of my career, I feel very prepared. I'm very stable and with a great motivation.

I am where I want to be in this club, in this country, in the domestic cups, I feel a bit frustrated I am not playing Champions League. I don't hide, I chase Sir Alex's record in the Champions League for matches as a manager. I am around 130 matches.

Hopefully it is only one season I am not there. When I say we, obviously the club is more important than myself, Manchester United is more important than myself and we have to make sure July 2017 this club is where it has to be in the Champions League.

What is the realistic aim this season? Simply to compete or to win?

It depends on the way you want to face it. I was never very good playing with the words or hiding behind words and hiding behind philosophies. I never tried to be good at that.

I was always much more aggressive in my approach with the risks that can bring. It would be easy and even honest and pragmatic to focus on the last three years on the fact that we don't qualify for Champions League and so on and so on and be quite pragmatic to say let's work and try and be back to the Champions League, try and be back to the top four, try and be back to the Europa League.

I prefer to be more aggressive and say we want to win and I can anticipate any one of you will come later with a question about style of play and a question about what is before and I can imagine one of these questions is around the corner and I can anticipate by saying you can win a short competition, a couple of matches without playing well but you cannot win competitions without playing well.

What is playing well? It is scoring more goals than the opponents, conceding less, making your fans proud because you give everything and you win. It is everything at the same time.

It is an aggressive approach by myself. I want everything. Of course we are not going to get everything but we want to.

Do you have a point to prove after last season?

There are some managers that the last time they won a title was 10 years ago. Some of them the last time they won a title was never.

The last time I won a title was one year ago, not 10 years ago or 15 years ago so if I have a lot to prove, imagine the others.

But the reality is that was never important for me. I play against myself. That is my feeling many times. I feel I have to prove not to the others but to myself. I would never be able to work without success. That is my nature and I have always to find the reasons why I have always many questions towards myself and the people working with me.

I could approach this job in a defensive point of view by saying the last three years the best we did was fourth. I can't go. It is my nature.

I work in some big clubs before. Obviously Manchester United by the social point of view is a completely different dimension but the reality is that when people have year after year a certain kind of menu, the menu has to change for better or worse.

Manchester United for many years, success was just routine and in this moment the last three years are to forget. I want the players to forget. I don't want the players to think we have to do better and finish fourth. Finish fourth is not the aim.

This is what I do with myself. I am 53, I am not 63 or 73. Maybe you are tired with myself because I started at such a young level. I am a young manager. If I don't go for big I am in trouble. The reality, I was in trouble for the last five months.

Are more changes needed?

I don't know. I think the third player will be official when? Soon.

I can try to make you understand the profile. We made a nucleus of four priorities, four positions to give a certain balance to the squad, to give a certain push in terms of quality and the qualities I need and want. Especially the ones with more vision.

I am more a manager that likes specialists and not so much the multi-functional players because I am very clear in my approach. Multifunctional players are like one or two, when you are in trouble you need someone who can fill but basically I want specialists.

We decided four targets. From these four, we have three and until we don't have the fourth, we are still working hard, myself, the structure, Mr. Woodward, the owners, we are working hard.

When we have the fourth I breathe and then the market will be open. We are not going to get the fourth on 31 August, we will get the fourth before then.

There is something for me, that the players I keep are all happy. Imagine first match I don't select somebody, he gets disappointed he has the chance to go to another club. If he leaves, somebody else has to come in.

There is a fundamental market and there is a supplementary market. We are doing well. We are getting the players we want and now we have the third.

Does the biggest challenge come from Pep Guardiola at Manchester City?

I think Leicester's legacy was not just the happiness around the country. The legacy was we are in a competition where 20 teams are fighting for the title. That is their legacy.

Next season if you have another team who win the first five matches, you consider them candidates. It is over the time you say they will collapse in December.

To speak about one manager, one club, one enemy, I hate the word in football and life, I don't think it is right. It is one thing to be a in a two-horse race like I was in Spain or in Italy it was three teams fighting for the title, then that kind of approach makes sense.

In the Premier League it doesn't make sense at all. If you focus on one opponent, the others will be laughing so I am not going to be part of it.

I am Manchester United manager with all the respect to all the other clubs in the country especially one that was my house for seven years. I share so many special moments with their fans. I am the manager of the biggest club in the UK. I am going to focus on our job and our club.

Thanks to what Leicester did. One of their legacies is to change forever the competition.

You have often been criticised for not giving youth a chance. What will your attitude be at Old Trafford?

I have no time to answer it. To answer it would take 10 minutes. I knew that was coming. You know how many young players I promote to the first team from academies? 49.

Do you want to know who they are? I can give you that. I promote 49 players from the academies from the clubs and with two factors, sometimes you promote players because you don't have another chance because you have so many injuries.

That is one factor and the second factor is when you are not playing for big targets, it is easier to bring them up.

My record of injuries is very, very low. Even in many years from the Champions League studies about every team, my teams were many times the teams with less injuries.

I never promote players because of need, I did it because of conviction and decision.

Last year was the only season of my career when I was not fighting for the title winning or finishing second or third once so it was never a situation of stability and no pressure to promote players. I did 49.

Some of them are big names, they are today Champions League winners in the Euros, playing for national teams and 49 is a lot. So one lie repeated many times sometimes it looks true but it will never be true. 49.

If you want the names, I give you the names.

Why did Ryan Giggs leave the club?

About Ryan, let me finish. I never run away about my responsibility. It is not my responsibility that Ryan is not in the club.

The job Ryan wanted is the job the club decided to give me. Ryan wanted to be Manchester United manager and the owners, Mr. Woodward, decided to give the job to me.

Like 2000, I decide I want to be a manager. For many of us, we start as assistant coaches and for many of us, arrives the moment we make a decision.

So when you are speaking about did I offer him a job. He could be what he wanted in the club. The club wanted to give him any important job in the club.

It happened with myself in Barcelona in 2000, I had a contract for another two years. It was not easy to go to another fight. For Ryan it is not easy to go the step from assistant to manager, it is the step to leave his house of 29 years.

He was brave, he is honest, so good luck so if one day he wants to come back when I am here, I will never say so and if one day the club offers him the chance to be manager, I think it will something natural and the consequence of his success in his career.

Have you had any advice from Sir Alex Ferguson? Did you speak to him?

Yes, bring the umbrella. Yesterday I couldn't believe it was raining in the training ground. It was great advice.

The second advice was to bring my typical bottle of wine. Now we are going to have many occasions to be together.

At the moment Sir Alex is on a bit of a holiday at the Euros so I cannot see him this week but when his holidays are finished we will have lots of time to meet. He will always be welcome to the training ground and we will have a lot of time to share our personal stuff.

His opinion is important to me, the same way so many legends love this club and they are in the pundits industry and every opinion will be important to me. I will try and learn from them.

What role will Wayne Rooney play?

In football there are many jobs. There are many jobs on the field.

The one that is more difficult to find is the guy who has put the ball in the net. The players change during the years their qualities, their characteristics.

It is normal a player at their age change a bit but there is something that will never change which is the natural appetite to put the ball in the net.

Maybe he is not a striker, not a No 9 anymore but for me he will never be a No 6, playing 50 metres from the goal. You can tell me his pass is amazing but my pass is also amazing without pressure.

To be there and put the ball in the net is the most difficult thing. For me he will be a 9, a 10, a nine and a half but never a 6 or an 8.

Mourinho sanctioned the signing of 34-year-old Ibrahimović and thinks he will be the ideal complement for 18-year-old Rashford; and this 'old and new' strategy possibly the reason why Rooney is behind them both. "Thirty-four is his age plus 18 Marcus Rashford's age," Mourinho said in an interview with MUTV. "Thirty-four plus 18 divided by two is the perfect age for a football player. So our two strikers are exactly in the perfect age, because 18 is not the perfect age, 34 is not. So I think they can be an amazing complement for each other."

Rashford, a graduate of United's academy, was thrown in during an injury crisis, scoring twice on his debut against FC Midtjylland in the Europa League, then featuring regularly and scoring eight goals in 18 appearances across all competitions. He ended up with an FA Cup winners' medal, earning a call-up to the England squad for the European Championship after having scored just a few minutes into his senior international debut against Australia.

Ibrahimović signed off his fourth season with PSG by scoring 50 goals in 51 matches, helping his team to the domestic Treble of Ligue 1, the French Cup and League Cup.

Maybe they will be a complementary pairing.

Mourinho believed that Ibrahimović's experience and haul of trophies will prove invaluable.

"Zlatan is Zlatan. He wins year after year," he added. "His records are absolutely amazing. His passion for the game is incredible. A man of his age, with his CV, to come for the biggest challenge of his career at the biggest club he has ever played for and the most difficult competition he has played in. He's an amazing player."

They worked together during a season at Inter Milan and had an exceptional relationship, with Ibrahimović later declaring that he would have been willing to die for him.

Mourinho continued: "This is the beautiful thing when you a coach a player and then a few years later you have him again. It's beautiful because it means the relationship was fantastic on a personal side of view and was great too. A few years later we are back together and I'm so happy with that because I know what he can bring."

Mourinho was certain over Bailly's ability to play in the first team straight away. He told MUTV: "I could compare him with some players I've had previously but I don't want to do it because obviously the other boys play for other clubs. But he is a player who we believe has all the attributes. He is very strong physically and very fast. It's not so easy to find a fast player when you have quite a big body; he's a heavy guy, a tall boy who's really fast. He comes from a Spanish culture where the first phases are important so technically he's very good. For some periods, he played right-back and, because playing in the right-back position demands more from an attacking point of view, it's good for a centre-back to play some periods as a right-back. My only question mark at the moment is one I have to help him delete - the question mark of someone who has never played at such a big club with so many responsibilities and so many expectations. So is Eric ready to come here and start performing from day one? I don't know. It is a question mark but my job is to delete that question mark as soon as possible and give him the stature, brain and personality to play for Manchester United."

Mourinho noted that United's England players would accompany the squad on their pre-season tour of China, not a scenario he expected as England were embarrassingly eliminated by Iceland at the last 16 stage of the European Championship, forcing early returns for Rooney, Rashford and Smalling. So, Mourinho would be taking England players to the Far East, although they would not feature in International Champions Cup friendlies against Borussia Dortmund and Manchester City. "I am taking the English boys - that I wasn't expecting but they're coming. I will take them but I'm not going to play them. What is more important is to work, to be together, to live together 24-hours every day during the week and finally when you come back from China is when the others are waiting for us. Then we will be together for 10-12 days before the Community Shield. Fifteen-17 days before the first game against Bournemouth and it's a difficult situation especially for a new manager but we can't run away from it. This is what we have and we have to try to do the best we can."

Before leaving for China United will play a pre-season fixture against former FA cup winners Wigan, providing an opportunity to look at several young players recommended by coach Nicky Butt. Speaking about the worth of pre-season matches, he said; "They are very important but they are not important to win. They are important for different reasons. For example the first game against Wigan I am going to have some players I don't know very well and bring into the first team. Kids like Tyrell (Warren), Axel Tuanzebe. I don't know them well. I just trust Nicky Butt and his judgment. Obviously I have to work closely with them (the youth coaches) and trust them. When they say 'we have a few players that in a couple of years they can be first-team players', I have to work with them and give them the chance to know me and accelerate their progress."

Mourinho offered his notebook out at the end of his press conference, but that was ruined after a glass of water was accidentally knocked over. "Forget it!" Mourinho snapped. But it wasn't some Machiavellian plot to deprive the media of the facts. In fact the club quickly produced a reprint.

He then privately recounted the names and the list was later sent out with more than the previously suggested 49, finishing instead with 55. On it were either academy products or players under the age of 21 he had given debuts to at their new clubs. He was clearly determined to make his point.

Robben cost Chelsea £12m in the summer of 2004 having starred for Groningen and PSV as well as at Euro 2004. The Dutchman had made his international debut 18 months before making his Chelsea bow and was being chased by the world's top teams - including United. Mario Balotelli is also on the list having already made his debut for Inter Milan by the time Mourinho took over in 2008, although he did flourish under him, playing 70 games in two seasons.

Mourinho also pointed to a number of youngsters at Real Madrid, including Raphael Varane, Casemiro, Alvaro Morata and Jesé. "Some of them are big names, they are today Champions League winners or in the Euros, playing for national teams and it is a lot," Mourinho had stressed in his unveiling media conference. "So once more, one lie repeated many times, sometimes it looks like it's true but it will be always a lie. So for many times, many of you - with or without intention - that is not the point, I don't care about it - but it was not true. My record of injuries is very, very low. Even in many years from the

Champions League studies about every team, my teams were many times the teams with less injuries in the whole of Europe. So I never promote players because of need, I did it because of conviction and decision. And last year was the only season of my career when I was not fighting for the title."

The 55 players on Mourinho's list:

BENFICA (2)

Diogo Luis

Made debut against Braga in 2000. Last played for Cypriot side Apollon Limassol in 2009.

Geraldo Alves

Centre back made just five league appearances after debut in 2000. Now with Astra Giurgiu.

UNIAO LEIRIA (2)

Nuno Laranjeiro

Became a first-team regular for União Leiria and also played for Portugal U21. Now with Fatima

Joao Paulo Andrade

Another player to cement first-team spot at União Leiria and even captained team.

PORTO (6)

Carlos Alberto

Opened the scoring in 3-0 Champions League triumph over Monaco in 2004. Five caps for Brazil.

Bruno Morais

The striker made just 17 league appearances during seven years with Portuguese giants.

Pedro Oliveira

Has played in Italy with Modena and also made five appearances for Portugal Under 21s

Reinaldo Garcia

He played for Porto for six seasons then moved to Spanish roller hockey where he became the star for Liceo La Coruna.

Joca

Retired from football in 2004 and is now assistant manager at Espinho.

Hugo Luz

Struggled for first-team action and went on to play in lower divisions of Portuguese football.

CHELSEA - FIRST SPELL (10)

Arjen Robben (U21)

Signed as a highly-rated winger but struggled with injuries. Now starring for Bayern Munich.

Lassana Diarra (U21)

Also played under Mourinho at Real Madrid. Now back in France with Marseille.

John Mikel Obi (U21)

Made first appearance in 2006. The 29-year-old Nigerian remains at Stamford Bridge.

Sam Hutchinson

Had a loan spell in Holland with Vitesse Arnhem. Now impressing with Sheffield Wednesday.

Jimmy Smith

Was highly-rated but failed to live up to the hype. Currently with League Two's Crawley Town.

Michael Woods

Signed from Leeds in 2006, but again failed to live up to expectations. Now playing in midfield with Hartlepool.

Anthony Grant

Made just one league appearance at Stamford Bridge. The 29-year-old is now playing for Port Vale.

Ben Sahar

Signed from Hapoel Tel Aviv but was unable to hit the ground running. Back in Israel with Hapoel Be'er Sheva.

Steven Watt

Scottish defender begun his career at Aberdeen. Now playing in non-League with Hastings.

Lenny Pidgeley

The goalkeeper had tough task of getting ahead of Petr Cech in pecking order. Now 32, he was last at Forest Green Rovers.

INTER MILAN (7)

Davide Santon

Went on to play in the Premier League with Newcastle before return to Inter last year.

Marko Arnautović (U21)

The Stoke City star is now starring in the English top-flight after arriving in 2013.

Alen Stevanovic

The winger failed to cement first-team spot in Milan and is now playing for Partizan.

Mario Balotelli

Didn't make his debut under Mourinho but the then 19-year-old played 70 matches in two seasons.

Luca Caldirola

The 25-year-old Italian centre back is now with Werder Bremen after failing to make league appearance for Inter.

Giulio Donati

After failing to make the grade at Inter, he went on to player for Bayer Leverkusen and is now with Mainz.

Rene Krhin

Made five league appearance for Inter. A Slovenia international, he is now playing for Grenada.

REAL MADRID (21)

Raphael Varane

Signed from Lens in 2011 for £8.5million. Now a regular at the heart of the Real Madrid defence.

Alvaro Morata

Made debut in 2010 after progressing through Real's B team. Sold to Juventus in 2014 but bought back this summer.

Casemiro

Signed from Sao Paolo for £4million in 2013. Now a regular under Zinedine Zidane.

Nacho

Made debut in 2011 after coming through the B team. Still at Real and a Spanish international

Jesé

Debuted in 2011. Still at Real in a support role.

Josélu

Scored on his one and only La Liga appearance in 2011. Now at Stoke.

Tomas Mejias

Another to make his La Liga debut in 2011. Now back-up goalkeeper under Aitor Karanka at Middlesbrough.

Omar Mascarel

Made his debut in 2013. Spent last season on loan at Sporting Gijon.

Fabinho

Made his debut in 2013 on loan from Brazilian side Rio Ave. Never moved to Real permanently and now at Monaco

Pedro Mendes

Made debut in the Champions League while on loan from Sporting Lisbon in 2013. Now at Rennes.

José Rodriguez

Made his debut in 2012 in a Copa del Rey game. Moved from Galatasaray to Mainz this summer.

Denis Cherishev

Came through the B team and made debut in 2012. Joined Villarreal this summer.

Pablo Sarabia

Replaced Cristiano Ronaldo for his debut in 2010. Joined Sevilla from Getafe this summer.

Juan Carlos

Debuted in 2011. Was on loan at Malaga, from Braga, last season.

Diego Lorente

Made his Real debut in 2013. Was on loan at Rayo Vallecano last season.

Alex Fernandez

A youth graduate who debuted in 2011. Was loaned to Reading from Espanyol in 2015/16.

David Mateos

Debuted in the Champions League against Ajax in 2010. Now playing in the MLS with Orlando City.

Jesus Fernandez Collado

Goalkeeper signed from Numancia and debuted in 2011. Now on the bench at Granada.

Antonio Adan

Youth graduate, debuted in 2010. Now a regular at Betis.

Fernando Pacheco Flores

Goalkeeper debuted in Copa del Rey in 2011. Now first choice at Alaves.

Jorge Casado

Another to debut in 2011. He's now playing in the Spanish second division for Ponferradina.

CHELSEA - SECOND SPELL (7)

Kurt Zouma

Joined Chelsea for £12million from St Etienne and debuted in 2014. Played 33 times for Chelsea last season.

Lewis Baker

Hailed by Mourinho, Baker debuted in 2014. Has been on loan at Sheffield Wednesday, MK Dons and most recently feeder club Vitesse Arnhem.

Dominic Solanke

Became Chelsea's youngest Champions League player on his debut in 2014. Another on loan at Vitesse.

John Swift

Made his debut on the final day of the 2013-14 season. Was last on loan at Brentford.

Ruben Loftus-Cheek

Made his debut in the Champions League in 2014. Signed a bumper new deal at Chelsea last season.

Andreas Christensen

Debut came in the League Cup in 2014. Was player of the year at Borussia Monchengladbach while on loan last season.

Bertrand Traore

Made his debut in 2015 after red tape saw him loaned to Vitesse. Played 16 times for Chelsea last season.

Mourinho's backroom staff were confirmed with, as expected, trusted lieutenant Rui Faria becoming assistant manager. Mourinho first met Faria at Barcelona before he worked as Mourinho's fitness coach during his time in charge of União de Leiria in Portugal and followed him to Chelsea (twice), Inter Milan and Real Madrid. Coaches Silvino Louro, who has been with Mourinho for more than a decade having started out as his goalkeeping coach, was named as one of four coaches. Ricardo Formosinho and Carlos Lalin (who also previously worked with the manager) and Emilio Alvarez were confirmed as members of the coaching staff along with analyst Giovanni Cerra.

United's commitment to overhaul their scouting department saw ex-Rangers coach Tommy Moller Nielsen (a Dane who also spent a year at Aberdeen) signed with the intention of being the 'eyes and ears' in Scandinavia. Nielsen worked for Everton, West Brom, Bolton and Nottingham Forest and will concentrate on the region predominantly for youngsters coming through. He coached under Sir Alex Ferguson's friend Walter Smith at Ibrox as well as Dick Advocaat.

United were making more than 15 new appointments in their scouting division after a review into the club's structure that was ordered by executive vice-chairman Ed Woodward with head of development John Murtough. The role of scouting auditor - aimed at heading up the operation without actually watching any football - was still being advertised.

Nielsen, 54, said: "I am a coach and wanted to coach again, but it is a very exciting and interesting job, I need to start. I get to work with football at the highest level and I am very pleased." Neilsen would be sent to the Rio Olympics on his first scouting mission.

MOURINHO'S TRUSTED ASSISTANTS:

Rui Faria: The 41-year-old followed Mourinho to Porto, Chelsea, Inter Milan and Real Madrid after initially working with him as a fitness coach at União de Leiria. He received a four-match stadium ban in April 2014 after aiming abuse at Mike Dean.

Silvino Louro: Worked with a range of top keepers including Petr Cech and Julio Cesar but now taking a general coaching role. The 57-year-old worked with Mourinho at Porto, Chelsea, Inter Milan and Real Madrid.

Ricardo Formosinho: Scouting role. The 59-year-old worked under Mourinho at Porto. Managed 21 clubs during his own managerial career.

Carlos Lalin: Fitness specialist. Similar role at Chelsea.

Emilio Alvarez: Will look after David de Gea, Sergio Romero and the goalkeepers.

Mourinho soon allowed a glimpse into his new office at Carrington after posting a picture on his Instagram account. With wall-length windows, it features a fitted television storage unit and spin bike, which the manager was pictured sitting on. On the TV screen there appears to be footage of his new captain, Wayne Rooney, who is addressing a camera while standing on a training pitch.

On a glass wall in the office, three of his four Guinness World Records certificates are visible, taking pride of place on the bottom windowsill.

His record achievements are: Most Points in a Premier League Season (95), Most Champions League titles won at Different Clubs (two), Youngest Manager to Reach 100 Champions League Games (49 years 12 days) and Most Games Unbeaten at Home in the Premier League (77).

Chapter 9

THE PRE-SEASON

The prospect of the most explosive season in Premier League history was the perfect antidote to the worst ever England performance in tournament football at Euro 2016.

All the world's top managers were in the Premier League with the arrival of Pep Guardiola at Manchester City and Antonio Conte at Stamford Bridge after the exploits of unfancied Italy at the European Championships, along with Jürgen Klopp at Liverpool. Even the Championship will feature Rafa Benitez at Newcastle United battling to get back to the elite.

The class of the managerial titans will be none bigger or more headline generating than in Manchester where José vs Pep will reverberate around the world and back again.

Incredibly the Premier League urgently needs to re-establish its credibility as the most powerful in the world after the debacle of the national team at the Euros in France.

Led by the Manchester United skipper Wayne Rooney, and scrutinised by the likes of Mourinho, it was a 'shambles to shame' and just about everything in between when it came to the team representing English football. The pundits dug out every possible negative description to paint a picture of abject failure at Euro 2016, and quite rightly so. It was bad, very bad, so bad, that there are no adequate words to describe it. So little point of trying to find a new one; it doesn't exist.

Regrettably, from a personal point of view, it is an all too familiar scenario having been there when Graham Taylor suffered similar anxieties to poor old Uncle Roy Hodgson when England were beaten by the USA. I can recall my Daily Mirror headline screamed out when Howard Wilkinson took over to take the team for the one and only time..."IS THIS THE WORST ENGLAND TEAM EVER." The answer came pretty quickly with another embarrassing performance and result that, yes, it was indeed the worst by some distance.

On this occasion, though, the real shame of losing to Iceland is that this new England team is packed with young fresh talent that might have actually had a chance. That chance was denied by a combination of players who caught the sense of the indignation that awaited them back home if they made themselves into comical figures by daring to lose against little Iceland, and consequently froze like the proverbial rabbit caught in the headlights when staring defeat in the face in that sterile, scared second half performance. Bring home the clowns. The nation voted Brexit and England quickly exited the Euros as well. Another tournament wasted, another opportunity missed and let's forget about Greg Dyke's plans of winning future World Cups. There will be another 50 years of hurt unless there are some fundamental changes behind the scenes.

Inevitably Uncle Roy quit with his trusted lieutenants Ray Lewington and Gary Neville - the 'Three Musketeers' denied the chance to face hosts France in the quarter-finals. We all can't wait until Neville is pushing the buttons on his electronic chalk board back in the Sky studios telling us all about tactics after proving an absolute dunce with his fist managerial job in Spain and now culpable along with all the coaching staff in the way England were out-thought by Iceland part timers. Give it up Gary!

And now the FA has to give up its succession policy with Gareth Southgate possibly poised to succeed Hodgson for just more of the same. The early list of managerial favourites dished up by the bookies and rolled out on both ITV and BBC made for depressing reading until pundits on Match of the Day came up with the name of Glenn Hoddle, slipped in at the end at 20-1 when his name didn't appear on the ITV list, even though he is one of their key co-commentators. Hoddle was the last English coach of an England team to put together a national side worthy to wear the shirts and might even have gone on in France to have won the World Cup. They were better than Argentina even with 10-men after David Beckham was sent off, eventually succumbing to yet another penalty shoot-out exit. Hoddle has the best ratio of results other than Sir Alf Ramsey and Fabio Capello, and was the only English manager sacked for non-footballing reasons. Hoddle has been reluctant to return to management for many years now, but wouldn't say no if his country came calling. He consistently describes that feeling with England as "unfinished business". Hoddle needs to be removed from pontificating on England for ITV to helping mould the young English talent, develop some new ones, and help behind the scenes as the first 'Technical Director' of the England team, if not the actual coach, in a new way of doing things, a new direction, rather than a like for like replacement for Roy Hodgson.

Rio Ferdinand said before the tournament that Hoddle was the coach he thought had any notion of how to build an England team, and while Hoddle sits with ITV, Rio and Alan Shearer do the same job on the BBC. All three should be part of the new vision for an England team that is led by a man of vast experience in major tournaments as the coach, and Shearer and Ferdinand as leaders of that dressing room. That should be the brains trusted, trusted to take England forward, rather than a groan of FA councillors swanning around enjoying the hospitality but playing zero support to the England manager. Of course that will never happen. Just look at the blind leading the blind, the men who are charged with selecting the new England manger. Well, at least the former Manchester United executive David Gill, the one-time Old Trafford executive, is among the three wise men on the election panel who will canvass opinion from within the football industry.

But all that is soul searching, and indeed heart-breaking, about the England national side will be put to one side as the partisan and intensely competitive Premier League gets underway, galvanised by the best managerial brains in world football.

Much of this momentous Premier League campaign will be concentrated in Manchester; a 'Tale of one City'. While Pep Guardiola was a game-changing signing for City, United trumped them with José Mourinho.

It's going to be a blockbuster of a season that's for sure, and it will not be the let-down that it was for England at the Euros.

Chelsea defender Kurt Zouma wants to see his former manager succeed at United.

Zouma, who was signed for Chelsea by Mourinho, says: "It's crazy to see José at Manchester United. The Premier League is the best in the world. The best managers in the world are all here. It means every game will be even tougher. There will be many great games. It will be strange to play against Manchester United with José as their manager. That's the life of football. I hope he does well there. But of course I hope he loses against Chelsea. José sent me a text to say good luck when I was having my operation. Everyone has been very supportive."

José Mourinho geared up for the new season fully prepared. He shared an image via his popular Instagram account of his desk and said: "Now is time to enjoy!!! Produce pre-season training sessions..." Mourinho was using an iPad, coloured charts, a Blackberry, a watch and a personalised pencil case featuring the United badge and the 'Special One's' face were also placed on the desk.

Details of Mourinho's first game at Old Trafford were confirmed as the Wayne Rooney testimonial v Everton on 3 August.

Wayne Rooney announced the plans for his testimonial match, between United and Everton, and he was described by José Mourinho in the same press release as "England's best player for over a decade." He wanted the 30-year-old forward to remain a central figure in a team he was completely overhauling.

Mourinho has a tried and trusted formula of building his teams around senior, long-serving figures, as he demonstrated with John Terry and Frank Lampard at Chelsea.

In a period of upheaval following the retirement of Sir Alex Ferguson, the captain seemed to be one of the few constants.

Talking about the testimonial game that launched a year-long initiative to raise £5m for children's charities, Rooney said: "For me there could not be a more special testimonial match. Manchester United and Everton are the only clubs I have played for as a professional footballer. I am happy to say now that, whatever may happen in the future, I will never play for another Premier League club. I owe United and Everton everything for giving me my footballing opportunities. Through the Wayne Rooney Foundation I want to put something back, and say a heartfelt thanks to everyone at these great clubs who helped me in my career. Everton and United, along with my family, gave me the support and opportunity to help me achieve my goals and dreams."

The match would see Mourinho's new United at Old Trafford and he said: "Wayne is and has been England's best player for over a decade and this game will be a fitting tribute to everything he has achieved. I'm looking forward to what will be a very special night for us both. I'm sure the fans will make this a memorable occasion and help Wayne to raise a lot of money to help support vulnerable children."

The European Championships may have been in full swing, with the mouth-watering prospect of England taking on Gareth Bale's Wales hogging the media limelight, but there was still room for analysis of the Premier League fixtures announcement, none more so than that early prospect of the Pep vs. José show.

José Mourinho gets his league managerial career at Manchester United off the ground at Bournemouth's Vitality Stadium on the opening day of the season and he will want to make it a winning start, as his preference is to make a whirlwind start, lead from the front, and never let anyone catch him. His Old Trafford debut is the following weekend with the visit of Southampton, where he would want to have six points on the board and already be setting the pace.

Guardiola gets a relatively straightforward start to life in the Premier League, kicking off at home to Sunderland before travelling to Stoke, then it's home to West Ham before the Manchester derby with Mourinho, then it's back to more gentle fare with Bournemouth and Swansea.

So, September 10 was the date to ring in your diary as Guardiola's Manchester City travel to face Mourinho's Manchester United. It might be pleasant on the surface, particularly after they will have already faced off in a pre-season encounter on their China tour, but everyone knows deep resentment will be simmering under the surface. It is anyone's guess what will happen and who might fancy a touch of the old 'mind games', but expect this fixture to be a defining moment in the race for the championship crown, even though the season is still very much in its embryonic stage.

Back-to-back trips to Liverpool, on October 15, and to his old club Chelsea seven days later, will ensure that Mourinho doesn't stray very far from the spotlight; was it ever any different?

How will he be received by Chelsea fans who used to worship him, who sung his name well after his dismissal last season? Now he's managing a team who are title rivals, and not much love lost between the two sets of supporters. But Chelsea fans are a rare breed who welcome back their heroes irrespective of issues that might sour relationships. Chelsea fans love him, and will miss him, and mourn not just his departure but their loss being Manchester United's gain. While hard to take, they won't forget what he did for them.

December appears to be kind to United, but the New Year sees Mourinho's side travelling to West Ham's new Olympic Stadium on January 2. Untied have come unstuck in east London before, but Mourinho will pay little attention to history and will be looking very much toward the 'squeaky bum' time of the business end of the season and will have a keen eye on the Old Trafford fixture with Liverpool.

If United have designs on regaining their place at the top of the Premier League come May, then they will have to navigate a couple of tricky trips to north

London in the closing weeks with Arsenal and Tottenham both hosting Mourinho's side, but it will be home from home for the new United manager who still has a property in west London.

Ahead of all that, though, Manchester United were finalising their pre-season matches:

The final overseas game was announced as that friendly in Sweden to face Turkish giants Galatasaray as part of the Club's Tour 2016, presented by Aon.

However, before the short trip to Scandinavia, José Mourinho's men would compete in the International Champions Cup in China, facing Borussia Dortmund in Shanghai on Friday 22 July, before the match against rivals Manchester City in Beijing on Monday 25 July.

Commenting on the Club's summer plans, Manchester United's Executive Vice Chairman, Ed Woodward, said: "The team has a valuable combination of domestic and overseas games against tough European opposition. Playing games across a number of countries allows our tremendous fans the opportunity to watch the team play, and importantly the number of games allows the manager and team the best opportunity to prepare for the coming season."

Chief Executive Officer of Aon Sweden, Jacob Schlawitz, stated: "At Aon, we are working with our partners to help them empower results and sustain success on their journey to greatness. We are proud to be a presenting partner of the Manchester United Tour 2016, and look forward to welcoming the Club to Sweden."

Following the games in China and Sweden, Manchester United will face Everton at Old Trafford on Wednesday 3 August in Wayne Rooney's Testimonial Match, followed by the Community Shield tie against Leicester City at Wembley Stadium.

José Mourinho refused to temper expectations as he reiterated his desire to win everything his team competes in, making it perfectly clear during his unveiling at Old Trafford that simply qualifying for the Champions League will not satisfy him.

In an interview with *Inside United* in conjunction with Adidas, Mourinho stated that he believed the Premier League champions could require fewer points than ever before. The lowest total stands at 75 in 1996-97 - won by United - with Leicester reaching 81. "I'm not humble when I talk about targets, I'm quite aggressive on that," Mourinho said. "I want everything and everything is to win matches, play well, score goals, don't concede goals... everything. I want everything. I know that we are speaking about a hypothetical situation which is very difficult to reach but I want everything."

He felt the huge sums of money pouring into the Premier League and lack of fear when facing traditionally bigger clubs will see the division become even tighter. "If you look at the Euros and you see what Wales have done and what Iceland did, I think football is changing," Mourinho added. "It's not just about the amazing economic situation that every club in the Premier League has now, which allows them to buy well and buy expensive and good players to compete for the biggest prizes. It's not just about that, it's also about training methods, preparation and mental preparation, and also nobody is afraid of anybody. In the past you could smash opponents, if you were one of the best teams, 5-0 or 6-0 and win 10-15 matches in a row. I think these times are over and fewer points will win the title. Even with a handful of defeats you can be champions because the profile of the competition has changed."

He revealed his like for lunchtime kick-offs - good thing as well since United play before two o'clock in four of their opening six games. "I love the early kick-off," he said. "I love to wake up early in the morning, go for breakfast, go to the bus, go to the game, play the game and win if it's possible and go home and that's it - game over. I don't like to wait for matches. In my time in Spain (at Real Madrid) I had some matches where we played at 10pm and I had one Super Cup match against Barcelona which started one day and didn't finish until the next day! I hate this."

Mourinho spoke glowingly about the "50-metre walk" from Old Trafford tunnel to dugout on match days and referenced his "relationship with Sir Alex Ferguson".

He was also "expecting a lot" from the club's supporters. He had a message for the supporters, declaring: "I understand that they expect a lot from me but I also expect a lot from them. There is no chance we will be happy if we are not together and I think the passion (they have) for this club is really amazing. It's a new chapter in the club's life. We have brought a few new faces in, we will keep some others but, in the end, it doesn't matter who the manager is, it doesn't matter who the new players are or who is staying or leaving, it's Man United and Man United is much more than any one of us. The passion the fans have is for the club and I feel that I am a club man. I am going to do my best to be happy and to make the people happy."

Pogba was in Los Angeles for the 2016 ESPY (Excellence in Sports Performance Yearly Award) award ceremony where he spoke in Spanish to the Spanish language channel, ESPN Deportes. During the interview, three replica shirts were pulled out of a bag one and he was asked to give his views.

The first was a Juventus shirt, next Real Madrid and then Manchester United.

Juventus: "This is my team, my family, where I am playing. I am happy there, I play football, and do things I wanted to do when I was small."

Madrid are "the white house - which won the Champions League this year, a great club."

United. He joked "I don't know this one." He then described his former club as "my first club, my first family."

After being asked what he would do if Mourinho called, he replied: "My response would be 'I don't know.' I don't know when. We will see. For the moment, I am here (Juventus) and I am happy here. I don't know where I want to go."

Pogba was asked which of the three replica shirts he would prefer to wear: "I'll take three."

How much of a challenge faced Mourinho at Old Trafford was merely emphasised as Antonio Conte, the 10th Chelsea manager of the Roman Abramovich era, gave his first media briefing at Stamford Bridge ahead of his own challenge to clear up the mess left behind by the 'not-so-special one' in his final season in west London.

Last season's debacle at Stamford Bridge was not just bad, it was "very, very bad" according to the man who quit the Italian national job for his first taste of English football.

"From last season we can learn a lot," said Conte. "It is not easy but you can restart and find a new way. It is very strange to win the title and then, only one year later, you are out of the Europa League and out of the Champions League. The club don't like this. Nor do the players because history says in the Abramovich era Chelsea are always in the Champions League. It is important to get back very soon, to fight for the title, to be there at the end of the season. It is important to be back in the Champions League. Chelsea is a great club and a great club must play in the Champions League. Some might think Chelsea are not favourites for the title and I think they can be right after last season. Also, you can see that we have signed only Batshuayi. But we are ready.

We are talking within the club and we know the team needs to reinforce. In the coming days we can buy one, two, three, I don't know how many players. We can reach our target to reinforce the team and go closer to the teams that seem to be higher in the table than Chelsea. It is not easy because there are teams with a lot of money to invest in the market. I know this year won't be easy. The Premier League is very competitive. We are under-rated and we might slip under the radar but I hope there is a small flame flickering here that can hopefully grow into a blazing inferno."

Conte called Carlo Ancelotti for information and planned to call Claudio Ranieri for further advice from fellow Italians familiar with the demands of Abramovich. "I am not afraid if the club sack me," said Conte. As for pressure, he said: "I was born with pressure, it's the norm. The manager is like a tailor, who must make the best dress for the team. You have to respect the characteristics of the players. I am a worker. I know only this road to win. I know only this verb: work, work, work. The players are ready to work and fight. They know last season was very, very bad. Not bad; very, very bad. Every single player knows this and wants to change the story. They want to remove the past. After a bad season there is a bit of sadness in all the people who work for this club and also in the fans. For us the most important thing is to concentrate in the present, to work and to build a great future. To work with passion and enthusiasm and transfer this to our fans. If we remain in the past it is not good for us."

Obsessive and intense, Conte is compared to Mourinho, still revered by Chelsea fans despite being sacked for a second time last year by Abramovich. "There are certain managers who are winners, on that I would agree with you," said Conte. "Some coaches have a winning mentality besides their working methods and philosophies. There are winners in football, but not everyone has that in them. Those who do are indeed special."

But, Mourinho was compared to the magic of Dynamo if he can conjure up the title at the first attempt. United legend Andy Cole knows Mourinho has a history of making an instant impact when he takes charge, but Cole, who collected 121 goals for United over six years, spoke to BBC Radio Manchester: "If José Mourinho comes to Man United and wins (the Premier League) in the first season I think that would be like Dynamo the magician. It would be fantastic. He's under no illusions how tough it's going to be to come to Man United and try and win the Premier League at the first attempt. Fingers crossed we have a better season than we did last season."

Cole won the treble with United in 1998-1999, but insisted that the main target should be Champions league qualification "Finishing in the top four has got to be a must. New manager and new players as well, it should be a good season."

Cole knows the importance of facing high level opposition before the season to fine tune the team. "It's pre-season - you've got to get up to speed when it comes to playing in good competition games, that's the test you want. You don't want to be winning games 10-0 in pre-season. You want a good stern test and they'll get that."

Mourinho was busy making changes at the Carrington training HQ, where he had removed the spy cameras installed by Van Gaal to monitor training performances of his Manchester United squad. The new manager instead wanted installed giant nine-metre high floodlights on the first-team squad car park. United had to ask for planning permission to make them the latest new fixture at their 44-hectare Aon Training Complex. United say the existing lights are not bright enough and will be removed, and that there is "a continual need to update the training centre in order for it to maintain its status as a world class training facility and meet the expectations and requirements of Manchester United, a world leading football club" and the lights are needed to improve vehicular and pedestrian safety on the first-team car park. A path was laid to enable the players to walk straight to their motors.

Mourinho is a players' manager and the upgrades were made to impress United's stars, who were said to be delighted when the cameras were taken out as they saw them as an unnecessary intrusion which characterised Van Gaal's reign.

WIGAN CHEER

José Mourinho was feted by the large United support of more than 7,000 who turned out at Wigan for the opening pre-season game.

Manchester United: Johnstone, Fosu-Mensah, Bailly, Blind, Shaw, Carrick (Capt.), Herrera, Lingard, Mkhitaryan, Memphis, Wilson Subs: Mata, J. Pereira, Blackett, Jones, Tuanzebe, Varela, Januzaj, A. Pereira, Valencia, Young, Keane.

José shook hands with all his players and the officials at the end. Juan Mata, whom he sold to United in 2014 while at Chelsea, got an arm round the shoulder before the full embrace. The new manager patrolled the touch line, angry, passionate, as usual, in huge contrast to the sedate style of his predecessor, and that hands-on involvement was welcomed by the travelling fans.

Mourinho insisted he does not want a cult of personality to be built around him, preferring the supporters' plaudits went to his players rather than himself. The inevitable first chants for Mourinho came within 60 seconds of kick-off.

"What I found was unbelievable for the first time in my career. The support for a friendly like this was like it was a crucial Premier League match. Unbelievable," he said. "I would prefer them to go with the players. I prefer them to go with the team, I prefer them to go with Man United. They are the ones on the pitch and they are the ones who need support and if I could tell them that, I would tell them directly: first the players. I'm the last one after them. But it is nice to feel welcome and that they are behind the team. It is nice to feel they liked the things I liked."

José and his coaching staff had prepared for their first match of the new era over dinner at a Brazilian steakhouse Bem Brasil in Manchester's Deansgate, a five-minute walk from The Lowry Hotel, where the new United boss was staying. A hooded Mourinho shook the hands of well-wishers on his way for the evening out. His every move in Manchester was shadowed by the paparazzi, and he knew that his every move at Wigan would be under intense scrutiny even though it was a 'meaningless' pre-season friendly made even more meaningless with 13 players still absent due to their international commitments.

"Meaningless!" Not when Mourinho is concerned. Every players' performance would be an indicator as to their chances to be a part of the new regime. The new boss could still select a strong 22-man squad for the first of five pre-season friendlies before the FA Community Shield fixture with Leicester at Wembley. A victory in this stadium in 2008 signalled another Premier League title under Sir Alex Ferguson whilst defeat, in 2012, sparked a collapse which resulted in the side being pipped to the title by rivals Manchester City.

United were a little bit late again, not arriving until just before 12:30, an hour before kick-off. No panic before a pre-season friendly, but amusing after the problems they endured towards the end of last season at Tottenham and West Ham, the latter being forced into a delayed start because of the chaos outside Upton Park.

Incredibly, 7,000 United fans travelled to witness the start of the Mourinho era and he informed MUTV on the eve of the match that he intended to make seven changes at half-time, but not Eric Bailly. "Mkhitaryan is comfortable as he speaks English fluently, but Eric is a bit different as he can't speak English and he speaks with those who are French and Spanish so for him step by step.

He has to get used to wearing a heavy shirt here. I will aim to give him 65-70 minutes. He needs to feel it and he needs to start communicating."

On Luke Shaw's return, Mourinho added: "The worst thing in football is long term injuries. The kid was great this summer working every day at the training ground for this. I was expecting a few limitations, bit of weight and a bit less sharpness but the physical and mental point of view is good." Shaw returned from a 10-month injury lay-off since suffering a horrendous double fracture of his right leg last September and played the first half against the Latics. After the game Mourinho added: "When I found Luke Shaw in the training ground, it was a surprise for me because I thought he cannot be ready. But he did fantastic in the summer, sacrificed his holiday, staying in the city and training every day. He is trying hard and was mad to play more than 45 minutes but for me, it's better 45 safe than more, so let's go step by step."

Shaw's participation was a massive bonus for the new manager. "From now on I'm just going to look forward and carry on doing what I did last year from the start," Shaw said. "Everyone helped from the club and from outside the club. My family and friends played a massive part in it. Obviously I have said it before, but here's a big thank you to the staff here who have looked after me really well and have got me back on the pitch."

He feared his career was over after he suffered that horrific double break of his right leg in September 2015, resulting in seven months on the sidelines following the challenge from PSV Eindhoven's Hector Moreno in a Champions League tie in Holland. "When I did it, the first thought that went through my head was, 'Am I going to play football again or how long am I going to be out for?'" said Shaw, who made an emotional comeback in front of his family at the DW Stadium. "It wasn't too much about the pain because I could deal with that. But, yeah, there was a fear about how long it was going to take or if I was I was even going to be back playing football. But as I went through it (the recovery process) I knew I was coming back and I'm looking past it. I'm just looking forward now. My leg feels great, I just want to push on in this pre-season and get fully fit. It is the best feeling ever. When I had my first game on Saturday against Wigan I felt so much emotion, the way the crowd were with me, with the cheers when I had my first touch. That meant a lot to me and my family were there to see it. It's the best feeling."

Boyhood Chelsea fan Shaw nearly joined Mourinho at Stamford Bridge before moving to United in a £27m deal from Southampton two years ago, so he was naturally looking forward to working with him. "Of course when I was younger

I did support them (Chelsea), but I don't think it's a special thing for me. Of course, I was very happy with the appointment, I was really looking forward to working under him. We've done a couple of weeks now. I've spoken to him a couple of times, and all the players have talked as well. We are going to be challenging for every title that we can go for this season. It's a fresh new start with a new manager. We're bringing in some great players, and maybe there's a couple more to come. We all feel strong as a group, and with the tactical side of what José wants to do, we're practising in training and hopefully we can take that into games and show a very strong side."

Asked if the signings of Ibrahimović, Mkhitaryan and Bailly - and the possible arrival of Pogba - left some playing for their futures at Old Trafford, Shaw replied: "I don't know. You've always got to play for your future because there are always going to be players coming in. We're at Manchester United so there's always going to be people coming into your position, so you've just got to get used to that. Everyone has looked normal, no one looks like they could be leaving. No-one speaks about that. They keep it private but everyone looks normal and is enjoying the training we're doing at the moment."

When asked by MUTV in the pre-match interview about working with several youngsters, Mourinho added: "I like the atmosphere, their enthusiasm and I would have liked everyone but that is amazing to work with them, they're young and want to work in a good atmosphere which is great. I want them to play and train against real opposition, so I will play 11 players in the first half and make seven changes at half-time. I want to keep the other three or four for the rest of the game. Next week we have Borussia Dortmund and Man City; we go again with the same players so they are going to face good teams with every player needs to be ready for these matches. If you ask me for three points today or three against Bournemouth, I want three against Bournemouth, but we have to compete and see players that I don't know so well."

Sir Alex told Mourinho to have a look at those coming through the Under 21s - Andreas Pereira the most gifted - and former coach Paul McGuinness hailed him this week as well. "At the moment, he's got to learn how to fit into the team and how to be a team player," McGuinness said. "But he has the belief and the ego to be a top player and, importantly, the talent to go with it. He's got the running power too."

As promised, Mourinho made seven changes at the interval with Mkhitaryan one of those not re-emerging for the second period. The 'Red One' spent much of half time signing autographs. Jones slotted in at centre-half with Daley Blind at left back. Valencia in at right back for Fosu-Mensah, with Adnan Januzaj on one wing, Young on the other, and Will Keane just behind Wilson. Mata lined up alongside Ander Herrera in the centre of midfield as Carrick was replaced. Jesse Lingard was also taken off.

Wigan keeper, Jussi Jääskeläinen, tried to play the ball out from the back, but his pass was presented to Juan Mata, who supplied the assist for Will Keane to score the first goal of the Mourinho era. Andreas Pereira collected the second. Blind and Herrera made way for Guillermo Varela and Tyler Blackett. Axel Tuanzebe and goalkeeper Joel Dinis Castro Pereira were the final substitutes as Bailly and Johnstone went off.

Mkhitaryan glided past defenders in the No. 10 role but he also missed the best chance when Lingard, following Mourinho's orders, crossed from the flank after a neat one-two with Herrera. Mourinho commented: "Mkhitaryan is a top-class player and currently at the best stage for a footballer - 27/28 years old. He is magnificent the way he thinks about football, he thinks very quickly and it's so sweet how he touches the ball. He can play in different positions behind the striker. He doesn't have the sharpness yet but he is performance was very positive.With Eric the way the fans showed how much they liked his performance when I changed him is enough. Of course he is a very young boy coming from a very different environment, but you could see what he is at this moment."

Two players under threat, Mata and Blind, impressed. Blind proved his ability at centre-half and left-back. Mourinho was more than satisfied with what he had seen. "It was very good," he said. "The result was not the most important thing obviously but we prefer to win than to lose. I could see things, I could see that they started identifying things and trying to play my football. We had great periods in the first half, we had good situations to score a couple of beautiful goals. In the second half we scored early and then we had the understanding of the game to play with stability and to keep possession of the ball and to control the game very well."

Pereira played the second half, showing classy touches and an impressive range of passing in central midfield, as well as getting into the box for the second goal. Mourinho was impressed: "Andreas has lots of talent - he has incredible vision and an incredible technique."

The 20-year-old was pleased too. "I can play in other positions but I enjoyed that role a lot," he added. "I'm very happy that I scored in this game, and yeah, it was not a bad strike at all."

Pereira was keen to be a part of Mourinho's plans. "I think it was very important for me to get some minutes and show the manager and show the team that I can help them," he said. "I am very happy that I could help. I want to show the manager, to show the people around the club, to show the players that I can help this season. It's very important for me. I want to show this in training and just keep working hard."

Pereira found opportunities limited under Van Gaal despite making his first-team debut two years earlier and was now hoping to make a significant impression on Mourinho on the tour of China. "We're very excited and we want to do the best," he said. "We want to win titles and you want to win things too so hopefully this season is our season. It's very important for the tour that we can get our team together and prepared for the season. When you play against a high-level team you can test yourself more, so you are ready when you come back to Manchester. They will be tough games even though they're friendlies. We have to prepare well and do everything to win, so they will be important matches for us. I have been to China once before and it'll be nice to visit again and play in front of the fans. You can see that football is a huge part of the culture there and it is very nice to see such passion."

Pereira was impressed with new recruits Mkhitaryan and Bailly: "They're very good lads so they fit in our team well. Hopefully they can help us this season."

Mourinho could already see things taking shape as he wanted: "Players tend to play the football their managers want them to play, they tend to adapt to it and I could see the players trying to go in the direction I want them to go and doing things I want them to do, from a defensive point of view and an attacking point of view."

He was handed, and warmly accepted, a couple of cakes including a Portuguese custard tart by a United fan just outside the DW Stadium, which prompted him to post a picture on his ever-increasingly active Instagram account.

Mourinho later reinforced how impressed he'd been by the level of support from the fans as he told MUTV: "Best of all was something that I never had before which was a friendly match which I could call a training session against opposition and yet there were so many supporters who gave permanent support to the team." He added: "There was the manifestation of happiness (from them) about a few things they could see in the team which was absolutely fantastic. As I said in my press conference I will try to give them everything and I'm sure they will continue to give amazing support to the team."

Soon afterwards Mourinho reiterated that the England trio of Rooney, Rashford and Smalling would travel to China but not feature in the games against Dortmund and City. "In China I will play with these guys that have been training for 10 days and the Rooneys and Rashfords and Smallings, these guys are coming to China without training, so I am not going to play them. I have two training processes, one for those that are close to condition and one process for the players coming back from their holidays."

Ibrahimović had been given an extended break ahead of the new season, missing United's China tour. But his manager still took time out to comment upon, and offer an insight into, his recently acquired striker. Speaking to Adidas Front Row, Mourinho said: "Zlatan? Three words - he's a winner, he's a goalscorer, he's funny. He's a funny guy. You need to understand him to use this word to describe him. He's a funny guy. If you don't know him maybe you think some quotes a bit arrogant. He's just a funny guy. I would say that. Funny, winner and goalscorer. I was so happy to go for him and obviously he's happy to work with me."

José Mourinho can become the new Sir Alex Ferguson at United, according to Claudio Ranieri, who says Leicester should be 6000/1 to retain the Premier League title.

Ranieri and his players famously defied odds of 5000/1 last season to win a first top-flight title in Leicester's 132-year history, but the Italian believes they should be even bigger outsiders this time around given the commitments of a debut Champions League campaign and the arrival of new managers at three of the league's biggest clubs. Ranieri's compatriot, Antonio Conte, took over at Chelsea, while José and Pep were installed on opposite sides of the Manchester divide.

"Mourinho can be the new Ferguson," Ranieri said in an interview with Gazzetta dello Sport, "He will not stay 26 years, but he will leave his imprint. Antonio and Chelsea are made for each other. Guardiola seems to be the right man in the right place."

Zlatan Ibrahimović told Eric Cantona that becoming the prince of Manchester United is ok, but he now wants to be "God" of Old Trafford.

Cantona, nicknamed "The King', sent a tongue-in-cheek message explaining that Ibrahimović would not be able to wear his crown but could still become "prince" at United. "I admire Cantona and I heard what he said," Ibrahimović is quoted in the Swedish tabloid *Aftonbladet*, "But I won't be King of

Manchester. I will be God of Manchester."

Cantona, though, welcomed Ibrahimović to the club and offered him the No. 7 shirt even though it was currently owned by Memphis Depay. Ibrahimović had yet to be officially assigned a squad number when Cantona offered his old number - a shirt the Frenchman helped make famous along with George Best, Bryan Robson, David Beckham and Cristiano Ronaldo. In a video for Eurosport, Cantona said: "I have a personal message for Zlatan: You decided to go red. It is the best choice you ever made. When you walk into the Theatre of Dreams. When you can feel the ghosts of the legends that have been here before. When you score that first goal right in front of Stretford End. When you hear the crowd chanting your name. When your heart beats so strong that it bursts out of your chest. When you feel that you will love them as much as they will love you. You will know, my friend, that you finally made it home. Just one last thing, there can only be one King in Manchester. You can be the prince if you want to. And the No. 7 is yours if you are interested. That is my welcome gift to you…The King is gone! Long live the prince!"

Maybe the new King had yet to arrive! Pogba? If indeed he'd arrive at all. According to the Independent, United delayed announcing the squad numbers for the new season as they awaited the outcome of the Paul Pogba transfer saga. The Sun suggested United refused to be forced into a situation where they might have to refund fans if their squad numbers changed.

In fact, speculation was rife that a host of top names would be sold off to make way for the new arrivals in the new squad. There was a modest start to the clear out with Eintracht Frankfurt signing Guillermo Varela on a season-long loan. The Uruguayan defender, 23, arrived at Old Trafford from Peñarol in 2013 but had to wait until December 2015 to make his senior debut. He has since made a total of 11 appearances for United, as well as spending a year on loan with Real Madrid's Castilla side. Varela featured in the pre-season friendly win at Wigan but would not travel with the squad to China, instead completing a switch to Frankfurt, with the deal running through to June 30, 2017. Eintracht finished 16th in the Bundesliga last term and only preserved their status in the German top-flight with a play-off victory over Nurnberg.

Preparations for the Tour of China were beginning to take shape with the only major outstanding issue being the matter of a world record bid for Paul Pogba to complete the team building.

Rio Ferdinand was critical of how Manchester United let Pogba go describing it as a very costly, a "huge, huge error". Ferdinand, who was at the club when

Pogba departed, branded it wrong to let a player leave who hadn't fully realised his potential. "This is potentially the £100m kid at 23 years old, he's got huge potential. The thing that stood out for me when I first met him other than he ability was his personality," the former central defender told the BBC. "This kid wants to be the best, he started this tournament (Euro 2016) very anxiously, like a kid who had something to prove after he'd been hyped up and was worthy of that hype but he's grown into this tournament (for France). Didier Deschamps has got to take credit as he's put him in a deeper role and we've seen what tools he's got in the bag, from his range of passing, playing through the lines into the centre forward, he looks more composed and has more time in that position. He's really grown in stature in the tournament and they rely on him in many areas. He's the poster boy of this tournament, there's a lot of pressure on his shoulders and he's got a fantastic future."

Ferdinand knew that he was showing signs of being a top quality player when under Ferguson. "His star quality was undoubted. There was not one person in that changing room who wasn't sure. Everyone in that changing room knew that him leaving was a huge, huge error."

The vastly experienced Michael Carrick believed his side's pre-season clash with rivals Manchester City will add an extra edge to preparations for the new Premier League campaign with the arrivals of José Mourinho and Pep Guardiola set to give "added spice" to the meeting between the two teams.

Carrick, who had recently signed a new Old Trafford deal, was confident that the new United boss and City rival Guardiola will spice up what is already one of English football's biggest rivalries.

United faced City as part of the International Champions Cup in Beijing and Carrick told the club's website "I'm sure there will be a little bit of added spice for a pre-season friendly. It'll be great for the fans out there to witness. The support we get out there is incredible so the atmosphere will go up a notch I'm sure."

Of course, it might only be a 'friendly', but it would give one of them an early edge in their personal contest between two of the most charismatic managers in world football.

"Pre-season is an important time for the team and for the players, making sure you get to that level that you need to be at for the start of the season," Carrick said.

Before facing Manchester City, United meet Borussia Dortmund in their tour opener, with new signing Henrikh Mkhitaryan up against his old side. Dortmund finished second in the Bundesliga, and reached the German Cup final, with Carrick believing Thomas Tuchel's side can provide a useful barometer for the new United under Mourinho.

"They're a terrific team who did well in last season's Bundesliga and I'm sure it'll be a good game for us," added Carrick, "Playing against them will allow us, to a certain extent, to judge where we're at. It's difficult to predict exactly what the games will be like because a lot will depend on which players are on display. But we know the games will be tough as we're talking about two great teams here. I'm sure they will be great games to watch."

Andreas Pereira hoped to go on the club's pre-season tour of China in order to establish himself with the new manager. The 20-year-old had a successful trip to the United States the previous summer, scoring his first senior goal in the friendly against San José Earthquakes and impressing with his creativity, but struggled for opportunities under Louis van Gaal; excluded from all but one of the last 17 squads of the Dutchman's reign. Speaking to ManUtd.com, he said: "It was a very good first pre-season with the team for me. The weather was great in America and lent itself to some really good training sessions and the games were played at a high level. I learnt a lot, but mostly that you have to represent your club always in the best way, both on and off the pitch, and that you must always be professional. The goal was really special, but for me just being with the team and seeing all our fans was great. When you play against a high-level team you can test yourself more, so you are ready when you come back to Manchester."

"They (the opponents) will want to prepare for the season too, so they will be tough games even though they're friendlies. We have to prepare well and do everything to win, so they will be important matches for us. I have been to China once before and it'll be nice to visit again and play in front of the fans. You can see that football is a huge part of the culture there and it is very nice to see such passion."

A few weeks earlier he posted a fitness video on Instagram, sending a strong message to the new manager he was ready for the new season.

He wasn't the only youngster to post their gym efforts online, Adnan Januzaj and Timothy Fosu-Mensah did the same. The footage showed Pereira doing a number of fitness drills, including skipping and shuttle runs. Pereira had also spoken positively about the arrival of Mourinho, and was optimistic about his chances of more game-time as well as playing for Brazil at the Rio Olympics. Speaking to *Globo Esporte*, he said: "We look forward to working with him (Mourinho) and very happy to, because he is a great coach, one of the world's best. We are prepared to work with him and have a great season."

Smalling wanted his team-mates to be dominating games straight away. "The tour is going to be a great test and it's great to be able to play high-calibre teams," Smalling told United's website, "From the off, we want to get up to that standard where we are dominating the very best of teams, so it's good to be playing them so early on in our pre-season programme.

Mourinho headed for Manchester airport for United's pre-season tour of China, filmed leaving his office at United's Carrington training headquarters dressed in the club's tailored dark suit - but a seemingly innocuous picture has led many supporters to believe that Pogba is on his way back to Old Trafford.

Manchester United executive vice-chairman Ed Woodward wasn't in the travelling party to China, but expected to join the tour later presumably following formal talks over a proposed move for Pogba, with the club expected to open with an offer of around £86million. However, Mourinho's wife Matilde posted a picture of her husband walking through his office on his way to the airport, and a partly filled tactics board left beady-eyed followers questioning the identity of one of the names.

The board appeared to show half of a formation with players legibly listed in seven positions.

David de Gea, unsurprisingly, appears to be the first-choice goalkeeper, while Luke Shaw and Chris Smalling are placed at left-back and left-centre-back respectively. Anthony Martial is on the left-wing, with Wayne Rooney behind the striker.

Interestingly, Marouane Fellaini is named as a second-choice in centre midfield, but the name above his is illegible. Many fans on social media have excitedly suggested that it simply has to be Paul Pogba, United's primary summer transfer target. So, has the manager already found space on his team sheet for the Juventus midfielder? Has Matilde given the game away?

In the short clip posted on the manager's Instagram page, he can been seen shouting "Vou embora!" ('I'm off', in Portuguese) before heading for the exit, with the caption: "China!!!!! Here we go!!!!" Matilde is also "ready for Beijing", where Mourinho is set to work on a 4-2-3-1 formation.

It wasn't too long before Ladbrokes announced the suspension of all bets on Pogba's move to United. Ladbrokes spokesman Alex Apati said: "As far as we're concerned all bets are off when it comes to Pogba making the move to United.

Ladbrokes, @Ladbrokes: BREAKING: We've suspended betting on Paul Pogba signing for Man Utd #MUFC

The betting also suggests he could make an immediate impact as United start what many believe will be a title-winning season. According to *Tuttosport*, Pogba would sign a "crazy contract" lasting five years that will double his current salary. Yet, Juve rejected an £85 million (€101m) package attached with £15m (€18m) of performance bonuses, insisting on £101m (€120), plus a further £8m (€10m) in add-ons. Twitter went into overdrive following reports Pogba's move had been completed. In fact, a barber in Miami fuelled Twitter fever further when he posted an image in which he was seen giving Pogba a haircut, and continued to tweet claiming the "Frenchman is moving to Man Utd."

Mourinho was without much of the spine of his new team, while many were still being rested after a long season culminating in Euro 2016. He had yet to complete his target of four key signings but Massimiliano Allegri confirmed Juventus were in talks with United over Pogba. The coach of the Serie A side was speaking ahead of their International Champions Cup friendly against Melbourne Victory: "Pogba is a Juventus player at the moment but we don't know what is going to happen. The club are looking after negotiations."

Pogba, though, is worth nowhere near £86m according to Paul Scholes, who played and trained with him for a brief period during their time together at Old Trafford. Scholes was quite rightly scathing in his assessment of current transfer saga. "I just don't think he is worth £86m," the ex-England international told *Sport Witness*. "For that sort of money, you want someone who is going to score 50 goals a season like Ronaldo or Messi. Pogba is nowhere worth that kind of money yet." Scholes' memories of a young Pogba are as an exciting talent who expected too much, too early. "He was a very talented young player, I played with him and I knew how good he was," he said. "He played for the first team maybe once or twice, but from my understanding he was asking for too much money. For his age, he was asking for far too much for a player who hasn't played first team football. OK, he has gone on to great things. I think certainly there has been a lot of improvement. He needed to improve if he is going to be a player worth £86m."

Juventus completed the signing of Croatian winger Marko Pjaca from Dinamo Zagreb for £20m. Allegri said: "He is another quality addition so whatever happens with Pogba, we will be in good shape." Juventus also agreed to pay the £78m buyout clause for Napoli striker Gonzalo Higuain. Talks were underway between the clubs with *Sky Italia* reporting the Argentina international underwent a secret medical in a Madrid clinic. Higuain scored 38 goals in all competitions for Napoli last season, who finished runners-up to Juventus in Serie A. His signing represented a major coup for the Italian champions as they looked to strengthen despite the loss of Alvaro Morata and the expected departure of Pogba. Higuain agreed a four-year deal worth up to £8.3m a year with bonuses after tax. Juventus will pay the fee in two instalments of £39m, though it was not dependent on Pogba's transfer as the Italians are a wealthy club with funds to spend regardless of whether Pogba was sold.

Mourinho announced his squad for the two-game visit to the Far East. David de Gea boosted United's squad for those two blockbuster friendlies. Mourinho and his squad were decked out in black suits for their long haul flight. Rashford, Mata, Memphis, Lingard and Rojo all posting selfies from inside the plane. Mata took time to meet fans before boarding, while the fit again Shaw and Mourinho's assistant Rui Faria signed autographs for waiting supporters. Rooney and Rashford joined the United squad at their Carrington training base earlier, linking up with United and their new manager Mourinho for the first time.

Mourinho was involved in an exchange with one autograph hunter at Manchester airport. According to onlookers, he remonstrated with the individual over the extent to which he has been followed since returning to management, saying: "You every day at my hotel."

United Squad in full for the tour of China:

Goalkeepers: David De Gea, Sergio Romero, Sam Johnstone

Defenders: Eric Bailly, Daley Blind, Timothy Fosu-Mensah, Phil Jones, Paddy McNair, Marcos Rojo, Luke Shaw, Chris Smalling, Axel Tuanzebe, Antonio Valencia

Midfielders: Michael Carrick, Ander Herrera, Adnan Januzaj, Jesse Lingard, Juan Mata, Memphis Depay, Henrikh Mkhitaryan, Andreas Pereira, Ashley Young

Strikers: Will Keane, Marcus Rashford, Wayne Rooney

Marcus Rashford was particularly eager to impress Mourinho on this pre-season tour. "It means a lot to be going," he told the club's official website. "It's an opportunity to show the manager what you've got and you have to take the opportunity when it comes. It would be a massive experience especially with the players that could be going as well. I've got a lot I can learn from them." Rashford was clearly excited to be a part of the trip to the Far East, where United have a huge fanbase, ahead of his first full season. "It's crazy to see their support. The training part of the tour is a big thing and getting used to the players and the personalities. I'm really looking forward to it."

José Mourinho gave up his business-class seat and sat in economy for the 12-hour flight as there were not enough seats to accommodate all of his coaching staff, so he gave up his luxury seat and privileges and 'suffered' the journey in the more modest economy cabin. Of the 30 business-class seats on United's chartered flight, 25 of them were taken up by the squad and VIPs including Sir Bobby Charlton and his wife, with not enough to cater for Mourinho's six-strong staff. So he decided to sit with his coaching staff and the rest of the club's touring party for the entire flight.

Immediately after leaving Shanghai Pudong International Airport Mourinho took his squad to the training field at their Century Park base.

United had been delayed by more than an hour clearing immigration at Shanghai airport and were taken through the back entrance of their hotel, disappointing more than two hundred fans who had gathered at the front.

Rooney confirmed: "I'm excited. I think it's going to be a big season for us. The appointment of José Mourinho is a fantastic appointment. The signings we've made have been fantastic. Hopefully we can have a good start to the season and be successful at the end of it. I've only had one day (with him) before we came out but it was a very good training session. Look at the teams he has been at before and the success he's had. We're hoping he can bring in that success to us."

Rooney admitted he was under pressure to prove himself all over again at United under the new manager. "I think you always feel pressure when you play for Manchester United," said Rooney at a Gulf Oil event in Shanghai at the start of the eight-day tour. "It's one of the - if not the - biggest football clubs in the world. Always you feel you have to prove yourself each season. Of course there's pressure, there is always pressure to be successful."

At the usual chaotic event at United's team hotel in central Shanghai, Rooney began the press conference by being asked about his favourite traditional Chinese dish (he answered "foo yung") and ended it by saying goodbye to his audience in Mandarin.

Mkhitaryan and Ander Herrera were also present alongside United ambassador Denis Irwin. Mkhitaryan struck an equally positive note: "It's a great opportunity for me to play for United, one of the biggest clubs in the world. I'm very happy to be here and play for this team. I will do my best to help the team win. We'll do everything to win titles. Of course it's going to be difficult but let's have a good preparation and then we we'll see."

Mourinho tantalisingly flashed his clipboard featuring possible formations and tactics:

Axel (Tuanzebe)   Smalling   Jones   Rojo

Depay

Lingard   Mata   Mkhitaryan

McNair   Pereira

Young   Carrick   Herrera   Januzaj

Rooney

Rashford

[obscured]   Blind   Bailly   Valencia

Supporters who were given access to the Gulf Oil event had the opportunity to take pictures of Rooney, Herrera and Mkhitaryan but were prevented from getting closer to their heroes at the end as club security staff hurried the players out of the hotel suite.

Meanwhile, David Beckham tipped Mourinho to be a success describing his arrival at the club "a great move". Becks believes Mourinho's experience of winning titles all over Europe will help him return United to the summit of the game in England. "I fully expect it to work," Beckham said in an exclusive interview with Sky Sports News HQ. "With José leaving Chelsea and now coming back into the Premier League with United, for me it is a great move. I had huge respect for Van Gaal, but it did not work out the way people expected it to. But I think at the end of the day, now it is a new start for United. We have had a couple over the last three or four years, which is not the Manchester United style, who are used to a manager like Sir Alex Ferguson being in there for so many years."

Mourinho had won trophies at every club he coached and that winning experience Beckham thinks will prove decisive. "We have had quite a lot of change over the last few years," he said. "So now with José in there, he knows what he wants and how to get it, he knows how to win titles. I think that is what Man United definitely need to get back to and they need to get back to being feared again. Because we were always a club - and are still a club - that when teams come to Old Trafford, they know they are going to be up against it and they know they are probably going to lose. So that is what we need to get back to."

Beckham feels Mourinho can win the Premier League in his debut campaign at United. "I am going to have to say United," Beckham said when asked who will win next season's title. "I will always be on that side of the fence."

Sam Allardyce was appointed as the new England manager and naturally Mourinho was asked of his opinion. "He is more than ready," Mourinho said of the former Sunderland manager. "He is a good motivator and can create a good team spirit." He added: "I wish him the best. I promise to try and supply him players and try to make sure the English players are always available in good condition." Allardyce is second only to Redknapp as the most experienced English manager in the Premier League, in terms of games managed - Allardyce has overseen 467 matches to Redknapp's 641.

England captain Wayne Rooney declared that the Football Association made a "good appointment" by naming Sam Allardyce manager. Rooney, England's all-time leading goalscorer, was part of the squad knocked out of Euro 2016 by Iceland in June. "He will probably bring a different way of playing to England," he said. "Hopefully it's a good way and we can be successful under him." The 30-year-old confirmed that he had no intention of retiring from international football. "Am I going to carry on?" said Rooney, who scored 53 times for England in 115 appearances. "It was asked of me after the Euros, but yes, I'll be there."

NUMBERS GAME

Ibrahimović was handed the coveted No. 9 shirt at Manchester United, with previous occupant Anthony Martial moving to No. 11. He has varied between numbers eight, nine and 10 throughout his career, but with all three taken upon his arrival at Old Trafford, he was expected to have settled for a different number. But Martial has moved to 11 meaning Adnan Januzaj now has the No. 15 jersey. Juan Mata keeps No. 8 and Rooney remains on No. 10.

Ibrahimović was quick to post an image of No. 9 on Instagram, writing: "I chose the number 9."

A few days later, Anthony Martial released social media profiles with pictures of himself wearing the United No. 9 shirt and launching his new business naming it 'AM9' - which uses his initials and his squad number from last season.

Martial announced his new brand on his social media channels, uploading new profile pictures on his Facebook and Twitter accounts. On Facebook, he changed his cover photo to a picture of him in the No. 9 shirt during last season's FA Cup semi-final triumph over Everton, where he scored a dramatic last-gasp winner to seal his side's place in the final, going on to defeat Crystal Palace at Wembley. The No. 9 is emblazoned across all of the striker's social media accounts and is even displayed in his Instagram username, Martial_9. Martial's choice of pictures led to hundreds of fans making comments about the squad number changes, with many speculating whether he was unhappy losing the No. 9 shirt to Ibrahimović.

United's other summer signings, Bailly and Mkhitaryan, took No. 3 and No. 22 respectively. The numbers were provisionally announced by United with James Wilson, Tyler Blackett and Guillermo Varela notable omissions. The 20-year-old striker Wilson was expected to join Fulham on loan, while Varela was signing for Eintracht Frankfurt on a season-long loan in Germany. Blackett, who like Wilson is a fellow England Under-21 international, was widely tipped to depart the club.

One notable absence was No. 6, which was being kept free for Paul Pogba. He notably wore the same number in his early days at Juventus.

Mourinho warned Juventus that there were other options if they fail to sign Pogba as United raised their offer for Pogba to £92m, but United will also pay the player's agent, Mino Raiola, up to £18.4m to conclude the deal. United made a second offer, their first offer of £87m plus add-ons was rejected during a meeting with United's executive vice-chairman Ed Woodward and the Juventus directors Giuseppe Marotta and Fabio Paratici as well as Raiola. The deal hinged on Juventus demanding that United pay the whole of the agent's fee, around 20%; United had already agreed to pay their half of the agent's fee.

Juve originally said that they would only let the player go for £100m but will now accept £92m if United pay Raiola's fee. United have also agreed to buy Pogba's commercial rights and pay him an extra £4.2m a season, taking his earnings to £290,000 a week.

Real Madrid had been in contact with Juventus to try to hijack the deal but United and Raiola were confident that the player will sign for the Premier

League club. Barcelona director Ariedo Braida confirmed that his club were priced out. Braida admitted Barça were interested in bringing Pogba to the Nou Camp, but he stressed that the club could not justify spending the type of money that was being demanded. "Clearly when you talk about figures that go over €100million, you need to reflect on them," Braida is quoted as telling Italian broadcaster, *Canale 21*. "It all comes down to the TV rights that brought in a lot of money and completely changed the logic of the transfer market. Clearly all players are overrated to some degree or another at this stage. We know Pogba, he is a player who proved to be very strong and, for a while, Barcelona were interested, but clearly the dynamics changed and once the figures reached a certain point, we were no longer interested. It's hard to keep up at some stage, because you don't only have to consider the price of the transfer fee, but also the player's salary. Over the course of five years, that can amount to tens of millions."

Mourinho would not deny United's interest in Pogba but there are also two other targets who fit the 'profile' of the fourth summer signing he wants to complete his rebuilding job at Old Trafford. Nemanja Matić, who played under Mourinho at Chelsea, was one of the options, with Paris Saint-Germain's Blaise Matuidi the other.

Speaking about his interest in Pogba before United's pre-season game against Borussia Dortmund in Shanghai, Mourinho said: "I don't confirm and I don't deny. I cannot tell. First of all, because I don't think it's correct to speak about players from other clubs. He's a Juventus player, not a Manchester United player. The only thing I can say is that my board, my directors, did fantastic work to do 75 per cent of the job I asked them to do. I asked them for four profiles of players. I gave them a few options and they did for me 75 per cent of the job in Ibrahimović, Mkhitaryan and Bailly, and we just have 25 per cent to do before August 31. So we are in a great condition to do what I consider will be a great market for us. So we are calm, we know the profile of player we want and we have three faces to fill that profile. I am really confident Mr. Woodward and the owners will get the profile of player that I think the squad needs to have a good balance."

Mourinho explained why he had given his No. 9 an extended leave, comparing his treatment with a tailor-made suit. Mourinho, who knows the player from their time together at Inter Milan, was happy that he has tailored the Swede's pre-season work after consulting his backroom staff. "The best suits are the suits by measure, right?" said Mourinho. "Suits by measure should be better than if you go to a shop and buy a size that fits you well or not so well. I do the same for the players. There are not two players the same. My decision with Zlatan is a consequence of many hours of study, analysis and discussion with my staff. Although he was out of the Euros one match before the English guys, everything is different. The body is different, the mind is different, the personality; the time he needs to adapt and have holidays. Even things you don't have to know, which is to prepare in a different way. At the training level we try to do suits by measure, perfect for the person. The way I'm building the team, it is more important for me the players from other positions than the one that I think is going to play as the striker. I need to change the profile of this team in relation to other dynamics, and the striker will be the easy one to finish the puzzle."

Inevitably, Mourinho faced the media ahead of his first major pre-season game where he discussed his hopes for the club, how he has always felt drawn to Old Trafford, breaking a career habit and staying longer than three years, being reunited with Ibrahimović, and why Mata still had a future at the club.

The media 'grilling' took place at United's team hotel in Shanghai:

What are your first impressions of the group of players after taking over at United?

"As we know, not every player is here working yet. There are quite a few but I was impressed. I'm not surprised because I think, at this level, players are professional. They want to work. But I was impressed with the way they were working. Even here we have had two training sessions where it's very easy not to work well. It's very easy to be affected by the weather, to be affected by the pitch which is dry and slow. It's very easy to say 'I've got jet lag, I didn't sleep very well'. Yesterday we arrived, had lunch and commercial duties, but the training in the first session was fantastic.

So the attitude is very good. The appetite is very good. They want to work, they want to improve, and they need to work a lot really because the most difficult thing in football that I've found during my career is when I go to a new club and I need to change the dynamic; the way of thinking, things that the players do automatically. Maybe some managers who go after me at clubs find the same thing if they're not happy with the dynamic of the team.

This is quite hard for the players because they become quite automatic in their way of thinking. So to change some dynamics is not easy. They must be very focused, but the players are giving all of this.

The last couple of days (Wayne) Rooney, (Chris) Smalling and (Marcus) Rashford have brought a different plus in quality because they replaced some players who stayed back with extra players of quality.

On Sunday, even before we arrive back in Manchester I will send two of my coaches to start working with the other players, so they'll start working on Sunday. Step-by-step we are going to do the puzzle, but it's easy to feel that they want it and that's very important."

What about Zlatan Ibrahimović, can he still have an impact in the Premier League at the age of 34?

"Yes, because first of all I know him very well. I always think there's our age in ID terms, but then there's our real age. Because, for me, the real age is not the age on your ID. That's just a date when you were born.

The real age - the real ID - is your body, your brain, your attitude. And this guy is young, his body is amazing. The way he grew up playing the sports he did before football - especially martial arts - he was prepared in terms of his muscles and the mental point of view in a different way to the traditional football player, his DNA, his motivation.

Let's be honest, he's very rich. He's made money all his career, he's won a lot of things. You only come to the most difficult championship in the world if you feel you can do it. If you don't feel you can do it, you go to America, China, stay in the French League one more season.

So the guy wanted this one more challenge. When I told him that I had won in England, Spain and Italy and he hadn't - that he'd done Spain, Italy and France - he thought 'ah, I want to go. I want to win every one'.

So his motivation is high. His body is amazing. On Sunday he is going to start a specific programme we have prepared before he joins our group on the Thursday, so he has five days just for him. So I expect he is going to be very good for us."

Will the squad feed off those qualities that Ibrahimović has?

"Sometimes people say the team has no leaders, it's this, it's that, but what we need is everybody with the same kind of mentality. I like communication and push them to communicate. I give a lot of instruction in training.

It's difficult for me to do the same in matches so I need guys on the pitch to read the game, to understand what we want. Zlatan is going to be one of them, and I feel already that we have guys to do the same. I don't think we're going to have a problem at that level. We have lots of quality.

When I see our group in the attacking areas: Zlatan, Rashford, Rooney, (Henrikh) Mkhitaryan, (Juan) Mata, all the wingers we have, I think we have lots of quality in attack to produce good football and score goals."

Do you think it was your destiny to manage United?

"The only thing I thought is that every club I was at, I was always playing against Man United - with Porto, Inter, Real Madrid, always; Champions League matches, big matches. Then with Chelsea, matches to decide the title, FA Cup finals, Community Shields. I've played so many times against Man United and what I felt was - and you know this is not easy with me - so many matches and no problems. It's very difficult to play against a club so many times and I have no problems. Not a yellow card, not a red card, not an offensive word. I won a lot of times but I also lost and there were not any negative comments."

There were when you first played them with Porto!

"That was him (Sir Alex Ferguson) not me! It was him, not me. So I always had that good feeling, for sure, and I think the fans feel the same.

I remember playing at Old Trafford and the way to the dugout was always nice. It was never like in other stadiums. There was always a connection.

Then can you end up being their manager one day or not? I always felt that what has to happen, happens and it happened so.

I think it's more important for the club and the fans than me - I think that is the way I have to look at it. The club is much more important than me, the fans are much more important than me, so it's not for me. I'm not working for me, I'm working for the club, for the fans. That's the way I look at things.

Can it be nice for my career to win trophies in every club? That would be amazing. To be champion in every club would be amazing. But that's an individual, selfish perspective that I don't want. I work for the club. The club brought me here because they trust me. I have the feeling - of course not everyone I guess - that the majority of the supporters they trust me. They believe that I can help the club. I have the feeling that the players want me.

I'm not saying they didn't want Mr Van Gaal, I'm not saying that. I'm saying that since I arrived I feel that they are very fine with me and my way of leading and my way of work.

But I want just to see my things in this way of perspective, and let's enjoy the season because a big season is waiting for us."

In terms of the size of the club and the job facing you, how does United compare to your other clubs?

"I don't want to compare because I want to respect every club. I work for every club. It doesn't matter the dimension of the club, it doesn't matter the objectives, it doesn't matter the responsibility. I always work the same way, giving everything.

I was lucky enough to work in some of the biggest clubs in the world and of course Man United doesn't need words from me for everybody to know what Man United is.

That challenge comes in a stable moment in my career, lots of experience, so I feel it comes in the right moment. I feel very calm about the job."

What is Juan Mata's future at Old Trafford considering that you sold him to United when you were at Chelsea?

"I sold because he asked for that. Nobody in my previous club wanted to sell or push him. No, it was his decision. He was not the first option, but he was playing every game. I never let Juan Mata out of my selection of the 18, but he was on the bench a few times.

We had a proposal from a big club like Man United. We thought in the club that the proposal was very much acceptable, that it was very good proposal for that period, three years ago. In this moment, the numbers are going crazy, so numbers that looked very high three years later it looks very cheap.

But he wanted to leave and my philosophy is I don't want players that want to leave. I want players that want to come and want to stay. So we sold Juan to Man United.

But I think since the first day everything is clear between us. There is space for him. He's a talented player and I don't promise places to anyone. I promise respect and I like him, so if he wants to stay - and I think he wants to - until this moment I don't have one little sign that he wanted to leave.

So I think he wants to stay and, yes, there is space for him and, yes, I think he can be useful to the club."

Is Paul Pogba worth £100million and do you think you'll get him from Juventus?

"I don't speak about players from other clubs. He's a Juventus player. If any club wants one of my players and it speaks about him I would not be happy.

So Paul Pogba is a Juve player and what we are trying to do we are trying to do in an honest, correct, institutional way.

The only thing I can say to you is we did 75 per cent of our market. We established four important target profiles - not faces but profiles - and we got three of them at the very early stage of the market.

Now we have 25 per cent of our market to conclude until August 31, and that player is not the only one. It's a profile we have, we have options for that profile, and we're going to get a fourth player. But maybe it's not the one you think."

If you get that fourth signing, how close will United be to challenging for the big trophies?

"Yeah, I want to challenge."

Can you challenge? Can United be in the title race in May?

"I don't know but I want. I'm not going to hide behind three bad seasons, three bad championships, behind two seasons not even with fourth place. I'm not going to hide behind that. I'm not going to hide also in that fourth is a target and everything better than fourth is amazing for us.

No, I want to win the title and I want my players to feel it. If at the end of the season anyone is better than us, then great. But now in this moment, before the flag to start the race, I'm not going to say we don't want to win."

When do you want to make that fourth signing?

"As soon as possible, but until August 31 that's fine."

Will Wayne Rooney remain your captain?

"Of course."

You said at your second unveiling at Chelsea that you could build a dynasty there. Can you see yourself staying at United longer than three years?

"I'm not at Chelsea because the owners didn't want me. If he (Roman Abramovich) wanted me I would still be there.

I have the contract I have and for that the owners are happy. To give me a new contract I will be happy to do that because that is what I want at this moment in my career, but I think it depends on many things.

I will try to do my work to make the owners realise that I am the right guy for this job. But in this moment I've just played Wigan."

Shortly afterwards at a training session, whilst mingling with supporters, Mourinho was presented with a Chelsea shirt to sign. The shirt was not immediately obvious but when he saw it was a Chelsea shirt he shook his head and moved on to the next autograph hunter as an official quickly stepped in to move fans with United merchandise to the front of the queue.

United's 2015 FA Cup triumph was the first piece of silverware the club won since Sir Alex retired as manager in 2013. Under the Scot, they won 13 Premier League titles, five FA Cups and two Champions League titles in the space of 26 years. In an interview with the BBC prior to the Dortmund game, Mourinho made it clear it was time to forget the past both the good ad the more recent bad when he commented: "It is very important to forget the past three years and to focus on good times. I think that's what everybody wants at the club, it is what every fan around the world wants but at the same time I think it is intelligent to understand that times are different and realities are different. I don't think it's possible for Manchester United to win so much in the next 20 years than in the past 20 years. There was a very important evolution in our Premier League. I want to bring the motivational levels up and bring the confidence back, but be intelligent and know the reality we face in the Premier League is different than 10, 20 years ago."

Rooney was four goals adrift of Sir Bobby Charlton's club record of 249, but was part of the disappointing Euro 2016 with England in the summer, playing as a midfielder. Rooney was the subject of two failed transfer bids from Chelsea when Mourinho was manager in 2013. "I am quite surprised with so many question marks around this guy," said Mourinho. "He is the club captain, he is the manager's captain, he is the players' captain. I trust him a lot. I think he's going to be a very important player for me and no problem for him."

Rooney, meanwhile, compared Mourinho to Sir Alex, with United's captain relishing working under the Portuguese as he did when the Scot managed the club. Rooney joined United from Everton in 2004 because Ferguson was in charge and he won all but one of his major honours while playing for him. He believes Mourinho can have a similar impact on his career. "I came to Manchester United because I wanted to work under Alex Ferguson and then in the latter years (with) what Mourinho has done in football, in Spain and Italy and England, he is a manager who you want to play under. He is one of the best around and to learn from what he brings it's going to be exciting for me to try and learn under a manager such as himself. I've been working under the manager for the last few days and the sessions have been very good. It is exciting, he is one of the best managers in world football and he has a clear idea of what he wants. I'm just looking forward to playing for him now."

Mourinho stated publicly that Rooney will play as the No. 10 after operating in midfield under Louis van Gaal. "It's almost like a free role and I am excited to play it," Rooney said. "He said to me about playing No. 10. That is something I've now got to work on and get myself in the right position to score goals. I have scored goals all through my career and I have no doubt in my goalscoring ability. Hopefully I can do that this season. I like to be involved in the game and I am now playing for José who, straight away, has no fears about players coming deep if they want to. It's a different way of playing, a different manager, different ideas and if I can bring my game and qualities to this team, then I know I can create chances and score goals."

Rooney played as the main striker for a while last season with little success and was then injured halfway through the season. When he returned LVG switched him to playmaker where he had a much greater impact and far more success. He admitted that when Van Gaal was in charge goals were harder to come by. "As the striker in the last couple of seasons, it has been difficult with not creating many chances. It will be the same as the England record. It will be a huge honour to become record scorer at this club. I have no doubt that it will happen this season. It will be a huge moment for me."

Despite the plan not to play on the tour Rooney, he wanted to be involved against Manchester City. "I feel good so I want to get out back playing and I am sure I will play some part on Monday," he said.

Rooney has his testimonial at Old Trafford against Everton. "I am delighted to have been at this club for such a long time and I am really pleased the club have granted me a testimonial which will raise a lot of money for children's charities so I am in a privileged position to do that," he said.

BORUSSIA DORTMUND 4-1 MANCHESTER UNITED

Mourinho refused to be overly concerned after the 4-1 defeat to Borussia Dortmund in Shanghai, which saw new signing Henrikh Mkhitaryan net United's goal, making the score 3-1 just before the hour mark.

"It was like Formula 1 against Formula 3," said Mourinho. "They are much sharper, so it was difficult to judge." He argued Dortmund had shown their pre-season preparations were at a more advanced stage. "One team started training a month ago and played four games," he said.

For those reasons Mourinho insisted that he can't judge his players on a 4-1 defeat just yet.

A weakened United team stalled in the stifling heat, but it was an embarrassing way to start the club's tour of China. "My thoughts are simple," said Mourinho. "I know that in pre-season the team that is at an advanced stage of preparation looks far better than the other team. It happens year after year. Some good teams lose to a big result. I think it's too obvious. After 10 minutes we know that one team started training 10 days ago and played one match, and the other team started one month ago and played already four games. It's so easy to see the difference of intensity and sharpness. For us it was very difficult. In the second half we were better and we were more adapted to the game. I think 3-2 would be more natural than 4-1 but they showed the good quality they had, individually and collectively. They showed that they are in a much advanced stage."

Asked if he could judge his players on that performance, Mourinho added: "Well it's a combination of factors. But to be fair, I don't think I can analyse them with this difference of power. At the moment the engines are completely different. At the moment they are much sharper and you can see that easily, so it's difficult to judge my players. Even in these circumstances it's quite easy to get three or four or five of them that you can see under difficult circumstances that the quality is there. The mentality and personality is there. It's easy for me. But, no, 10 days of work, people are really tired, the match is against high quality opposition and in a much more advanced stage of their preparation. It would be unfair to make any kind of decision. But day by day they start winning my trust and start winning their positions in the squad and in the team. But the reality is that even in this situation we have six players that stayed in Europe plus Smalling and Rooney - we are speaking about eight players not yet involved. Obviously there are some players here who are not going to stay in the squad, so the squad will be different than we are in this moment."

Mourinho dismissed suggestions that such a heavy defeat would have any bearing on his transfer plans. He added: "We are completely convinced of our market. I said in the first press conference at Old Trafford that our market has a fundamental part, and that part is four players - one central defender, one midfielder, one striker and one creative player. When we finish that fundamental market we are balanced. Maybe today you don't feel it but no Ibrahimović, no

Fellaini, no Martial, no Schneiderlin. Lots of them that are not here yet. Then the market will be open until August 31. Sometimes things happen that you are not expecting and we have to react. But our fundamental market is 75 per cent done and when we sign one midfield player that crucial work will be done."

An error-prone United side were three goals down inside an hour before Mkhitaryan pulled one back, against the club he left for Old Trafford, and then conceded a fourth towards the end of this International Champions Cup encounter.

Mourinho learned a great deal about players from a match played in 102 degree temperatures on a dry pitch and in front of a less than capacity crowd at the 57,000-seater Shanghai Stadium. Memphis Depay showed he is not a central striker, and Phil Jones and Sam Johnstone were others to be replaced after a dismal first half.

Chelsea had a disastrous pre-season a year earlier that quickly saw their defence of the title disintegrate and while the new manager would have liked a winning start, he had pointed out in the build-up to the game that the Germans had the advantage of five extra pre-season games and several more weeks of training, and it certainly showed in the stifling heat.

Antonio Valencia, United's captain for the night, put a stray back pass wide of goalkeeper Johnstone who had to dash across to prevent it from rolling into an empty net, and then dribbled around Pierre Emerick Aubameyang on the edge of his six-yard box. As Johnstone screamed at Valencia Mourinho made a note on his pad; it was unlikely to be complimentary.

Dortmund took the lead in the 20th minute through Aubameyang's free kick from 25 yards. Johnstone should have held it as it dipped over the wall and straight at him. Instead, he spilled it several yards to his right where Ousmane Dembélé was following up. Johnstone made amends by blocking Dembélé's low shot, but Gonzalo Castro was able to clip the ball over Eric Bailly standing on the line.

United's big chance of the half fell to Jesse Lingard when he robbed Marcel Schmelzer of possession and went through on goal. But he never looked confident, and fired a low shot tamely at Roman Weidenfeller. Dortmund went further ahead from another mistake in the 36th minute as Jones was penalised for handball, giving Aubameyang the opportunity to easily beat Johnstone from the spot.

Mourinho made four substitutions at half-time, sending on Sergio Romero, Marcos Rojo, Ashley Young and Marcus Rashford for Johnstone, Jones, Depay and Lingard, and United were certainly brighter in the second half. However, they conceded a third goal just moments after Mkhitaryan had gone close, as Dembélé completely bamboozled Rojo before hammering a shot past the helpless Romero.

At least United pulled a goal back within two minutes when Rashford - who had only had one training session since returning for pre-season - dummied the ball into the path of Mata and he squared it for Mkhitaryan to slot home. The Armenian and Blind then made way for Januzaj and McNair after Dortmund made seven changes in one go. But the final goal went to Castro who beat a static defence and Romero in the 86th minute.

Ander Herrera agreed with Mourinho that United were at a much earlier stage of their pre-season preparations, but he stressed: "We are Man United and we should win." He added: "They are a very good team and have already played four games. That is one of the most important things when you play four games but there are no excuses. When you have played four or five you can see that you arrive one second before your opponent. I think we are improving, we are building a fantastic team. New guys are very comfy on the pitch but we are a team, we want to all be fit as soon as possible. Yesterday we trained two times so we can feel it on the pitch! I think we know what we have to do. Every player is very clear. We want very aggressive players in the midfield, we want to attack and I think we are going to see a very offensive Man United but of course we need to be compact we can do that as well. I don't want to talk about the past. The most important thing for Man United are the things that are happening now. We want to get the ball to attack and create as many chances as possible. You have seen we had some chances but we are just not fit enough yet. (We need to be) compact, attack, aggressive and finish the chances. The most important thing is later because we are Man United and we have to win everything."

Manchester United (4-2-3-1): Johnstone (Romero 46); Valencia (A. Pereira 74), Bailly, Jones (Rojo 46), Shaw; Blind (McNair 65), Herrera; Mata, Mkhitaryan (Januzaj 65), Lingard (Young 46); Depay (Rashford 46)

Subs not used: Tuanzebe, Keane.

Goal: Mkhitaryan 59

Booked: Bailly

Borussia Dortmund (4-2-3-1): Weidenfeller; Passlack (Larsen 46), Sokratis (Bartra 61), Bender (Merino 61), Schmelzer (Burnic 63); Castro (Leitner 85), Rode (Sahin 63); Dembélé, Ramos (Mor 62), Kagawa (Hober 64); Aubameyang (Pulisic 64)

Subs not used: Burki, Bonmann

Goals: Castro 19, 86 Aubameyang (pen) 36, Dembélé 57

Booked: Sokratis

The following morning United officially launched their new Adidas home kit of 'two halves' via Twitter. The shirt features a design in which, divided vertically, each side of the jersey has a different hue, with one a crimson red colour, and the other a scarlet red.

In the second year of their partnership with United, Adidas has taken cues from the north-west side's illustrious history, with the two-tone red split design evoking the yellow and green two-tone Newton Heath kit of 1878. United were formed that year as Newton Heath LYR Football Club by the Carriage and Wagon department of the Lancashire and Yorkshire Railway (LYR) depot at Newton Heath.

The official coat of arms for the City of Manchester was the basis behind the idea for the honeycomb graphic that knits together the two red block designs on the shirt. It was inspired by the worker bee which appears in the crest and originates from the Industrial Revolution, in which Manchester played a significant role.

Speaking at the launch of the new kit design in Shanghai David de Gea was confident United will challenge for the Premier League title as they enter a new era under "winner" Mourinho. De Gea has been enthused both by the summer acquisitions and appointment of Mourinho, with the player so often linked to Real Madrid clearly excited by the season ahead at Old Trafford. Asked if United are capable of challenging for the Premier League this term, De Gea said: "Of course, of course. I think we signed top players, really good players. We are Manchester United and we want to fight for everything. I feel for the fans, for the club and the players (that something exciting is coming) - you feel like (it is) a new era. I think the club is really strong now. The players, we want to everything and hopefully we can do it."

United's player of the year for the last three seasons further added: "He (Mourinho) is a winner - he is one of the best managers in the world and we feel it. We are really comfortable with him. He is a strong character but he makes jokes. It is good for us to laugh and I think he is a really good manager."

De Gea hoped Ibrahimović's cutting edge will add an exciting new dimension to United's attack. "You know he is a top player, he is a top striker. He is a killer and hopefully he plays his best in Manchester."

The extreme heat and humidity had not stopped Mourinho's men from often training twice a day in sweltering Shanghai. "With the heat, with the humidity, it is really tough but we enjoy China," said De Gea, who watched the International Champions Cup loss to Dortmund from the sidelines. "It is my first time here. It is really hard training but we enjoy it a lot. It is unbelievable the fans in China. It is really crazy, but it is good for us. We enjoy it a lot. Of course (the tour brings us closer together), with a new manager and with new players. Of course we need to train, train and try to be a compact team. The key in pre-season is to try to be fit as soon as possible and then go to the Premier League and try to win."

Guardiola's Manchester City were next in the first ever Manchester derby on foreign soil and, while it was only a friendly, De Gea was keen to secure the bragging rights at the Bird's Nest. "It is not the same, playing away from your country, in China against City," he added. "But it is always a special game and of course we are going to try and win."

Mourinho had been speaking to Portuguese newspaper *Expresso*. Asked if he'd tried to win the Premier League immediately, Mourinho answered: "It is logical... and difficult, very difficult, but Manchester is Manchester. The history is amazing and I feel it's my mission to give my best." Asked which club would challenge United, he explained that Chelsea had a squad who were champions, and have a great coach, and added: "Liverpool grow with another great coach. Arsenal, which is the prototype of stability, has the same coach for years and years in a row." Mourinho also picked out Manchester City because of the investment in their squad over the years, and said that Leicester City can't be ruled out, especially given that they've kept Jamie Vardy, despite the advances of Arsenal. Mourinho believed the Premier League more is now very competitive, with even smaller clubs able to spend, and refuse, big amounts of money: "All the Premier League teams have a fantastic economic potential. So in this league is possible that a newly promoted team can buy a player for €20m."

As Manchester City landed in China ahead of their pre-season tour, the Manchester derby set to be played in Beijing was in danger of being called off with severe thunderstorms forecast to hit China. A United spokesman said: "The organisers are working very hard to get the game to go ahead."

JOSÉ VS PEP. UNITED VS CITY. THE BUILD UP

On the eve of the first 'English' clash between Pep and José, it was clear that Mourinho was back to his best, demanding the title in his first season at Old Trafford. Three weeks from starting his eighth Premier League season, and his first away from Stamford Bridge, he was still a manager and a man in a hurry.

As he prepared for the show down with Guardiola he revealed that he was given a three-year target to win the Premier League but his confidence was back to its optimum as he believed he could do it in just one; as he had made an instant impact at other clubs.

United finished seventh, fourth and fifth since last winning the Premier League, but he called them "untouchable" in terms of prestige.

In an exclusive interview in The Sun, he explained how he told executive vice-chairman Ed Woodward and the Glazers during contract negotiations of his desire to bring immediate success back to the club.

Mourinho told SunSport: "No ultimatum. No demands. Just tranquillity to play and work my three-year contract. The message from the owners and Mr. Woodward was this: 'Get your three years, do your work, improve the team and bring us back where we belong during a three-year period'. My message was that I wanted to win the title in the first season."

His route to success was to change the mentality of his players into title contenders. He said: "I want to be champion. To say before the season starts that the top four is the target? The top four is not the target. We want to play to be champions. If during the season we realise the points difference doesn't allow us to fight for the title, we are going to establish a new title and when you can't be champion the next target is to finish top four. But day one, I don't want to hide behind a bad season or no Champions League football to say we want to finish top four."

Looking ahead to the new season Mourinho was far from happy about playing on Thursdays in the Europa League, and so with no help from the Premier League the tournament will be used for experimentation and to give fringe and young players their big chance. "You need to rotate players". Mourinho further added: "The Premier League doesn't make any favours for you. You play Thursday and then I don't think they are going to play us Monday, they are going to play us Sunday and probably at 12 o'clock. It is the worst. For the Premier League it is the worst. It is much easier to be a Champions League team. Obviously it is much easier to be what Liverpool were two years ago, no Champions League and what Chelsea are next season with no Champions League. One complete week to work every week, that is a dream. That is a dream for a manager who wants to improve his team. So we are in the worst possible situation. But in this moment I want my players to think 'every day I want to be champion and want to fight for the title'."

Mourinho has been working overtime from 'Day One' to get the preparation right for the new campaign. He said: "I go there at eight in the morning and leave at 7pm. Dinner and sleep. I really don't know Manchester and I'm not worried about it. It is the club dimension and the training ground, the facilities and the conditions. That is my world."

Louis van Gaal's style alienated the fans but winning is the vital ingredient for Mourinho, not fancy football. He said: "People weren't so happy with the fact they could smell during the season that Manchester United would end outside qualifying for Champions League football. For a giant club like United it is a big thing. From a prestige point of view Manchester United is untouchable and it is not because of one season outside the Champions League that we are not at that level. United are very powerful economically, commercially, and it is not because of one season outside the competition that we are going to be affected by that. But Man United is Man United and last season was negative from a Premier League point of view. We want to go back for better results and the best way to go for better results is to play well. When people say this team doesn't play so well and wins, I never believe it so much. To win so many times, you need to play well."

Mourinho knew that Paul Scholes and other key ex-United legends had been instrumental in Louis van Gaal losing his credibility during his period as coach, and the new manager had a tough task reining in their very public with such high profile platforms on which to express their controversial views. He would accept criticism, in fact, he invited it. At times, even, it sounded more like a challenge to deliver it in person at the training ground.

Roy Keane, Gary Neville, Ryan Giggs, Rio Ferdinand, Owen Hargreaves, Michael Owen as well as Scholes are top TV pundits, who haven't held back. "At this club you find legends from five years ago, legends of 10 years ago, legends of 15 years ago and legends of 20 years ago," Mourinho said in The Sunday Times. "Their voice becomes very powerful. That is something you have to understand. When people belong to the club history, they are different to a normal pundit. You have to look at them in a different way. You have to be respectful with these guys. They are so powerful in the fans' world that they can influence positively or negatively. The fans love them, so when they are positive they can unite and when they are negative they can create a more difficult situation.They are working and have to try to be honest and independent. So, myself, as Manchester United manager cannot ask them, 'You belong to our history, you are here to help.' You have to accept that if they are happy with the team they can elevate the support; if they are not happy maybe they can disturb and make things more difficult. I would say to them, 'You are welcome at the training ground.' Any time you want to give an opinion, welcome, it is your house, it is your home and you can be back when you want."

But Mourinho is wise enough, and sufficiently long in the tooth to know that the only thing that silences the critics is winning, whether they are the clubs legends or the journalists themselves. It is a results driven industry. Even something that should be quite routine, such as a pre-season friendly, now takes on enormous significance.

Rather worryingly, United's flight to Beijing from Shanghai was forced to make an emergency landing more than a 100 miles away as bad weather continued to affect their pre-season tour of China, which was now becoming more chaotic the longer it went on. Memphis Depay revealed in a video posted on social media that the plane had been diverted to Tianjin as United travelled to the Chinese capital to take on rivals Manchester City. "We're lost somewhere," said Depay as he stood on the tarmac with two air stewardesses. "We had to make a quick landing. We tried to fly to Beijing but the weather is a little bit bad so we had to land somewhere else. Now we're waiting until the weather gets a little bit easier so we can land. I hope we can leave soon so we can prepare ourselves for the game against Manchester City."

Mourinho confirmed that one or two planes carrying United's players from Shanghai to Beijing had to make an emergency landing in Tianjin due to the bad weather, and those on board did not arrive for dinner at the team hotel until 1am. He said: "We were supposed to fly in two different planes and share half of us in one plane and half of us in a second one. The ones in the first plane were lucky because the plane was great and we landed safely and we were in the hotel in good conditions to have dinner. The second group was unlucky. The plane was not good, they had a storm and had to land for about a couple of hours. They sought to come by bus, then they got the plane and they arrived in the hotel to have dinner at one o'clock in the morning."

The game at the Bird's Nest Stadium had already been in some doubt following downpours in Beijing and there was a forecast for more showers before kick-off. As a consequence City switched training to the nearby Olympic Sports Centre in the morning and United planned to do the same for the evening session.

The early bench mark for the fans' feel good factor would be the outcome of this much anticipated clash in faraway Beijing.

Granted, it might only be a friendly but the eyes of the world would be on the two managers as they face each other for the first time since a bitter feud during their respective Barcelona and Real Madrid careers.

Pep Guardiola intended to kick off his renewed rivalry with José Mourinho with a polite handshake and a smile, expecting it to be reciprocated. "It's a friendly game, a really friendly game," Guardiola told a news conference. Asked if he would shake Mourinho's hand, he confirmed: "We are polite guys - why not? Why should we not shake hands? No reason why. He will want to win and so will I, that's all."

He then added, "I saw United's game against Dortmund - it's too early to know how they will be. I'm pretty sure they will be stronger than in previous years. Of course with this manager and with the good players they already had - I'm sure they will buy new players too - they will be a strong team."

There was, however, deepening concern in both City and United camps about the Bird's Nest Stadium pitch after more heavy rainfall.

Guardiola wanted to get through the game without any injuries. "We didn't see the pitch but there is a lot of water in the last days so we understand it's not in a good condition but okay we're going to adapt and adjust. It's our second game of preparation - the most important thing is that the players are not going to be injured. We know the humidity for the training is not ideal but we also know that it's so important to come here to know the people and to play a good two games against amazing teams like United and Dortmund. We don't want to expend too much energy in training because of the humidity but we stay here, we play, and then go back to Manchester for two more weeks of preparation before the first official game."

Mourinho condemned the state of the pitch in Beijing and agreed that players avoiding injury is more important than the result. Both teams trained at the nearby Olympic Sports Centre due to concerns over the surface at the Bird's Nest which faced another 24 hours of heavy rain before kick-off. City's deputy groundsman Craig Knight had been in China for the past 10 days, at City's expense, to try and sort out the problem, which started with a fungus affecting part of the pitch.

Parts of the surface were re-laid with new turf but that was damaged by heavy rain, so 70 local staff worked around the clock to try and fix the problem. Mourinho was asked for his thoughts on the conditions."I think Beijing is unlucky because the pitch is very bad. The pitch and the conditions of my players are more important than results in pre-season. It's not a problem for me to lose matches in pre-season. It's a problem for me, bad conditions for my players to train and bad conditions for my players to play. So if you ask me my objective for the match tomorrow I only have one: take the players home safe without any kind of injury. It's not the conditions to play a good game of football, but we have to play. We cannot just run away and disappear and not play. So we have to play and try to be lucky. Normally when you say lucky you say lucky because you want a good result. The result I want tomorrow is to go home without injuries and that is the luck I want."

Mourinho hoped both teams hold back rather than risk hurting themselves chasing a meaningless pre-season victory, adding: "City versus United for me is Old Trafford or the Etihad or a cup final at Wembley, not a friendly. It was a friendly before we knew the conditions. After we know the conditions, it's maybe a double friendly. I just hope the players keep that balance and there are no problems. I repeat, if it was a friendly then it becomes a double friendly because no injuries, play calm, play safe, go home, keep the preparation next week. I think Man City have here all their players. We have six, seven, eight which stayed in Europe, so what I want is to go to Manchester and start training with the whole group and play Galatasaray and Everton before we play Leicester and try to be in the best possible condition for the Premier League. Tomorrow is the last day and it's over."

Guardiola took charge of his first City game as they lost 1-0 to Bayern Munich in their first pre-season friendly of the summer. Delph came on as a second-half substitute. "It was our first game, because of that we're trying to implement the systems we've been working on. It's not going to happen overnight but the boys are switched on and eager to impress the new manager - we're all really enjoying our football."

"The best manager in the world" suggested Fabian Delph as the 'friendly' became increasingly focused on the two managers. He learned more in three weeks under Pep than he has throughout the rest of his career. He struggled during his debut season after moving from Villa, but Guardiola's methods were having a positive impact on him. "The first three weeks have been amazing. I've learned more than I have throughout my whole career," he said. "It is a big statement but it is the truth. Every manager has their own methods, their own systems of play - there's no two alike. I believe we've got the best manager in the world here at City - already in the first two to three weeks I've been so impressed with what we've been doing - the different systems, the intensity of training, his man management skills - it's been brilliant for me. It's so intense - high pressing, very energetic. It's been tough but it's been very, very good. The manager has a lot of different systems and it is all about learning different positions. I am on a big learning curve. If that can keep going I would be very happy. I don't think I will be a centre-back but you will be pleasantly surprised."

Even in a short space of time, Gaël Clichy was talking up City's prospects as much as they were under Mourinho at United.

The former Arsenal full back said: "In a short period of time, he's shown us how great he is. Of course, being great doesn't mean having results, but everyone is looking forward to this season. The young players are improving, we're improving. We don't want to say too much because one manager isn't going to change the whole club, but of course he's going to change a lot of things."

Clichy has played under Arsene Wenger, Roberto Mancini and Manuel Pellegrini, but Guardiola's distinctive style is unparalleled. "Each manager has their own philosophy. I've been with Arsene Wenger and it was a different philosophy. Roberto Mancini was a different philosophy. We all know the way he wants to play and it's not for me to tell you what he wants. It's very good. It's very impressive. It's fresh and he has new ideas. It's not going to be easy because we are starting from zero and the way he wants to play. Having a great manager and great players is not enough and you have to work hard and we start the season as strong as possible."

Clichy came on as a second-half substitute in the defeat to Bayern Munich but despite United vs City being just a friendly, the players were all motivated for the first ever meeting between the sides outside the UK. "He (Pep) wants us to be proud when we wear the shirt" Clichy said. "He wants us to play good football, the way he sees football. His philosophy is the priority. For sure, we want to win every game, but in the end we are here to learn from him. If we can win these games, that would be fantastic, but our focus is on Sunderland."

City captain Vincent Kompany had an extended training session on his own and then sat out the main session the day before the game.

He suffered a succession of injuries, culminating in a groin problem that ruled him out of Euro 2016, so there was bound to be caution especially given the number of times he returned, only to be sidelined again almost immediately.

Guardiola declined to put a timescale on his recovery. "What happened in the last two years has been so difficult for him and the team," said Guardiola. "The important thing is not when he will be fit, it is to be sure he is fit. He needs to play one week, then another, training regularly, every day. If the doctor says he is fit for the first game against Sunderland great. If it is the Champions League qualifiers in August great. If not, September. If not, October. The moment the doctor says he is ready he will be with us."

JOSÉ VS PEP. UNITED VS CITY. CANCELLED

Manchester United, @ManUtd: Due to recent weather events, tournament organisers & participating clubs have decided to cancel tonight's International Champions Cup game.

7:39 AM - 25 Jul 2016

A statement from the ICC read: "The International Champions Cup China, Manchester United vs Manchester City match is cancelled due to the extreme weather events in Beijing over a multiple day period. The Committee and both teams make the decision together in the interest of player safety."

Both City and United said "tournament organisers and clubs" decided to cancel the match after rain had fallen overnight and there were forecasts of more heavy rain on the day of the match. Organisers later said the match would not be rearranged. So, the first meeting of the respective managers in a Manchester derby since taking charge will now take place on 10 September in the Premier League.

Executive vice-chairman Ed Woodward defended the decision to call off the game, but suggested they would return in the future. The game was cancelled less than five-and-a-half hours before kick-off as Woodward insisted that it would not affect plans to come back in future. "It's extremely disappointing not to be able to play the game in this amazing stadium, but the recent torrential rain would have caused problems anywhere in the world and has left the pitch unplayable. We know our fans in China will, like the players and staff, be saddened by the cancellation of the match, but I am sure they appreciate that the player safety has to be the top priority. I am sure we will return to the Bird's Nest in the future to give them the chance to see the team in action."

Tragically, and of far greater concern, it was reported that floods in north and central China had killed at least 150 people with scores missing and hundreds of thousands forced from homes. It certainly placed the sporting matters into context.

"The cancellation was made in the interest of player safety and comes following extreme weather events in Beijing over a multiple day period, that have left the playing surface in a condition deemed to be unfit for play," a statement said. "The conditions experienced in Beijing on 19 July and 20 July were reported as being some of the most extreme weather conditions the capital of China has experienced in recent history."

In a video posted on United's Twitter account, Luke Shaw said: "Just a little message from me that the game has been called off. Obviously I know you're all disappointed and as players we're all disappointed too. We came out here to play here in front of all you fans because we know how much you love us all. We're so sorry and if we could change it, we all want to play right now but that is the final decision and we can't play. Hopefully we'll see you all soon."

In another video, Juan Mata said: "I know you are all disappointed but I wanted to say thank you for all your amazing support here in China. In Shanghai and now in Beijing, we really felt that you love the club, love United. So we are really disappointed because we were looking forward to the game. But I'm sure we will be back really soon."

Vincent Kompany admitted it was a huge disappointment, but agreed that the conditions were "just too dangerous". Kompany would not have played against United because he was recovering from injury. He said: "It's sad for us, it's sad for our fans. Obviously it's disappointing because we looked forward to playing a derby in Beijing for a long time. We had our groundsman working for 10 days on the pitch, but the conditions were just too dangerous for the players. It's sad to call it off, but I think mainly we want to thank all the fans for their passion and for the way they've received us in Beijing since we've been here. We're moving on now to Shenzhen to play against Borussia Dortmund now, so it's not finished for us in China, but obviously it's a big disappointment for us. It's been a special experience and everything in China has been greater than life itself almost. It's been a truly a unique experience and it's hard to put it into words when a big event like this is not happening, but I do feel it's not the last time we will come to Beijing. If we're patient, like Chinese people are, then good things will come around again and we'll be here again. There're things in life that you don't control and, as we say in Manchester, we just get on with it, and

I think it builds up for the next time we come around for an even bigger event. In the meantime we have to get on with it, we move on to Shenzhen, and I'm sure we'll have plenty of time to get some good game-time in and obviously see our fans over there. I've been looking forward to Shenzhen as well, it's close to so many great cities as well - Hong Kong, Macau - and it's against really good opposition in Borussia Dortmund. We saw how they played against Man United. I might be watching it from a distance still at the moment, but there's a lot to learn out of games like this, so I'm looking forward to it."

Manchester City subsequently flew on to Shenzhen to play Dortmund, and chief executive Ferran Soriano echoed Woodward's comments about returning to China. The club sold a 13 per cent stake in the City Football Group to Chinese investors for £265m last year back with extensive plans in the Far East. Soriano said: "We are very disappointed not to be able to play for our supporters here in Beijing. The players have been working hard in training to prepare for an exciting derby. We know how much everyone was looking forward to the game, but we understand that this bad weather is beyond anyone's control, and that the rain has made it totally unsafe to play on this pitch. It has been a pleasure and an honour to experience such a warm welcome from the people and supporters here in Beijing, and we remain committed to playing here in the future."

United were left to fly out of Beijing and return to Manchester as planned.

Because the game was cancelled there were not enough matches played in the tournament for there to be a winner of the 2016 International Champions Cup.

The cancellation capped a chaotic 24 hours for United.

Mourinho's planned news conference had to be scrapped as too many people tried to get into a room which was deemed too small and too hot, so he was forced to address the media by the side of the pitch. It was the club's decision to move the press conference outside and away from the room which included around 80 members of the media crammed into a small space. The press conference in a stiflingly hot room initially looked as though it would be called off, although local media complained that Guardiola had turned up for his interviews earlier in the day. After discussions between United officials, their Chinese hosts and organisers Relevent Sports, it was then moved outside. Mourinho spoke to the club's TV station MUTV and then sat stony faced while a scrum of local media waited 50 yards away. He then agreed to take questions and spoke for 10 minutes. Hours earlier, Guardiola was handed a towel as temperatures reached unbearable levels inside the Olympic Sports Centre during his press briefing.

The match was unlikely to have been a sell-out due to the high price of tickets, £60-£300, with 50,000 sold for a game with a reduced capacity of 60,000. Even with their historical differences both managers were united in their condemnation of the pitch as their tours of China descended into farce. It's possible that United will consider heading to the States for pre-season in future under their new manager.

TAG HEUER TIME

Despite the on-field disappointments the commercial machinations continued to grow inexorably from strength to strength.

Manchester United announced their 70th commercial partnership, with watchmakers TAG Heuer, one of the first since José Mourinho became manager that further illustrates their status as the world's No. 1 commercial club and explains how they can splash on a new world record fee and salary to match on the likes of Paul Pogba. Let's face it, though, he's good, but not that good. He is not a Lionel Messi or Cristiano Ronaldo.

TAG Heuer features on digital advertising boards at Old Trafford. Bespoke timepieces will also be displayed around the stadium, in addition to the team's dressing room. Wayne Rooney, Marcus Rashford, Ashley Young and new signing Henrikh Mkhitaryan were all present to celebrate the club's new venture during the pre-season tour.

Manchester United's group managing director, Richard Arnold told their official website: "This key partnership has been struck at a very exciting moment in our history. Led by our new manager we're proud to be in China, where we enjoy vast and loyal support, preparing for an important season ahead. In TAG Heuer, we have a partner that will naturally be well-equipped to support us, not least because we share so much. Our rich history can be traced back to the same era; we've both overcome challenges and come out stronger in our quest for the highest level of performance. Our prestige is down to our unrelenting commitment to be pioneers."

'Gold Trafford' boast more partners than any other Premier League side including deals for nutritional supplements, ready-meals, outdoor apparel, casual footwear, in addition to the usual official kit supplier, plus an official feature film partner, beer, wine, and spirits. In fact, they could become the first club in history to earn more than £500million in a year.

A summary of their commercial partnerships:

Global partners:

Adidas, official kit supplier

Aon, Principal Partner

Chevrolet, Principal Partner

20th Century Fox, official Manchester United feature film partner

Abengoa, official sustainable technology partner

Aeroflot, official carrier

Aperol Spritz, official global spirits partner

Apollo Tyres, official tyre partner

Casillero del Diablo, official wine partner

Columbia, official outdoor apparel partner

DHL, official logistics partner

Epson, official office equipment partner

Gulf Oil International, official global lubricant oil and fuel retail partner

HCL, official digital transformation partner

HEROES, official formal footwear partner

Kansai Paint, official paint partner

Marathon Bet, official global betting partner

New Era, official leisure headwear partner

Nissin Foods Group, official global partner

Swissquote, official forex and online financial trading partner

Toshiba Medical Systems, official medical systems partner

Yanmar, official global partner

Regional partners:

A.P. Honda, official motorcycle partner for Thailand

Achilles Radial, official tyre partner for Indonesia

CHI, official soft drinks partner for Nigeria

Cho-A Pharm Co Ltd., official pharmaceutical partner for Korea and Vietnam

Donaco, official casino resort partner for Thailand, Cambodia, Vietnam, Laos, Myanmar and South Korea

Eurofood, official confectionary partner for Cambodia, Laos, Myanmar, Thailand and Vietnam

Federal, official tyre partner for Taiwan and China

Gloops, official social gaming partner for Japan

The Hong Kong Jockey Club, official partner

IVC, official wellness partner for China

Manda, official nutritional supplements partner for Japan

Nexon, official social football gaming partner in South Korea

Ottogi, official ready meal partner for Korea

Sbenu, official casual footwear partner in South Korea

Unilever, official male shampoo partner in Indonesia, Singapore and Vietnam

Media Partners:

Bakcell, official integrated telecommunications partner for Azerbaijan

Belgacom TV (11+), official MUTV broadcast partner for Belgium

Cable and Wireless, official Quad-Play partner for the Carribbean

DirectTV PanAmericana, official MUTV broadcast partner

Eclat Media Group, official MUTV broadcast partner for South Korea

Emtel, official triple play and MUTV broadcast partner for Mauritius

Fiji TV, official MUTV broadcast partner for Fiji

Globacom, official integrated telecommunications partner for Nigeria, Ghana, Republic of Benin

PCCW, official integrated telecommunications partner and official broadcast partner for Hong Kong

Portugal Telecom (MEO), official MUTV broadcast partner for Portugal

Sina Sports, official MUTV broadcast partner for China

Sky TV NZ, official MUTV broadcast partner for New Zealand

STC, official integrated telecommunications partner for Saudi Arabia

TM, official integrated telecommunications Partner for Malaysia

TrueMove H, official integrated telecommunications partner for Thailand

TV 2, official MUTV broadcast partner for Norway

VIVA, official integrated telecommunications partner for Bahrain and Kuwait

Financial Partners:

AFB, official financial services affinity partner for Kenya, Ghana, Zambia, Zimbabwe, Uganda and Tanzania

Banif Bank, official financial services affinity partner for Malta

BIDV, official financial services affinity partner for Vietnam

Commercial Bank of Qatar, official financial services affinity partner for Qatar

Danamon, official financial services affinity partner for Indonesia

DenizBank, official financial services affinity partner for Turkey

Emirates NBD, official financial services affinity partner for the UAE

Eurobank, official financial services affinity partner for Serbia

Invex Banco, official financial services affinity partner for Mexico

Krungsri, official financial services affinity partner for Thailand

Maybank, official retail banking partner for Malaysia, Singapore and Philippines

MBNA, official financial services affinity partner for the UK

Santander, official financial services affinity partner for Norway

Shinsei, official financial services affinity partner for Japan

Virgin Money, official financial services partner

Despite the flight home from Shanghai taking eleven hours, and touching down at 05.00, the squad immediately reported for training at the Aon Training Complex the following morning. Starting at 06.30, they trained for 2 hours before heading home. Mourinho was understood to be unhappy at the lack of fitness work the players had done over the last 72 hours but praised the commitment of his players, telling ManUtd.com: "They are a great group of boys and the intensity of the session shows they are very professional in their outlook."

Wayne Rooney tweeted a message to the club's fans after returning home from the pre-season tour: "Back home after a great pre-season camp in China. Thanks to all our fans over there for the brilliant support."

After sitting out United's pre-season trip to China, their new No. 9 caught up with his team mates in training in readiness to travel to Gothenburg for the match at Ullevi Stadium. The game against the Turkish side, Galatasaray, had been arranged once the deal for Ibrahimović had been signed, as the player's popularity in his homeland would all but guarantee a full house in the 43,000-seater stadium.

Henrik Larsson, a cult hero at Old Trafford when he joined United on a brief loan spell in 2007, expected Mourinho and United to get a good reception in Scandinavia. "United are big here, as they've always been," he told ManUtd.com. "It's in Gothenburg and I was at the game when United played Barcelona there a few years back. There were a lot of spectators then and I expect it's going to be the same again this time around. I still try to watch United as much as I can, whenever it doesn't clash with one of my own games here. I definitely try to watch as much as I can. I've seen a little bit of Marcus Rashford and he looks exciting. It is just a question of bringing him from talented prospect to a fully-fledged star."

Bryan Robson is excited about Zlatan's arrival and he hopes the Swede can make a similar impact to Robin van Persie, who joined United during the latter stages of his career in 2012, with 30 goals in his debut season to help Sir Alex's team win the Premier League title. "Zlatan is 34 and it would have been nice to get him at 28 or 29, something like that, but the way he played for PSG last year showed he has a lot to offer still and he looks really fit," Robson told MUTV. "I think back to Sir Alex's last year when everybody talked about Robin van Persie's age and his injuries when he joined, but he won us the title with his goals that season. Hopefully Zlatan can do the same. He will take the pressure off Wayne Rooney as well. Every time we've had a bad result the excuse is that Wayne didn't play particularly well. The pressure has always been on him to perform and Zlatan will take that away from Wayne a wee bit, so Wayne can relax and enjoy his game. Zlatan gave a great interview when the reporter told him that he'd previously described himself as 10 out of 10 and asked how he would rate himself now... Zlatan said 11 out of 10!"

Ji-sung Park worked alongside Robson on the club's trip to China, and the former Korea Republic captain agrees that Ibrahimović's confident personality will benefit the dressing room. "Yeah I think the club needs a big character like him," Park also told MUTV. "He has a lot of experience and then he can show his character in the dressing room and on the pitch. He can influence the players and particularly the young players. They can learn a lot from him and then show it on the pitch."

Ibrahimović turned down the chance to link up with David Beckham in the MLS to sign for United. He was linked with a move to the US, but opted for a one-year deal at Old Trafford, reuniting with former boss Mourinho. Speaking exclusively to Goal, Ibrahimović admitted that he rejected Beckham's offer to play for his new Miami-based franchise, which recently secured land for a stadium and hopes to join the league in 2018, such was his desire to play in the Premier League. "David is a good friend of mine, and he has asked me to play for his team," Ibrahimović said. "For now, I want to achieve big things with Manchester United, but I have a lot of respect for the MLS, and anything is possible."

Ibrahimović, however, declined to rule out a move to America in the future. "I am not ruling out the MLS," he added. "Once I had decided to leave PSG there were many offers, but with Zlatan that is normal. I know that teams from the MLS were interested, but the opportunity to play for Manchester United, and of course to work with my good friend José Mourinho again, was impossible to turn down."

He had no intention to retire. "I have a contract with Manchester United, but I feel in great shape. I feel as though I could play until I am 40. It is impossible to predict the future."

THE ROONEY ROLE?

Where the 'new boy' plays or rather who supports him in attack will largely determine where Rooney plays. Mourinho will also define where Rooney plays for his country, according to new England boss Sam Allardyce.

Rooney, 30, featured as a forward and in midfield under previous England manager Roy Hodgson during Euro 2016. Newly installed as Roy Hodgson's successor, Allardyce said it was too soon to confirm whether Rooney, England's record scorer, would remain as captain. "I still think Wayne Rooney has a massive place to play in the England side," said the 61-year-old Big Sam. "If José says he is not going to play him in centre midfield and he is playing up front and scoring goals for Manchester United then it would be pointless me bringing him into England and playing him in centre midfield."

With Rooney facing competition for a starting spot at Old Trafford, Allardyce said a player's club form will be important in him being selected. "I don't know until that happens with anybody, let alone Wayne Rooney," he added. "I hope there are standout players all over the place when the Premier League starts. I hope it's a hugely difficult task for me to pick my first squad because everybody is on really good form and playing exceptionally well."

Allardyce's first game in charge will be a World Cup qualifier against Slovakia on 4 September, and he hopes to have made contact with Premier League managers such as Mourinho and Pep Guardiola to "hear their thoughts" before choosing his squad. "We've got to try and help each other if we possibly can," said Allardyce, who has more than two decades' worth of domestic coaching experience. "It won't always be the case, the demands on Premier League managers and demand on me as England manager is bound to cause some conflict down the line because the pressures are far greater than ever before. So they are bound to want to protect their players and that is what I have to try and overcome with a little bit of give and take, hopefully."

Clearly, though, Henrikh Mkhitaryan was bought to be the support striker, thereby limiting Rooney's options.

Mkhitaryan was also a man on a mission, as he was seven-years-old when his father, Hamlet, died from a brain tumour. He brought his young family back from France to spend his final days in their home town of Yerevan, Armenia, having left a year before Henrikh was born following an earthquake that killed 25,000 and left half a million more homeless. Three operations failed to cure his illness. He died at the age of 33 in May 1996, leaving behind his wife Marina Taschyan, young Henrikh and daughter Monica.

Captain of Armenia, as well as his country's all-time top goalscorer and most famous footballing export, he gave an interview to the media sitting in a marquis in Shanghai's Century Park during the recent launch of United's new home kit. Micki to his team-mates is driven by the memory of his father. "Because of him, when we came back to Armenia it was my dream to continue his work and to be a good player also. He was my motivation because when

I was young he was playing football professionally, and I was always dreaming to go with him to the training ground. I couldn't understand that I would disturb him during training because I was a child. He was 33-years-old. It's a pity but life continues. I hope he's proud looking at me from the sky. I try to do everything to make him proud. I watched his videos many times when I was young but now they're just memories. I'm sad because I think he could help me with his words and support. But that's life. I'm trying to do everything with my family members and friends who are watching me playing every game. They try to help me to say where I did wrong and where I did well. It's very difficult when you grow up without a father because in the family you don't have a man who can give you direction and discipline. My mother was both my mother and father, so I'm thankful to her and all the people who were next to me at that time in a hard moment. So I think that life continues. My mother works in the Armenian Football Federation (as head of the national team's department), and my sister works at UEFA. We are a football family.'

Dortmund beat Liverpool to sign him for £24.4m in 2013, and he became a key figure in Jürgen Klopp's success story. Klopp is now at Anfield, and Dortmund team-mate Ilkay Gündoğan at City. 'It doesn't matter if he (Gündoğan) will be my rival, I will be happy to see him every day or any time he wants."

Ex-Dortmund player, Shinji Kagawa, recommended life in Manchester even though his spell at Old Trafford was disappointing. "At this club you have to try to do everything to show your best qualities, otherwise you will not be here anymore," added Mkhitaryan. "It doesn't matter if they bought me for 38m Euros or 40m Euros, I'm not guaranteed to play the games. I am always doing the maximum for myself because after my football career I want to sit down and think I've done something good - I won this title or that title, because that's the history. If you retire after your career, people will talk about your titles. So that's the most important thing in football. As a child, I dreamed of playing for one of the biggest clubs in the world. When my agent phoned to say I had an interest from Manchester United, I was very happy because it means I did something good in my life."

FROM NOISY NEIGHBOURS
TO WEIGHT WATCHERS

Meanwhile, over at City, Pep had banished overweight players from first-team training and banned junk food, imposing the strict discipline that was a hallmark of his time at Barcelona and Bayern Munich to make sure his players are as fit as possible for the new season.

Samir Nasri was one of those Guardiola ordered to lose weight before the 29-year-old can rejoin his team-mates.

Gaël Clichy discussed how anyone who failed to meet Guardiola's 'Weight Watchers' plan cannot work with the first-team squad "You often hear managers say being healthy is really important," said Clichy. "With him, if you're weight is too high, you're not training with the team. That's the first thing. You can hear it a lot but, for my part, it's the first time any manager has really done it. So we have a few players who are not training with the team yet. You have to know that if your weight is 60 kilos and you are on 70 kilos, then you cannot play football because you're going to get injured and get your team in trouble. That's important. He cut out some juice and, of course, pizza and all the heavy food is not allowed. Some people think that's normal but, in truth, it's not always like this. I know because I've been playing football for a long time. It's really refreshing and very exciting."

Guardiola reminds him of his former boss Arsene Wenger, that both men have "changed the way people see football." Clichy observed: "I think he's an ideal manager for any kind of player. The goalkeeper needs to be better with his feet, the centre-backs are improving and the full-backs are important. He said if he could play 11 midfielders, he would play them. So I guess for a midfielder it's unbelievable. And the strikers are going to score a lot of goals because we are going to create chances. I can even tell you that the assistant manager will improve. He's the kind of guy that if you're lucky to work with him during your career, he is someone you will remember for a long time because he's truly impressive. He's been a player also which makes a big difference. He's young so I think he understands how football is going with the new generation coming though. He told us, 'we're going to be friends for all the pre-season and I know that when I name the starting XI for Sunderland some players are going to be upset - from that moment, I don't know what to expect'. He just wants us to trust him, he wants to trust us, and I think it's the right way to start a relationship."

Clichy felt the players raised their game to impress Guardiola. "Any manager who comes into a new club brings an energy," he said. "Instead of giving 100 per cent you give 110 per cent just because it's a new manager and you need to show yourself. But, of course, he's bringing something different. He's bringing something he's been doing with Barcelona and Munich. Guardiola, Wenger, Mourinho, Big Sam, any manager who comes into a new club will bring this thing for the first year at least. All the players want to play harder and train harder. When you have someone like Guardiola, who has won so many trophies, then you have to adapt and quick. It's just normal, if you have a new boss you just want to impress."

And still the Pogba saga continued...

Massimiliano Allegri believed the £110m price tag on Pogba was not unrealistic. The Juventus boss was asked if the thought the price quoted was "insane" following the Old Lady's 2-1 defeat of Tottenham Hotspur at the Melbourne Cricket Ground. Allegri laughed, before saying: "That's what it is - I don't assign prices to players. Each player has a value - some are low and some are high." The Juve boss had repeatedly been asked about Pogba's status during his side's trip Down Under. At no point had he ruled out a move.

And now Real Madrid coach Zinedine Zidane refused to rule out hijacking United's world record bid. Pogba was thought to favour a move to Madrid as Zidane confirmed Real's interest on their pre-season tour of the United States. "In this moment we are still working (on a move for Pogba), and I cannot say anything more. Until August 31 anything can happen, but today he is not a Real Madrid player and I cannot talk about what will happen. I always say how things are, but now is not the time to talk about this. A lot of clubs are interested in Pogba. Real Madrid always want the best players. But we owe Juventus respect, and I can't say anything more out of respect."

Whilst that was slowly dragging on the fastest man on Earth, Usain Bolt, is expecting "greatness" from José Mourinho this season, as he sent Mourinho a personal message.

In a video clip he said: "Well José, it's Usain Bolt. As you know I'll be watching you this season and I expect nothing but greatness from you as I will bring greatness. So I'm looking forward to it. We need a championship."

Mourinho, who had already publicly declared he was targeting Premier League glory in his first season in charge, took to Instagram to thank the Jamaican sprinter, saying: "tks [sic] a lot champion. We all wish you more glory at the Olympics."

Usain Bolt also took time out to wish Jose Mourinho's new striker a big welcome. "Hey Zlatan, this is Usain Bolt. I just want to say welcome to the greatest team you've ever been in; Manchester United. [I'm] looking forward to the goals, I'll be watching you."

CARRINGTON CULL

The expected cull at Manchester United was ruthless as Mourinho, at the club's Carrington training base, told nine players they could leave.

Eager to whittle his first-team group down to 24 players before the start of the season, he divided the 'candidates' into 'potential United players' who will be made available on loan, and those who have no future and can leave on a permanent basis. All nine were informed personally by Mourinho.

German World Cup winner Bastian Schweinsteiger was the highest-profile victim of Mourinho's 'Clear-out Thursday'. Schweinsteiger endured a disastrous £7m move from Bayern Munich, mainly due to injuries, but had two years of a £160,000-a-week contract left; not easy to off load.

Almost simultaneously the Germany captain announced his retirement from international football. The 31-year-old midfielder had been part of the squad that won the 2014 World Cup in Brazil. He retires as Germany's fourth most-capped player of all time on 120 - behind Lothar Matthäus (150), Miroslav Klose (137) and Lukas Podolski (129). "I had the opportunity to experience moments that have been indescribably beautiful and successful," Schweinsteiger said.

Youngsters Cameron Borthwick-Jackson and Tim Fosu-Mensah, who both impressed under Louis van Gaal last season, were told they were not in the manager's plans, while Brazil Under-20 midfielder Andreas Pereira was told to gain first-team experience on loan in order to fight for a place at United in the future. Pereira was one of the first to see the manager and was told he still had a chance at United in the future. The Belgian-born midfielder signed from PSV Eindhoven in 2012 made two starts and 11 substitute appearances for United, his only goal coming against Ipswich Town in a Capital One Cup tie last season.

Striker James Wilson met with Mourinho before the tour to China and was told he was part of United's long-term plans, with the door left open for him to stay and play in the Under-21 side, or go on loan if he wanted as United had 12 clubs enquire. Adnan Januzaj, Will Keane, Tyler Blackett and Paddy McNair were the others on the hit list.

There was later some confusion, though, over the highly-rated defender Tim Fosu-Mensah. He was in fact in talks about securing his long-term future at the club despite being asked by Mourinho to train with the Under 21s rather than the first-team squad. There had been an outcry among the fans to keep the talented kid. United, however, assured the 18-year-old Dutchman they see him as an important part of Mourinho's plans, and negotiations were ongoing about a new contract to ward off interest from other leading clubs in Europe. Troubled by a minor calf injury, he had been training apart from Mourinho's main squad alongside Bastian Schweinsteiger, Will Keane, James Wilson, Cameron Borthwick-Jackson, Andreas Pereira, Paddy McNair, Tyler Blackett and Adnan Januzaj, and was assumed to be one of those on their way out.

Fosu-Mensah was only omitted from United's squad to face Galatasaray due to a minor injury concern. "Fosu-Mensah is not so much injured," Mourinho confirmed on MUTV. "But he has this little thing that we want to be careful with, given that he is young. He is separate from the group until he is 100 per cent back." Smalling was another absentee from the 23-man squad, with Mourinho confirming that he suffered a recurrence of a problem picked up last season. "Chris Smalling has had a recurrence of an old injury from the previous season," he said. "We shall see what happens, but already he is suspended for the first game against Bournemouth."

POGBA WATCH

Another day, another story in the saga. This time it was reported that Juventus are now prepared to allow Paul Pogba to join Manchester United for a world record fee of £92million plus £8m in add-ons, if United agree to pay the 20 per cent bonus due to the midfielder and his agent Mino Raiola. Even further add-ons may come into play if he wins the Ballon d'Or.

More or less at the same moment Pogba, himself, posted an interesting and perhaps cryptic or teasing picture on Instagram. The photograph was in black & white but with a red filter, clearly highlighting his red hat and red shoes - was this a hint towards his next destination?

SWEDISH DELIGHT

Zlatan Ibrahimović promised to give fans "what they want" as he prepared to make his debut when United faced Turkish giants Galatasaray in the pre-season friendly in the veteran striker's homeland of Sweden at the Ullevi Stadium. "Everybody has been waiting for that moment," he told MUTV. "There has been a lot of talk and to make my debut in my country will feel great. I think the fans are waiting for me to come back and they are waiting to enjoy not only me, but the team as well. Hopefully, we can give them a good game and, at the same time, we are in the preparation. We need to keep focused, to build up the physical part and the conditioning part but we will give them what they want."

Reflecting on his first week at the Aon Training Complex, he spoke highly of his new surroundings and team-mates. "Positive vibes. They seem to be good guys, quality players, they train very hard and, during the training, are very focused. The coach - he is direct, he is concrete, he says what he wants and the players are adapting. So there are only positive things. I believe in working hard. Not only in games but even in training. The way you train is the way you play in the games - that's my philosophy. Working hard, training hard and feeling good. Then you need to get the rhythm by playing games."

Wayne Rooney, meanwhile, believed Mourinho will reinstate a "winning mentality". Talking on Manchester radio station Key103, he explained how Mourinho's winning obsession had United "excited". Winning was a key note in his assessment when he observed: "He's made, in my opinion, great signings, they've gelled in really well with the squad so it's exciting times. It's always exciting when you get a new manager but to get a new manager in the stature of José Mourinho... he's first of all great to work under and he's brought his way of working and a winning mentality back to the club. I think Manchester United as a football club need to win. We have to win and he certainly has that winning mentality. He has that stature of winning trophies wherever he goes and we have to deliver for him so there's pressure on players, of course there always is at Manchester United but we're ready, we're working hard and I think this season we'll give a real challenge on all fronts."

The Portuguese had given his players the day off following their two-hour session at Carrington immediately after touching down from Asia. Sportsmail had been told United's stars were not put out by that unorthodox instruction and are buying into Mourinho's methods. "The training is tough, of course, it's pre-season so you'd expect that but we've enjoyed it," Rooney confirmed. "He's come in and he's been great with the players. The training has been hard but enjoyable. The players are ready, we're working hard, we know it's a big season for us."

Mourinho might have instructed nine players to find new clubs - either permanently or on loan - but Rooney believes his personal touches could give United an edge this year. Rooney added: "He's the manager but he has a balance both in terms of being a manager and then also being a friend to the players, so he has that balance right so you can see why he's been successful everywhere he goes."

Mourinho hailed his players' commitment to his worth ethic. "The players have been fantastic in their attitude," he said. "We have done a number of double training sessions, but I am not worried about them being tired on Saturday as the reality is we have to work and are looking at the (Galatasaray) game as one more training session because the players need minutes - we will need to recover from that too."

He also believes that his players immediately felt Ibrahimović's impact in training, setting the example others can follow. "With Zlatan you may see someone with a big ego, big self-esteem, but it is in a positive way," Mourinho told MUTV. "When he is with the group, he is humble and friendly to everyone - integration is good. Zlatan is a fantastic player and, immediately in training, we could feel what I call 'functional empathy' - people looking to him, him looking to connect with other players. He is an amazing link player, an amazing player. He could be anything on the pitch, not just a goalscorer."

Ibrahimović and Mkhitaryan were helped by their ability to speak English. "Zlatan and Henrikh are fluent in English and in many other languages," the United boss explained. "They are good guys and experienced guys. Eric doesn't speak English too well. But he speaks French and Spanish which makes it an easy position in this squad with all his teammates who speak those languages. He is coming up, step by step."

With Sweden gearing up for the return of Zlatan, fellow Swede and former Manchester City, Lazio, Sampdoria and England boss, Sven-Göran Eriksson, was convinced Ibrahimović is capable of having the same impact as Cantona. "You can't say for sure, of course, but Zlatan is the same type of charismatic figure as Cantona so it's entirely possible he could have the same effect on United as Cantona had all those years ago," he said in an interview with the Daily Mirror. "I am certain United will hope that is the case and if you buy a player like Zlatan you are getting someone who is capable of inspiring the players around him by the way he performs. Cantona did that and helped many of the young players at United at that time. Zlatan has had an impact wherever he plays because of his ability and his character, so a big club like United is an ideal stage for him."

Now coaching Shanghai SIPG FC in the Chinese Super League, he discounted the criticism that United were paying over the odds for an ageing superstar. "People who say that don't know Zlatan," said Eriksson. "He would never have signed for United if he didn't feel it was a challenge he could meet. Also you cannot ignore his relationship with José Mourinho. They have been together before and you cannot imagine he would sign him on sentiment. He must believe Zlatan can still perform at the very highest level, and I am absolutely certain he can and will. Zlatan still feels he has a lot to offer and I am certain he will make a big impact for United and on the Premier League."

The Galatasaray coach Jan Olde Riekerink predicted Ibrahimović will be a revelation in England. The Dutchman was a reserve coach at Ajax when Ibrahimović joined from Malmo in 2001. He said: "The moment I met him he was at the start of his career, now he is at the top and has developed as a world star. They can watch him and he will be a big role model."

A new angle on Ibrahimović was offered from the blue half of Manchester and, in the process, stirred-up the local rivalry between José and Pep. New Manchester City signing and clearly well-read, Ilkay Gündoğan, stated that even Ibrahimović knows Guardiola is the best coach.

City had unveiled Gündoğan alongside fellow new man Nolito, as cross-town rivals United announced the capture of Ibrahimović; who has made his dislike for Guardiola no secret and is an open admirer of Mourinho. Ibrahimović was scathing of Guardiola in his autobiography and has had plenty to say about his former Barcelona manager since, but Gündoğan said that even in his derisive attacks Ibrahimović had admitted that Guardiola is the best coach in the world. "Even the players who don't like him (actually rate him) and the best example is Ibrahimović." Gündoğan said. "I read in his book that he doesn't like him. But he says he is the best coach he ever worked with. This is really special to read, but he is being honest. It is the same thing I heard from the players at Bayern Munich. They told me the same - that he can improve everyone. That is what is possible."

IT'S ZLATAN TIME

Zlatan time turned out to be three minutes, 15 seconds.

Ibrahimović got his non-competitive debut off to the perfect start by scoring a spectacular overhead kick within four minutes of the game starting, that got José Mourinho enthused on the touch line, and inspired a 5-2 win in Gothenburg.

Galatasaray responded well to make it 2-1 before half-time, but Mourinho made a series of changes at the break and he got the reaction he wanted. Young striker Marcus Rashford impressed, winning a penalty which Rooney converted. The captain scored another from a cross before Mata capped the victory off with a close-range finish. Rooney, playing as a No. 10, scored twice in the second half in his first outing since Euro 2016.

The Zlatan Effect had already been working during his first few days of training with the squad, and it took just three minutes and 15 seconds to mark his United debut with a trademark goal. From Antonio Valencia's cross from the right the 34-year-old, with so limited pre-season training, connected with an overhead kick past that bounced past goalkeeper Fernando Muslera into the corner.

Ibrahimović's compatriots chanted 'Zlatan, Zlatan' during the 45 minutes he was on the pitch. "It was a good start and fantastic to score my first goal for United in Sweden," he said. "I had good support. This is my country. It is impossible to fail in my country."

He added: "There's something great being built here. If Pogba comes, it will be more interesting. Let's see."

After the 4-1 defeat against Borussia Dortmund and the Manchester City friendly being cancelled, Mourinho started with his strongest available line-up before making 11 changes.

Both the constitution and shape of his team were forming; 4-2-3-1 with Rooney behind Ibrahimović, Martial and Mkhitaryan either side. Rashford came on as a half-time substitute and notably made an impact.

Mourinho commented: "The players needed to play. Marcus did well and Ibra showed glimpses of what he can do. To train against opposition like this is the best we can do. I'm really happy with the mistakes we made as we can work on them."

Rooney was thrilled with the way it was all taking shape and the way he was slotting into the new look attack with Ibra. "He is a fantastic player and showed what he is capable of doing. It was a great goal and I am sure there will be many more moments like that from him. We have seen him do special things throughout his career and I am sure he will do that for us through the season. It's a great signing for us, with his experience, and he's been successful wherever he has been. Hopefully he will be for us as well. He's a nice fella, a normal guy. He gets on well with everyone, certainly on the pitch with the aura he brings with him."

After a difficult first 45 minutes Rooney, who wasn't one of the five changes made by Mourinho, improved to score twice in three minutes. "The plan was always for me to stay on in the second half. The important thing was the minutes. Of course you want to win, but the important thing is getting fit for the start. The manager has already told you and he's told me I will be a No. 10

and when I play in that position I know I will score goals."

United, without the injured Chris Smalling, had allowed Sinan Gümüş and Bruma to put the Turkish club ahead at the interval.

In the second half, though, Rooney volleyed in Valencia's cross, one of three assists for the attacking full back. Rooney then released Rashford with an outstanding pass and the teenager's speed earned a penalty which the No. 10 converted. Valencia set up Fellaini for a header to make it 4-2 after 62 minutes and after Rooney had been withdrawn, Mata burst into the area to convert Carrick's cross.

The Zlatan effect had begun straight away and with league titles in Italy, Spain, Holland and France, expectations were beginning to rise. "It's a massive help being with him day-in, day-out," concluded Rashford. "He's been amazing."

Mourinho was very happy with how United played, attacking with real intent and purpose in the second half, 2-1 down, before they scored four without reply to comfortably beat the Turkish side.

Irrespective of the score, Mourinho had instructed his players to focus on their fitness and get themselves as ready as possible for the new season. He explained: "Of course. I think everyone gave everything to improve. And even with the guys who came on at 4-2, I told them to forget the result, don't play like we are winning 4-2. 'You need this 30 minutes to play high tempo, high intensity, forget the 4-2'. That's what they all tried to do. Of course Marcus did well. Of course Ibra did show glimpses of the things he can bring us. But when I see guys like Fellaini, Martial, Schneiderlin, they trained two days and they can be here. I told them, 'Don't try to go with the intensity of the game, go with an intensity that makes you comfortable.' I prefer this way, I prefer that they are on the pitch so I am happy. I am happy with the opposition, they played already six or seven matches so they were in a higher tempo than us. I am happy with it all. And I am happy that out of such a big group we have just Timothy (Fosu-Mensah) and Chris Smalling with little injuries and apart from them, no injuries and everything looks like it's going well."

Manchester United: De Gea (Romero 67), Valencia (Darmian 67), Bailly (Jones 67), Blind (Rojo 67), Shaw (Memphis 67), Schneiderlin (Fellaini 45), Herrera (Carrick 45), Mkhitaryan (Lingard 45), Rooney (Mata), Martial (Young 45); Ibrahimović (Rashford 45)

Goals: Ibrahimović 4, Rooney 55, 58 (pen), Fellaini 62, Mata 67

Booked: Rooney

AND FINALLY (NEARLY)...

Paul Pogba (almost officially) perhaps became the most expensive footballer in the world by some distance when the summer's longest running transfer saga all but concluded with Manchester United agreeing a £100million 'package' with Juventus.

TOP 5 BIGGEST TRANSFERS:

Gareth Bale - Tottenham to Real Madrid £86m

Cristiano Ronaldo - Man United to Real Madrid £80m

Gonzalo Higuain - Napoli to Juventus £76m

Neymar - Santos to Barcelona £72m

Luis Suarez - Liverpool to Barcelona £63m

The world record transfer surpasses the British mark by an astonishing £40m - the previous record paid by a British club was the £59.7m United splashed out on Argentina winger Ángel Di María from Real Madrid in August 2014. The world record transfer fee had stood at the £86m paid by Real Madrid to Tottenham for Gareth Bale in 2013. Pogba had famously left Old Trafford in July 2012 after Sir Alex Ferguson refused to agree to Raiola's demands for an improved contract. Juventus paid £800,000 in compensation!

The 23-year-old would move to Old Trafford as part of a world-record deal - once agent, salary and administrative fees are included - making him the most expensive football player in history.

It was generally accepted that United would pay £92m for the Juventus midfielder while the Serie A giants are expected to foot the tax bill in a move which will lower the expectation on Pogba. Consequently, it was reported that Juventus would announce the transfer fee at £84.3m, just shy of the £86m Real Madrid paid to Tottenham Hotspur for Gareth Bale in 2013. Add-ons, however, would include a bonus to Juventus should Pogba renew his contract at United, and should he win the Ballon d'Or.

Pogba had, though, undergone a medical in Los Angeles after his recent holiday in Florida before 'agreeing' a five-year contract worth an eye-watering £290,000-a-week.

Pogba hinted at the move himself, signing a No. 6 United shirt while on his holidays in Los Angeles, sharing a snap on Instagram of himself at a theme park, joking in the caption: "Breaking news: Pogba undergoes medical check in Universal Studios amusement park California."

Raiola responded on Twitter the following day: "There is no deal done regarding Paul Pogba, lots of bla bla bla."

Adding on his Twitter page:

Mino Raiola, @MinoRaiola: Journalist = parrots. No deal done between clubs. It's a game between Italy press and UK press who announce it first and who is worse.

Pogba would become United's fourth signing since José Mourinho was appointed as manager, following the arrivals of Eric Bailly, Zlatan Ibrahimović and Henrikh Mkhitaryan. That would crucially complete his request "for four profiles of players"

Regardless of the move having been officially announced, the anticipated sniping began with Jürgen Klopp at Anfield. The German would rather build a team his way than splash £100m on one player. Klopp said: "If you bring one player in for £100m and he gets injured, then it all goes through the chimney. The day that this is football, I'm not in a job anymore, because the game is about playing together. That is how everybody in football understands it. You always want to have the best, but building the group is necessary to be successful. Other clubs can go out and spend more money and collect top players. I want to do it differently. I would even do it differently if I could spend that money. I don't know exactly how much money we could spend because nobody has told me, 'No, you can't do this'. If I spend money, it is because I am trying to build a team, a real team. Barcelona did it. You can win Championships, you can win titles, but there is a manner in which you want it. If you all swim in the same pool, the pool is too small if you all go for the same players. There are a lot of players outside that pool, good players on to the next step in their career. We try to find them." Klopp had brought in six players at a cost of £62m, including Sadio Mané, Georginio Wijnaldum, Joël Matip, Loris Karius, Alex Manninger and Ragnar Klavan. Klopp added: "I'm not interested in other clubs. They can do what they want and spend as much as they want. I don't know exactly how much we have spent. For five or six players we could have bought one player for the same money but I don't care. I have no influence on what other clubs do so why should I think about it? I am not the moral guardian of the league. It's all about perspective. I am pretty sure it will stop somewhere. Where there is money somebody else will take it. That's how it is in the football business. If we are convinced someone is the right player then we think about money. If we agree then we will do it but only then for the right price."

Arsene Wenger still refused to pay inflated fees by calling Pogba's £100m move to United "completely crazy". Despite, once again, being under pressure from supporters frustrated at a lack of transfer action to match the likes of United, City and Liverpool, Wenger was in defiant mood while in Los Angeles as Arsenal continued their pre-season preparations.

"I buy players that I think can strengthen our team," said Wenger. "Today we have to be very strong not just to buy to buy. There is always a wave of opinions. People are better informed today, they know all the players, they tell you always: 'You should buy'. When you ask who, they become much shorter." Commenting on Pogba's move to Old Trafford, Wenger said: "It is completely crazy if you cannot afford to pay it. If you can afford to pay it you can justify it. It is completely crazy if you compare it to normal life. That is for sure. But we live in a world where every activity that is worldwide makes a lot of money. Football has become a worldwide competition and that is why clubs can afford to do it. Does it make sense in the way the player can give you that investment back? Nobody ever could calculate. Since I am in this sport I always thought the record cannot go higher and I was always wrong. Maybe in a few years it will be 200, 300, who knows?"

Wenger defended chief executive Ivan Gazidis, under attack from supporters eager for Arsenal to spend more money: "I work every day with Ivan, believe me he is highly motivated to bring players in. Sometimes I have to calm him down. I believe as well this is a period where everybody wants to dream, and transfers bring dreams. But we live in a realistic world and part of our job is as well to rate the players we have inside the club. One of the values of our club is to give chances to players who deserve it."

Wenger vowed to try to bring the title back to the club in what could be his last season. "We had 18 teams behind us last year, we want to make sure we get 19 behind us next season. It's always been difficult, look at my hair and my wrinkles. I think I enjoy it because I am a competitor, I like to improve and move forward, it is a great challenge. I believe a big club is first about identity, values, despite all the money we talk about, and to make these values win. We focus on being faithful to our game. I am a long time at the club because I share the identity of the club. I want, in my final year of contract, not necessarily final year at Arsenal, to make sure these qualities come out in the club again and that we can win."

Arsenal's record transfers:

Mesut Özil - £40m from Real Madrid, 2013

Alexis Sanchez - £35m from Barcelona, 2014

Granit Xhaka - £30m from Borussia Monchengladbach, 2016

Chapter 10

THE DENOUEMENT

It's really hard to believe that it was back in 2011 when I was in Manchester at Rio Ferdinand's restaurant, Rosso, launching 'Manchester United 19', the book that chronicled all of the club's title wins, culminating in their 19th title, their record breaking League Championship.

Sir Bobby Charlton contributed the Foreword to the book, and legends such as Bryan Robson, Tommy Docherty and Wilf McGuiness turned out for the launch party. No one in that room, packed with so many connected to Old Trafford over several generations, thought for one moment that a barren spell was just around the corner. My thoughts were about updating the book with the 20th title, closely followed by the 21st! The 20th duly arrived in 2013, as for the 21st...

Sir Alex Ferguson stated that his brief was to knock Liverpool "off their perch", and more than 2,000 games and 25 season later, he finally did just that. But, of course, Sir Alex finally retired, in came David Moyes, then Louis van Gaal, and it went from bad to worse, with Old Trafford losing its identity, of 'attack, attack, attack' as the fans have consistently demanded over the years and the chant I've heard in nearly 40 covering football all over the world.

I've written a couple of books on Sir Alex and, of course, 'Manchester United 19' is a particular favourite of mine. I've also written four books on José Mourinho over the years. He is a favourite of mine as well!

José will have learned a great deal from his disastrous second spell at Chelsea. Invaluable experience in fact.

In my previous book on Mourinho, 'Farewell to the King', I went into graphic detail about how things had gone so horribly wrong and so quickly for the

'Special One', who looked far from special in the bottom half of the table. Guus Hiddink arrived to explain that owner Roman Abramovich was fearful that the slide would take them all the way to relegation.

The causes for one of the biggest ever collapses in defence of the Premier League title was traced back to accumulative errors pre-season; poor performances, late arrivals, the manager giving weary stars too much time off, and failure to land the 'big fish' transfers the manager had craved. Of course it had also long been levelled at Mourinho that he did an Alan Hansen - "you can't win things with kids."

Conte arrived at the Bridge from his exploits with Italy in the Euros and said he will actively seek to do the opposite. "There are many players with good prospects at Chelsea. I don't know why in the past only a few players have played with the first team," Conte told ESPN FC. "I love to play with the young players and to improve them. It's important to have good quality to improve and to show that a young player can play with the first team."

Mourinho had already tried to disprove the pre-conceived notion he doesn't give kids their chance by producing his long list, 'the 55', of instances of giving youngsters their opportunities at all of his clubs.

Equally, it is also true that he wanted English football's brightest young central defensive prospect in John Stones at Everton. Chelsea made four unsuccessful bids as Mourinho sought the long term successor to John Terry. The background to that was that Abramovich had ordered no more £50 million signings after being caught cold with the Fernando Torres fee he had authorised to Liverpool. Instead, Chelsea were left with issues in defence, combined with the additional failure to buy another striker, ending up with Falcao on loan.

Stones was part of the England squad at Euro 2016 but did not feature as they were knocked out in the last 16, yet former England coach Glenn Hoddle was a big advocate of grooming Stones earlier and having him ready for the Euros, which Roy Hodgson failed to do.

Stones made his debut for Barnsley in March 2012, 10 months before joining Everton for £3m. Now, Guardiola identified the Yorkshireman as the kind of central defender who fits his approach to the game. "Normally central defenders are strong in the air and aggressive," explained Guardiola. "But we need to have a good build-up to create easy passes in the midfield so they can create good passes for the strikers. I believe when the ball goes from the central defender to the striker as quickly as possible, it comes as quickly as possible back. That is why the players in that area need quality. By 31 August we will have the right squad to play how we want."

Guardiola used midfielders Javier Mascherano and Javi Martínez as central defenders while managing Barcelona and Bayern Munich, and he identified a City midfielder who could step into the back four if required. "Fernandinho can play in 10 positions," he said. "He is quick, fast, intelligent, aggressive. He is strong in the air and has the quality to play good build-up, can go right or left and can pass long."

So, with the 'Special One' replacing the 'Lame One' how might the 2016-17 season conclude?

Well, this is sure to be the most fascinating and closest Premier League season of all time and it is already getting many top pundits scratching their heads wondering how it will pan out, and I will also give you my forecast. While it will carry a warning not to place bets on my predications, I should say that I am often more right than wrong. That's enough of me patting myself on the back though.

Let me first share some expert analysis, firstly from Slaven Bilić.

Slaven Bilić excelled as an ITV pundit during the 2016 European Championships, and he's not a bad manager in his day job either. The West Ham manager made a very interesting observation about the fate of some of the world's top coaches, including that of José Mourinho and Pep Guardiola.

Bilić would love to break into the Top Four but the Leicester City example has widened the number of clubs with such ambitions. These, of course, include West Ham and with a big improvement in the playing style since the departure of Sam Allardyce and the arrival of the Croat, plus their move to the Olympic Stadium, expectations are growing in east London. By the way of going off on a tangent, Bilić would have made a far more worthy England manager than Big Sam, whom some Hammers fans dubbed 'Fat Sham' at Upton Park. Bilić's CV includes being an international as well as an international manager, while Allardyce hasn't even managed a team in the Champions League.

Anyway, wisely, Bilić shifted the pressure away from himself and onto one of the Premier League's big-name managers whom he argues is going to get 'slaughtered' when they finish outside the top four this season. He counted on his fingers the managers who will expect to be in the top four: "The managers like José Mourinho, Pep Guardiola, Jürgen Klopp, Antonio Conte, Arsene

Wenger, there are five of them and one has to finish fifth - if indeed they are the top five - and that one is going to get slaughtered. And they are all big names." Mauricio Pochettino didn't get a mention until Bilić remembered he had forgotten to mention him. Bilić also made the point that champions Leicester City will be aiming to avoid relegation as their priority. "Spurs will probably be unhappy to finish sixth," he said. "Everton, and all that. Therefore when we talk about Champions League, whatever, Europa League, mid-table, it is all very dangerous. Make no mistake. I am a confident, over-optimistic person but apart from the top seven clubs on paper everybody is looking forward to 40 points. And that includes Leicester also because we all know what can happen in the Premier League, with Newcastle. A massive club that spent £80m in two transfer windows went down so you better work hard and play good."

Antonio Conte was expecting a strong challenge from United with expectations on Mourinho sky high. Conte was deeply involved with a rebuilding project at Stamford Bridge and was making a series of significant signings as, indeed, were all his rivals. And, how all those signings gel would largely determine the fate of the clubs and indeed their managers.

The former Italian team manager at the Euros was well aware of the threat United will pose this season. "Mourinho is a top manager and is a winner," Conte said. "I know this - we know this. Now Mourinho is the manager of Manchester United. I think United is another team - I'm sure - will fight at the end to win the title. It's a very strong team with a good manager and good players but it's important for Chelsea to think of Chelsea. Not the other club, the other managers or the other players. (We need to) think of ourselves, because the most important thing is to think and to trust in our work, in our ideas and in our confidence. I think this is the most important thing now."

Dwight Yorke, talismanic striker and a leading member of the United side which secured a unique treble in 1998-99, believed Mourinho will help the club reclaim its place at the pinnacle of the world game. "Mourinho has the capability to restore the leadership quality of the squad. He is a great motivator. United can only benefit from his experience. The process for recovery is already underway and the team is more focused. Everyone is trying to impress the new manager and there is a lot of competition for the first team." Yorke felt the lack of goal threat was at an end, "We have signed Zlatan Ibrahimović. Wayne Rooney, Marcus Rashford and Anthony Martial are there too. I don't think it will be a problem anymore."

When Sir Alex arrived to "knock Liverpool off their perch" it was far simpler; the focus was on one club. Now José has to knock City and Chelsea off their perches, try to stop Liverpool under Klopp getting back on that perch, as well as being mindful of Arsene Wenger trying to make a point (or maybe a perch) at Arsenal.

For me, the season will be dominated by United and City, but Pep Guardiola will find the Premier League tough to adapt to at first, which will give United the edge under Mourinho who does know his way around the Premier League block. Beware Liverpool under Klopp and I can see them finishing in the top four. Chelsea will be a big threat with Conte in charge, so it will be tough for Arsenal and Spurs to make it into the top four. That would be bitterly disappointing to the extent that it could be the end for both managers in north London.

Mourinho has already stated that his target is to win the Premier League in his first season in charge at Old Trafford. The absolute bare minimum is Champions League qualification.

A hard-fought, close, tempestuous and defining season is to be expected. Hold on tight.

So, Manchester United, 2016-17 Premier League Champions - but don't bet on it.

Firstly congratulations to José Mourinho for landing the dream
job at "The Theatre of Dreams" and becoming The Red One
from all at Footba11legends! The Manchester United Legend Sir
Bobby Charlton was the first to coin "The Theatre of Dreams"
to describe Old Trafford and the phrase became synonymous
with Sir Alex Ferguson's exciting trophy winning teams.

Footba11legends trades in sports memorabilia, promotes sports Question & Answers with football legends and is currently working on an online fanzine.

José Mourinho is a brilliant appointment from the Old Trafford board and one which is designed to bring the coveted 21st League Title to Old Trafford for starters. José will become a Red Legend if he can achieve that in his first season at The Theatre of Dreams.

The appointment should be applauded by all football fans as it was made when certain sections of the media and public were focused on other events. José Mourinho from being the late Great Sir Bobby Robson's student is now truly one of the most charismatic, insightful and successful managers of all time. I'm sure Sir Alex Ferguson is confident that José Mourinho will enjoy the success which he himself brought to his beloved Manchester United.

Harry Harris is a true legend of sports journalism and I have enjoyed reading some fabulous books written by Harry over the years. The Ferguson Effect (before Sir Alex Ferguson was knighted), Manchester United 19 which included Bryan Robson being voted by former Manchester United players as the greatest Manchester United player of all time. My personal favourite so far is Hard Tackles and Dirty Baths which Harry wrote with George Best.

I have enjoyed meeting Paddy Crerand at a few events and listening to Paddy speak about the players who have become Manchester United Legends over the decades and who are remembered each home game by the singing corner faithful at The Theatre of Dreams.

I would like to take this opportunity to thank Paddy and Sir Bobby Charlton for personalising my 1968 The Manchester United Football Book No.3. It's something I treasure. The book captures Manchester United being the first English side to win The European Cup (The Champions League).

The away shirt worn in 1968 when winning The European Cup was blue as it will be for this season and the next couple of seasons at least. Perhaps in the 2017-2018 season José Mourinho's Manchester United will lift The Champions League wearing blue who knows.

José Mourinho understands the great tradition of Manchester United and embraces the challenge to ensure that the legacy and tradition continue under his guidance.

José Mourinho has applied his undoubted positive attitude and belief to be a winner. He instils this self-belief in the team's he builds and knows only too well that you cannot win League titles and Champions League trophies without strong characters and leaders on the field of play.

The players he develops grow in stature and perform to incredible levels. I wouldn't be surprised if he improves on the 18 clean sheets achieved by the team last season. José is a great believer in keeping the game simple, don't concede, score more goals than opposition and work for the team.

Bryan Robson and Steve Bruce epitomised the team spirit, character and leadership which brought Sir Alex Ferguson his first title at Manchester United and paved the way for other great leaders to follow.

I am looking forward to watching Wayne Rooney's performances in José Mourinho's Manchester United team. Wayne Rooney is maturing into an influential Manchester United Captain and leader both on and off the pitch. Wayne Rooney is a player that José Mourinho has always admired and I know the pair are excited to be working together.

José and his board have brought in some great signings to achieve the target to win the Premier League in José's first season as Manchester United Manager. My son Seb is a big fan of Zlatan Ibrahimović (goal scoring phenomenon) but his favourite Manchester United player is David de Gea (Seb is an aspiring goalkeeper). I agree that David de Gea is an inspirational goalkeeper and to keep the legendary Victor Valdés out of the Manchester United starting 11 is no mean feat.

I wish José Mourinho and Manchester United a great 2016/2017 season along with Aitor Karanka at Middlesbrough. (My home team)

I believe Aitor Karanka has the winning (and clean sheet) mentality which he no doubt honed when he was José's student and put to good effect at Old Trafford last year defeating Louis Van Gaal's Manchester United in The Football League Cup.

I am sure José enjoyed cheering his friend Aitor Karanka's Middlesbrough to promotion last year and will be wishing Aitor and Middlesbrough well this season except when playing Manchester United of course.

Good Luck to José Mourinho The Red One!

Ant Verrill

@footba11legends.

Double winner British Sports Journalist of the Year.

British Variety Club of Great Britain Silver Heart for 'Contribution to Sports Journalism'.

Double winner Sports Story of the Year; only journalist ever to win the sports story of the year accolade twice.

Total of 24 industry awards.

Appears regularly as an analyst on football related matters on all major TV News and Sports programmes and channels, including Richard & Judy and Newsnight, BBC News and ITV News at Ten, Sky, BBC Global, Radio 5 Live, Radio 4, LBC, and TalkSport, interviewed on Football Focus, numerous Football documentaries, appeared on the original Hold The Back Page and Jimmy Hill Sunday Supplement on Sky.

Arguably the most prolific writer of best-selling football books of his generation. Among his 79 books are the highly acclaimed best-seller 'Pele - His Life and Times', 'Gullit: The Chelsea Diary' and 'Manchester United 19'. Penned a dozen best-selling books on Chelsea, including 'All The Way José', 'Chelsea Century', 'Chelski'. Biographies on Roman Abramovich, Franco Zola and Luca Vialli.

Autobiographies for Ruud Gullit, Paul Merson, Glenn Hoddle, Gary Mabbutt, Steve McMahon, Terry Neill, and Bill Nicholson 'Glory, Glory - My Life With Spurs.' Biographies on, Jürgen Klinsmann, Sir Alex Ferguson, Terry Venables, George Best's last book, the best-selling 'Hard Tackles and Dirty Baths'.

Written one of the most influential football columns in the country for three decades, one of the best investigative journalists, arguably the best news gatherer of his generation. Previously: Chief Football Writer for the Daily Mail, Daily Mirror, Daily Express, Daily Star, & Sunday Express; ESPNsoccernet Football Correspondent, BT Sport.

H&H Sports Media Ltd with co-founder, former England, Spurs and Chelsea player/manager Glenn Hoddle, running Zapsportz.com & F30 Legends.

Director of Fleet Street Sport & Media Group Ltd, Chairman Niall Quinn, patrons Sir Michael Parkinson, Lord Herman Ouseley, Early Shrewsbury.

Latest books: 'José Mourinho: Farewell to the King', 'The Immortals' on Leicester City's Premier league winning season, 'Up Front: Kerry Dixon' and 'Down Memory Lane'.

RedStrike is an international partnership group of skilled consultants who are best in class in their chosen fields of sports & marketing.

RedStrike focuses on delivering intuitive & innovative solutions that use sport to connect brands with people in meaningful ways.

Fronted by Mike Farnan, former Managing Director of Manchester United International, RedStrike is very much an International Agency with offices in Chester, London, Kuala Lumpur, Dubai, Jeddah and Johannesburg.

RedStrike are marketing advisors to Scuderia Ferrari, another powerful red force, who like Manchester United have a mass global following of over 600 million people.

OTHER CLIENTS INCLUDE:

Macron, Globe Soccer Awards, Events in the Sky, Bottoms Up Beer, URUP, Mobilibuy, Dublin GAA, GAC Logistics, The Game, Metro Bank, Soccer Services, Story Stream, The All Blacks.

CONTACT:

T: 020 3356 2971
E: mike.farnan@redstrike.com

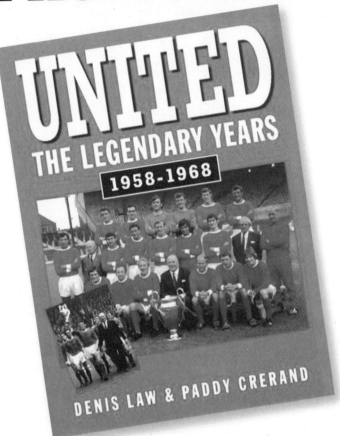